TOKSVIG'S
ALMANAC
2021

TOKSVIG'S ALMANAC
2021

*An eclectic meander through
the historical year*

SANDI TOKSVIG

First published in Great Britain in 2020 by Trapeze
an imprint of The Orion Publishing Group Ltd
Carmelite House, 50 Victoria Embankment
London EC4Y 0DZ

An Hachette UK Company

1 3 5 7 9 10 8 6 4 2

A CIP catalogue record for this book is
available from the British Library.

ISBN (Hardback) 978 1 3987 0163 2
ISBN (eBook) 978 1 3987 0164 9

Typeset by seagulls.net
llustrations by James Nunn

Printed and bound in Great Britain by Clays Ltd, Elcograf, S.p.A.

www.orionbooks.co.uk

To Elena and Marisa

Contents

In Praise of the Colour Purple – Women and Reading

Be warned, this book is full of crazy ideas and that's because I've been going mad. I've been going mad because I've been reading in order that I might know what I wanted to write about. My wife, who is a therapist, says I mustn't use the expression 'going mad' anymore. It is politically incorrect, so let me start again by saying I've been reading and it's making me troubled. There is a marvellous book called *Women Who Read Are Dangerous* and it quotes many an expert from the past who actually thought this. In 1791 the German theologian, Karl Gottfried Bauer, wrote, 'The lack of all physical movement while reading, combined with the forcible alternation of imagination and emotion,' would lead to 'slackness, mucous congestion, flatulence, and constipation of the inner organs, which, as is well known, particularly in the female sex, actually affects the sexual parts'.

Honestly I could hardly sit still after I read that; my sexual parts were so astir. Bauer himself had several children, including two simply listed as 'unmarried daughters', as if no greater disappointment could be imagined. Thank goodness those two hadn't been allowed to read. Why, they might not only have been spinsters but wanting to vote as well. Hard to believe but it was an actual argument against women's suffrage that the female of the species simply wasn't built for it. If we exerted our tiny little minds too much – reading or taking part in civic society – then we were risking the very thing we had been brought into the world for: our reproductive health. So, if you're a woman reading this – hang on to your womb, it's going to be a bumpy ride.

In the 19th and early 20th centuries the general consensus was that the human body contained a finite amount of energy. If women used too much brainpower then their ovaries would atrophy and no one wanted that. Reading could make women infertile and, worse than that, ruin men's lives. British women did not get the same voting rights as men until 1928. I have an original anti-suffrage postcard sent five years before, in 1923, which shows a man overwhelmed with cooking, cleaning and childcare while in the back room a disgraceful woman is reading. Whoever the sender is, their only greeting is the words 'A LAST WARNING' in large letters on the back.

According to William Sedgwick, one of the founders of the MIT-Harvard School of Public Health, thinking of any kind was especially dangerous for pregnant women. He declared, 'We must not forget pregnancy and lactation, both of which are a great strain on a mother's vitality. Any further strain, like the responsibilities of the suffrage, is bound to be harmful to both mother and child.'

What about the postmenopausal woman like myself? Surely reading might calm my addled brain? But not so. In 1913 Sir Almroth Wright, a British immunologist who we could have done with in times of pandemic had he not died back in 1947, used his no doubt excellent brain to write that vital contribution to British society – a strong letter to *The Times* newspaper. In this letter he declared that the menopause gave rise to 'serious and long-continued mental disorders developing in connexion with the approaching extinction of a woman's reproductive faculty'. He went on to write a whole book entitled *The Unexpurgated Case Against Woman Suffrage* in which he blathered on a bit more. It seems he was terribly clever about the human body and antibiotics but never really understood the uterus.

Fundamentally, the view was that no man should allow a woman in his life to go to the office, the ballot box or that terrible well of reading – a university. Women's heads were imagined to be filled with little more than puppies, hats and chocolates, and that was how it ought to be. The trouble with this image is that it overlooks a few critical points on the subject of women and writing. The first writer in the world of any kind that we know about was a woman. The earliest known poet whose name was recorded was **Enheduanna**, who lived in the Sumerian city-state of Ur in the 23rd century BC. She was a high priestess and her collection of work, known as 'The Sumerian Temple Hymns', makes her the first named author of any kind in human civilisation. An elaborate carved disc found in 1927 during excavations of the Sumerian city of Ur show Enheduanna as a figure of huge importance.

Enheduanna's very existence tells us that there were women writing, and therefore reading, more than 4,000 years ago in ancient Mesopotamia. Where else? Well, Japan. Over a thousand years ago there was a lady-in-waiting to Empress Shōshi of the Imperial Heian court called **Murasaki Shikibu**, also known as Lady Murasaki. She seems to have been quite a woman. Despite being Japanese, the Heian court used Chinese as their written language and women weren't supposed to learn it. Murasaki, however, seems to have ignored that rule and had a brilliant knowledge of Chinese classics. We know this because she wrote *The Tale of Genji*, the world's very first novel.

Murasaki seems to have had connections and that helped her be allowed to put pen to paper. Having a position of power was essential for early women writers. Enheduanna was a priestess and being left alone to a holy life has often been the key for early women writers. Back in the 1100s **Hildegard of Bingen** was the mother superior of a monastery in the Rhine Valley near Bingen in Germany. Here she was able to find the peace to write and she penned one of the first operas ever written. Then there's **Hrotsvitha of Gandersheim**, another nun, who a thousand years ago wrote plays and so on. Women writing and reading is not new. If you are lucky enough to go to Fontevrault abbey near Chinon in France, you can pay your respects to **Eleanor of Aquitaine**, who died in 1204. There is a splendid carving which shows her reading even though she is dead, while her husband King Henry II appears to be lying beside her wondering if he locked the front door.

There have just been too many phases where the world decided to try to put the female mind into some kind of small box. In general, the last hundred years have seen the education of women become disgracefully commonplace, but some of the misogynistic attitude towards it has stuck around. In 2013 someone took it upon themselves to change the list of American novelists in Wikipedia to a list of only male novelists, while women writers were moved into a subcategory. Thus **Harper Lee**, **Edith Wharton**, **Toni Morrison** and **Donna Tartt** were all bumped down into a lesser and more belittling list. They've since been moved back but that anyone had to bother seems to suggest they were, well, troubled by women being in control of a narrative.

Although Lady Murasaki's *The Tale of Genji* is a classic of Japanese literature, her name seems to have been a pseudonym. It's the Japanese word for the colour purple. Too many women's names have been lost over time so *Toksvig's Almanac* reinstates a few, as we go in search of patches of purple.

A last warning

There is a new complexity in writing about history which I struggle with. There are those who say that some stories can only be told by those with direct experience of them. This makes it tricky. I am a white lesbian from Denmark and if I only wrote about white Danish lesbians then this *Almanac* might be rather thin. Personally, I would love to have a fuller understanding of lesbian history as it is incredibly difficult to document. Finding other women like myself helps me to understand my place in the great pantheon of human experience, and I am always grateful to anyone who points me in the direction of a woman whose story I did not know.

It's also worth a note of caution that all the women in here are extraordinary but that doesn't mean they are all nice. There are serial killers as well as those who tried to cure disease because I've set out to present as wide a range of women as possible and, well, we come in all shapes and sizes. The result is that there are women included whose lives I couldn't possibly approve of but who are nonetheless interesting. I am painfully aware that I have not been able to even scratch the surface of the females who are worth reading about. I know someone somewhere will be outraged about the inadvertent exclusion of a vital story. The truth is we need thousands of *Almanacs*. I am merely trying to shine a light into a few of the many dark corners of history where women's stories lie, and hope others will pick up where I left off and discover more. We all need to hear as many accounts as possible and then each go off in search of our own understanding. With that in mind, please know that I am merely here as a signpost not as an expert.

History records many women who dressed as men, and you will find some of them here. From this distance it is impossible to know if these women dressed as men simply to take advantage of opportunities that were only offered to men, or if they felt that they were what we would now call a trans man. That makes it tricky when it comes to pronouns, as I'd usually ask someone what they preferred to be called, and a few hundred years gets in the way of the question. I've done my best here with the information that the, often limited, historical record offers.

The consequence of all this is that this book may be the most incomplete book you will ever have in your hands. Rather than that being a disappointment, I think it is unbelievably energising. *Toksvig's Almanac* is intended merely as a starting point for your own discoveries. Find a fabulous (or infamous) woman mentioned and, please, go looking for more of her story. The names mentioned are merely temptations. *Amuse-bouches* for the mind, if you like. How I would have loved to have written out in detail each tale there is to be told, but then this book would have been too heavy to lift.

In the literature of the Tamil people of India and Sri Lanka there was a poet known as **Avvaiyar** (ஒளவையார்). It translates literally as 'Respectable Woman'.

As is often the case with women in early recorded history we don't know much about her. She may even have been three women over several generations, but certainly there is a record of Avvaiyar writing as far back as the 3rd century BC. Her words of wisdom have been passed down to us.

'கற்றது கைமண் அளவு,
கல்லாதது உலகளவு'

I long to be able to read those marks on the paper but at least I can have the translation. Over thousands of years her voice still resonates as she reminds us:

> 'What you have learned is a mere handful;
> What you haven't learned is the size of the world.'

A couple of notes about dates

If there is ever date confusion then blame two guys from the past, Gregory and Julius, which sounds like a terrible double act. I'm going to precis here because there are more interesting things to write about.

The Egyptians were the first to try to make any kind of note of dates, then the Babylonians had a go, followed by the Greeks and the Romans, but the first calendar that anyone wanted to put up on the wall arrived courtesy of Julius Caesar in about 45 BC. It's possible old Jules was not brilliant at counting. His calendar had an inbuilt error of one day every 128 years, which turned out to be even more annoying than you might think. The error was down to someone miscalculating the solar year by 10.8 minutes, which is the sort of miscalculation my old teachers warned me about.

In 1582, Pope Gregory adjusted the calendar the way some men adjust their trousers. He seems to have been better at adding up and this updated model became known as the 'Gregorian calendar'. It decreed that the start of the year was 1 January, and because Greg seemed important most Western nations began celebrating the start of the year then. England and the American colonies, however, didn't want to be pushed around by Rome so they carried on in their own way for a while, celebrating the new year on the date of the spring equinox in March. Then, in 1752, they gave in, aligned with the rest of Europe, and switched to Gregory's way of doing things.

Not everyone was thrilled. The switch from Julian to Greg meant that, in September 1752, eleven days were effectively 'lost'. The English have a long tradition of having governments who are poor at communication. Instead of explaining the maths behind the change they simply announced that Wednesday 2 September 1752 would be followed by Thursday 14 September 1752. There are those who will tell you this caused riots with ignorant folk wanting their eleven days back, but it's probably not true. What people mostly didn't like was a 'popish' calendar whatever day it started on.

Anyway, I've done my best to be accurate about dates but if anything of note happened between 2 and 14 September 1752 I cannot be held responsible.

JANUARY

'January, month of empty pockets! ... let us endure this evil month, anxious as a theatrical producer's forehead.'

– **Colette**, French author, born 1873

Wolf Month

Let me draw your attention to *A Restitution of Decayed Intelligence*, which is the title of a book not an ambition of mine. It was written in 1605 by an Anglo-Dutchman called Richard Verstegan. Among other things, Verstegan tells us that the Anglo-Saxons called January *Wolfmonath*, or 'wolf month', apparently because it was the month you were more likely to be eaten by a wolf than any other. Good to know. (I'm not suggesting you read his book, although it is interesting partly because it contains the very first version of the story of the Pied Piper of Hamelin.)

January is named, of course, after the Roman god Janus. Let's start by being honest. Janus is the sort of name that might make schoolboys snigger. It's not a cuddly name, but then he was a god so perhaps cuddling was not top of his list. Janus means 'archway' in Latin, which, apart from being the name of an underground station in London, is not widely used for children these days. Romans seem to me to have been quite showbiz. Like so many of my fellow performers, they loved a good entrance and exit. They used to have freestanding ceremonial gateways called *'jani'*, after Janus. These didn't really go anywhere; they were there for symbolic comings and goings. It's a bit like the Queen opening parliament. It doesn't mean anything; it just makes everyone feel better. In Roman times you wouldn't have wanted to be a soldier heading off to war without passing through a lucky *janus* (I know it's childish but that just doesn't sound right). Janus seems to have got the god of doorways gig because he was the god of change and beginnings, so it seems suitable that he gets the first month of the year named after him.

NEW YEAR CELEBRATIONS

Happy New Year

Welcome to the beginning of a brand-new year. Been celebrating? Well, you're in good company although historically January was not always the time for it. That's because the month itself didn't turn up until the reign of Numa Pompilius in Rome, so somewhere between 715 and 673 BC. Before Numa the Romans had a calendar with just ten months in it. The year consisted of 304 days, with the remaining 61 falling in winter when no one could be bothered to mark them off. You know how it can be between Christmas and New Year. Then someone with a tidy mind thought, 'We really should account for those days', and January and February got added to the reckoning. Ironically, no one seems to have noted the exact date on a calendar. Strictly speaking, the first time in history that New Year's Day was celebrated on 1 January was in 45 BC because that's when the Julian calendar took effect.

Before January was a thing people still marked what they thought of as the 'new year'. Possibly the oldest of such shindigs that we know about dates to about 3,500 years ago. There may have been happy gatherings before that but, as is the way with history, if everyone was too drunk to write it down then somehow it didn't happen. So, the best we can do is go back to the ...

Babylonian Akitu

Babylon was founded in about 2300 BC so this is one of the oldest New Year celebrations. Perhaps because they had never heard of the month of January, the Babylonians of ancient Mesopotamia kicked off the new year in late March with the festival of Akitu. The date wasn't fixed but rather depended on the timing of the first new moon after the vernal equinox. The celebration lasted several days and was quite the religious affair. Statues of gods were paraded through the street so they could cleanse the place and get everyone ready for the return of spring.

The patron god of Babylon was called Marduk. He was their equivalent of Zeus or Jupiter; in other words, the king of the gods. Marduk looked human but dressed as a king carrying a snake-dragon because, well, he could and a spade because agriculture was everything. During Akitu the earthly King of Babylon would be brought before a statue of Marduk and stripped of his royal regalia. Then things got interesting if humiliating. The king had to swear he had done a good job; a high priest would slap him and drag him around by the ears to see if he would cry. Once royal tears were shed then Marduk was happy and the king could carry on. I can't see this making a comeback any time soon, although there are several world leaders who I think would benefit.

Chinese New Year

This is one that's still carrying on even though it began over 3,000 years ago during the Shang dynasty. Actually, it could have happened earlier but the Shang were the first in Chinese history to begin writing things down. The date is based on an old lunar calendar and is set each year according to the second new moon after the winter solstice, which I think sounds complicated. Basically, late January / early February. It probably just started with a bit of excitement about the new spring planting season, but human beings like a bit of storytelling so it soon had myths springing up about it. Here is a quick one:

Once upon a time there was a bloodthirsty creature called Nian. Nian appears to have had a rigid eating schedule, for this hungry beast particularly liked to prey on villages every new year. In order to frighten him away the villagers did several things – they made loud noises (which we all know beasts absolutely hate); the locals also decorated their homes with red bits and bobs and they burnt bamboo. Worked every time.

I don't think Nian turns up like he used to, it's not something you see on the news, but the bright colours and lights have stayed. The loud noises got even louder in the 10th century when the Chinese invented gunpowder and became the first to mark New Year with fireworks.

⤞ POEM OF THE MONTH ⤝

January by Edith Nesbit

WHILE yet the air is keen, and no bird sings,
Nor any vaguest thrills of heart declare
The presence of the springtime in the air,
Through the raw dawn the shepherd homeward brings
The wee white lambs – the little helpless things –
For shelter, warmth, and comfortable care.
Without his help how hardly lambs would fare –
How hardly live through winter's hours to spring's!

So let me tend and minister apart
To my new hope, which some day you shall know:
It could not live in January wind
Of your disdain; but when within your heart
The bud and bloom of tenderness shall grow,
Amid the flowers my hope may welcome find.

Edith was an English author and poet, born in 1858. She wrote about forty kids' books and really set the benchmark for modern children's literature. If you know her then most likely it's because she wrote *The Railway Children*, which became one of the great children's films of all time. I love that film and once embarrassed myself by saying, 'Get off the line, Bobbie!' to Jenny Agutter, the star of it. I also love that Edith was a political activist, which is a fine thing to be. She co-founded the socialist organisation the Fabian Society, on whose behalf she was an active lecturer and prolific writer during the 1880s, an era when frankly she should have been at home.

Sadly, Edith didn't have the best personal life. When she was in her early twenties, she married a bank clerk called Hubert Bland. I would have thought his surname alone should have been enough to make her think twice about a proposal, but she was pregnant and society was unbelievably judgemental about that kind of thing. It can't have been a happy marriage as Hubert carried on living with his mother. Once he finally left home he turned out to be less than bland. He would go on to impregnate Edith's friend Alice not once but twice, and to persuade Edith both to adopt the kids and let Alice live with them.

After Bland died Edith married Thomas 'the Skipper' Tucker, the captain of the Woolwich Ferry, a free service that crosses the same 1,500 feet back and forth across the River Thames in five to ten minutes all day, every day. Hard to think of someone more dependable. I wonder if the poem was for him?

Anyway, new hope.

Resolutions

While you're making any New Year's resolutions it's a good day to consider how much you want to go against the crowd in your daily decisions. It was on 1 January in 391 (or even 404, it's so hard to be specific) that a tourist called Telemachus was visiting Rome 'from the East', which is a big place. He popped in to see a gladiatorial fight in a Roman amphitheatre and was horrified. So horrified that he tried to stop it and was promptly stoned to death by the crowd. At least that's what some people say. Details are tricky from this distance because according to *Foxe's Book of Martyrs* (and who hasn't got that by their bedside?) first published in 1563, he was actually stabbed to death by a gladiator which upset everyone so they all went home. Either way, think before you valiantly insert yourself between armed men.

 — 1 January 1859 —

Dr Elizabeth Blackwell becomes Britain's first woman doctor
'It's not easy to be a pioneer – but oh, is it fascinating!'
Without some women standing up to be counted we would never have had the amazing female doctors and scientists who, among others, the entire planet has had reason to be grateful to in the last year or so. Hard to believe women were once thought incapable of anything other than being on the receiving end of medicine.

I was reading about **Dr Una Ledingham**, who was a proper new start baby as she was born on 2 January in 1900. A man called Richard Trail has penned a short biography of her on the Royal

College of Physicians website. It explains that Una was from London and received her medical training at the London School of Medicine for Women, a marvellous place of female education founded in 1874 by pioneering women physicians **Sophia Jex-Blake**, **Elizabeth Garrett Anderson**, **Emily Blackwell** and **Elizabeth Blackwell**. Una worked as a doctor from 1925 on and became an expert on the problems of diabetes in pregnancy.

Una seems to have been energetic in the extreme. She married a doctor and ran his practice as well as her own work while he was on active service in the Second World War. Everything I can find about her says she was forthright, which I would have loved. She stares boldly at the camera in the photo I have seen of her. Even in memoriam, however, this is not always a quality for which women are fondly recalled. Richard Trail, writing about her, says:

> In some ways she was her own worst enemy; only the discerning could appreciate her fairness, broadmindedness and deeply felt sympathy for her patients, under a rather hard exterior and a tendency to mar her brilliant conversational powers with an overpungent wit.

An overpungent wit.

How awful.

Perhaps that has been the problem down the ages. These damned clever women with their sharp tongues. Maybe that was an issue for **Agnodice**, the first female doctor in ancient Athens. She lived in the 4th century BC, a time when the Greeks thought you needed a penis in order to steady your nerve while helping someone. Women were allowed to be midwives but then someone suggested the midwives were helping their patients obtain abortions. After that, no woman was allowed to place her healing hand on anyone else's. In fact, it was so disapproved of that the penalty for a woman practising medicine was death, which certainly would make anyone think twice. Agnodice was clearly made of stern stuff. Her reaction was to cut her hair and disguise herself as a man in order to study medicine. The records suggest she even travelled to Egypt to learn her skills. The Egyptians seem to have liked women rather better and they had no problem with them becoming part of the medical profession.

Still dressed as a fellow, Agnodice returned to Athens and began to practise medicine. The female patients loved her. She became so popular with them (they may have known she was a woman) that she was accused by a group of men (who thought she was a man) of seducing them. She was put on trial in the Areopagus, a large bit of rock northwest of the Acropolis where court cases for serious matters were held. Here the Greeks tried murders and arson and serious cases involving olive trees. Forced to defend herself, Agnodice revealed that she was not seducing any women as she was one herself. Ignoring the fact that being a woman doesn't necessarily stop you seducing someone of your own sex, you have to imagine the shock bounced off the rock. The men threatened to execute her for breaking the law by practising medicine while pretending to be a man, but her female patients saved her. It seems they pointed out how Agnodice had been successfully practising medicine for some time now and that the male doctors were simply jealous. The court was shamed into pronouncing an acquittal. After the trial, the laws were changed so that women could practise medicine equally with men.

Different countries had varying attitudes to women being in the curing profession. The Italians were more chilled than the British. **Dorotea Bucca** held a chair of medicine and philosophy at the University of Bologna for over forty years from 1390, taking over the seat from her father. **Anna Morandi Manzolini** was a professor of anatomy at the University of Bologna in 1756, and no one should forget the **Women of Salerno**.

The Women of Salerno, also referred to as the Ladies of Salerno, were a group of female physicians in medieval Italy. They not only worked with patients but also taught and published medical works in all branches of medicine, not just those that applied to women. Check out **Constance Calenda**, an Italian surgeon specialising in diseases of the eye, who predated American and English women doctors by hundreds of years.

Of course, the world has moved on. My youngest daughter is a doctor in the British National Health Service and that wouldn't have been possible without those great women who went before her. This week we can celebrate Dr Elizabeth Blackwell who, on 1 January 1859, became the first woman to have her name entered on the British General Medical Council's medical register.

Born in Bristol, Blackwell began her career as a schoolteacher, but when an unwell female friend said she would not have suffered so much if she had had a woman doctor, Elizabeth decided to change careers. The problem was finding anywhere that would let her study. Only New York's Geneva Medical College would accept her, so she travelled across the ocean and, in 1849, graduated with her MD degree, becoming the first woman to receive a medical degree in the United States.

Her hopes of becoming a surgeon were dashed when her eye became infected through her work and eventually had to be removed. Undaunted, she went on to open her own medical practice in New York, developing the New York Infirmary for Indigent Women and Children as well as a medical college for women. She continued to visit Britain and helped found the London School of Medicine for Women, the very place from which the overpungent Una Ledingham would herself graduate.

I don't know what Elizabeth was like as a person except that she rather controversially at the time believed women were capable of sexual passions equal to men. Go girl. Some said she was acerbic. Perhaps she too had an overpungent wit but that was probably okay. Wit served her well. When she first applied to the Geneva Medical College the faculty thought they would ask the all-male student body what they thought. As a joke, the 150 men voted to let Elizabeth in never believing she would take up the offer. The joke was on them.

2 January 1922
Veronica Foster born

Aka 'Ronnie, the Bren Gun Girl', Canadian forerunner to American Second World War icon 'Rosie the Riveter'. She worked for the John Inglis Company assembling Bren light machine guns. Her image featured on propaganda posters encouraging women to serve Canada by working in munitions factories. After the war, she was lead singer with the dance band Mart Kenney and His Western Gentlemen.

3 January 1905
Anna May Wong born

Wong was the first Chinese American Hollywood movie star, gaining international recognition in everything from silent films, movies and TV, to stage and radio. She was born in LA's Chinatown where her parents owned a Laundromat. She struggled with being constantly cast in stereotypical roles.

4 January 1705
Madame d'Aulnoy dies

French novelist and writer, born in 1650 or 1651, who invented the term 'fairy tales' although she called them *'contes de fées'*. In her real life it's hard to tell fact from fiction. Certainly there were a lot of affairs, a good deal of intrigue and it's possible she was also a spy.

5 January 1947
Kathrine Switzer born

In 1967 Switzer became the first woman to run the Boston Marathon as a numbered entrant. It was against the rules so officials tried to grab her, but she finished the race. In 1972 women were finally permitted to run as official entrants.

6 January 1907
Maria Montessori opens her first school

Montessori was an Italian physician and educator. Today hundreds of schools bear her name and teach her educational methods. Her child-centred way of teaching was first developed for children with mental disabilities and then applied generally when she opened her first school, Casa dei Bambini (Children's House), in Rome for children from low-income families.

7 January 1955
Marian Anderson becomes the first African American woman to perform at the Metropolitan Opera in New York

Born in 1897, Anderson was an American singer of classical music and spirituals, and a very important figure in the struggle of black artists to overcome racial prejudice. In 1939, the Daughters of the American Revolution (the DAR) barred her from singing in Constitution Hall in Washington, DC, because they only allowed white artists. The then First Lady **Eleanor Roosevelt** was furious. She resigned from the DAR and helped arrange for Anderson to sing on the steps of the Lincoln Memorial. More than 75,000 people showed up to hear her.

True love bonus date: 7 January 1355
Inês de Castro, Queen Consort of Portugal, dies. Crowned queen 1361

Yes, you read those dates right. This case of star-crossed lovers got weird fast. In 14th-century Portugal, the king's son, Don Pedro, fell in love with Inês de Castro. There were only a couple of problems with this: for one, his father, King Afonso IV, did not approve, because Inês was illegitimate. Indeed, she came from a long line of illegitimate people which is a weird concept in itself. For another, Don Pedro was already married. Don's dad had arranged for him to marry a noblewoman named Constanza and Inês was Constanza's lady-in-waiting. When Don Pedro refused to stop seeing Inês, the king had her killed. Two years later Afonso died, Don Pedro became king and then it gets really odd. It is said that Don Pedro had Inês's body exhumed, clothed in royal dress, and placed on a throne so he could 'crown' her his queen. According to legend, he made the other nobles all kiss her hand as a sign of their devotion. I mean, it's love but ...

8 January 1867
Emily Greene Balch born
American economist, sociologist, professor and pacifist. She won the 1946 Nobel Peace Prize for her work with the Women's International League for Peace and Freedom (WILPF) based in

Switzerland. Due to the excesses of Nazism she did not criticise
the Allied war effort in the Second World War but supported
the rights of conscientious objectors.

9 January 1799
Maria Gaetana Agnesi dies
Italian mathematician, philosopher, theologian, born 1718.
Child prodigy. Wanted to be a nun but had to look after her
twenty siblings. The first woman appointed as a maths professor at a university although she never took up the post.
Also the first to write a maths handbook. In the later part
of her life she devoted herself to charity as the director of a
poorhouse she founded. She was buried in a mass grave with
fifteen others.

10 January 1903
Dame Barbara Hepworth born
Hepworth was an English artist and sculptor, part of the St
Ives colony of artists during the Second World War. She was
a rare female artist of her time who achieved international
recognition. Her museum and sculpture garden in St Ives is a
magical place.

11 January 1055
Theodora III Porphyrogenita becomes sole ruler of the
Byzantine empire
Born in AD 980, Theodora was joint Byzantine empress with
her sister Zoë from 1042. After Zoë's death she became the sole
ruler, and the last ruler of the Macedonian line.

12 January 1965
Lorraine Hansberry dies
Hansberry, born in 1930, became the first African American female author to have a play performed on Broadway, with *A Raisin in the Sun* in 1959. She was the first African American dramatist to win the New York Drama Critics' Circle Award. She died of cancer aged thirty-four, and inspired Nina Simone's song 'To Be Young, Gifted and Black'.

13 January 1886
Sophie Tucker born
Tucker was a Ukrainian-born American singer, comedian, actress, radio personality, known as 'The Last of the Red Hot Mamas'. Her hilarious act, in which her healthy sexual appetite was a recurring theme, made her one of America's most popular entertainers during the first half of the 20th century. *'I've been rich and I've been poor. Rich is better.'*

14 January 1841
Berthe Morisot born
French painter, part of the Parisian group who became known as the Impressionists. She and her sisters had their first art lessons in order to do a drawing for their father's birthday. She focused on daily life for her subject matter, which led to her work being underrated in its day. It enraged her: 'I don't think there has ever been a man who treated a woman as an equal and that's all I would have asked for, for I know I'm worth as much as they.'

15 January 1915
Fannie Farmer dies
American cookery expert, born in 1857. Author of *The Fannie Farmer Cookbook*, she had a paralytic stroke as a teenager which

meant she had to leave school. She was unable to walk for some years and took to cooking at her mother's boarding house. Aged thirty, she enrolled at the Boston Cooking School. She introduced standardised level measurements in recipes. Her other thrilling book titles include *Chafing Dish Possibilities*, published in 1898.

16 January 2006
Ellen Johnson Sirleaf elected president of Liberia
Born in 1938, Sirleaf is known as the 'Iron Lady'. Her election as the twenty-fourth president of Liberia made her the first elected female head of state in Africa. She served until 2018. Before that she spent twelve years in exile, working as an economist for major banks. She shared the Nobel Peace Prize in 2011 for her work on women's rights.

17 January 1647
Elisabeth Hevelius born
Hevelius was one of the first female astronomers. As a child she went to astronomer Johannes Hevelius because she wanted to study and he had the best observatory in the world in Danzig, Poland. They married when she was sixteen and he was fifty-two. When he died, she completed and published their jointly compiled catalogue of 1,564 stars and their positions.

18 January 1213
Tamar the Great of Georgia, Queen (and King), dies
Tamar the Great, born around 1160, was Queen of Georgia from 1184 to 1213. Because she ruled in her own right, rather than as the wife of a king, she also held the title of the king, so she was actually King Tamar. She consolidated her empire and had many cultural achievements. The Georgians still love her to this day.

19 January 1953
Almost 72 per cent of all American television sets tuned in to the sitcom *I Love Lucy* to watch Lucille Ball's character have a baby

Lucille Ball was a celebrated American actress, comedienne, studio executive and producer, born in 1911. She created and starred in *I Love Lucy* with her husband, Cuban band leader Desi Arnaz. The show was produced by their TV production company, Desilu, and she was the first woman to head such a company. The show is regarded as one of the best and most influential sitcoms in television history.

20 January 1863
Mary Meyer, homesteader, files for a homestead in Nebraska

There are no known birth or death dates for Mary but we do know it was on this date that she became the first woman to file for a homestead in the United States. The American Homestead Act offered free land to settlers if they promised to live on the land, build a home, make improvements and farm for five years. In fact, there were plenty of single women with or without kids who got their own land. It wasn't all *Little House on the Prairie*.

21 January 1862
Božena Němcová dies

Czech writer, born in 1820. Her novel *The Grandmother* (*Babička*) is considered an iconic work in Czech literature and is required reading in schools. A mother of four, she lived a life of poverty and died of exhaustion the day after *Babička* was published. Her image features on the 500 Czech koruna banknote.

22 January 1925
Fanny Bullock Workman dies
American geographer, cartographer, explorer and one of the first female professional mountaineers, Workman was born in 1859. She wrote about her adventures, using them to champion women's rights and women's suffrage. She was passionate about accurate measuring of climbing feats and an expert on climbing at altitude. She was among the first women to be admitted as a member to the Royal Geographical Society in London, although the admission of women was then revoked until 1913.

23 January 1918
Gertrude B. Elion born
American biochemist and pharmacologist, who shared the 1988 Nobel Prize in Physiology or Medicine. Her work led to the creation of the AIDS drug AZT. She also developed the first immunosuppressive drug to fight rejection in organ transplants. Elion died in 1999.

24 January 1862
Edith Wharton born
American novelist, short story writer, playwright and designer. One of my favourites. She was born at a time when women were just expected to get married and nothing else, yet she became one of America's greatest writers, with over forty books to her credit. She was the first woman to be awarded the Pulitzer Prize for Fiction.

25 January 1812
William Shanks born
A rare boy, but worth a mention. British amateur mathematician, Bill was addicted to calculating π to as many places as he could.

He devoted his life to it. He would sit each morning calculating new digits and then spend the afternoons checking his work. He supported himself by running a boarding school and, as British boarding schools used to be places of confinement rather than education, he had plenty of time for his hobby. By 1873 he calculated π to 707 places. Unfortunately, the final 180 calculations of his workings-out were entirely wrong. Fortunately, he died not knowing this, nor that in 1958 a computer would manage his lifetime of calculation in a mere forty seconds.

 — 26 January 1788 —

Arrival of the First Fleet of British ships at Port Jackson, New South Wales, Australia
Let's head down under and celebrate, for 26 January is Australia Day. Hoorah!

Time for some Australian trivia:

- It's the world's largest inhabited island and the smallest continent, but the largest continent occupied by one nation.

- It's the only English-speaking country where voting is compulsory. Nevertheless voter turnout is 95 per cent – 5 per cent still can't be bothered.

- It is the place where, in 1856 in Tasmania, the secret ballot box, a prized symbol of democracy, was pioneered.

- It is the home of the world's largest cattle station which, at 24,000km², is about the same size as Israel.

Finding Australian women to talk about is easy. Narrowing it down is hard so let's just take a bite of the apple. Literally. A

Granny Smith in fact. Granny Smith was a real woman, **Maria Sherwood**, who was born in Peasmarsh in Sussex, England, sometime in 1799. She was the daughter of a farm labourer and went into the farm labouring business herself. The apple doesn't fall far from the tree (I don't know how long I can do apple-related remarks) but, anyway, not surprisingly she married a farm labourer. He was called Thomas Smith. They were both illiterate and seem to have known nothing about birth control because over the next couple of decades they had eight kids.

Who knows what put it in their heads but, rather unexpectedly, in 1838 they emigrated to New South Wales under a government scheme to encourage settlers. They got a place in a fruit-growing district called Kissing Point where hardly anyone else wanted to live, partly perhaps because it was known at the time as the Dark Country. Thomas bought some land in a place called Eastwood and they set about growing fruit, while Maria made extra money selling homemade fruit pies in the local market.

Leap forward thirty years and you find Maria using a box of French crab apples to make her pies. She throws the leftover peels and seeds on to a compost heap and forgets about them. Then a few months later she notices a fledgling tree growing from the compost. She decides to look after it and it grows up to bear apples. Wonderful apples. Granny Smith apples. Maybe the discovery was an accident, but many men have been remembered for less. It would be others who would profit from this fruit after Maria's death, but her legacy lives on in the Granny Smith Memorial Park, the southern part of the farm where she lived with Thomas.

There are other great women called Smith of whom Australia can be proud. Women like **Fanny Cochrane Smith**, who was an Aboriginal linguist. She was born in December 1834 on Flinders

Island in Tasmania. The island used to have its own language and it is thought she may have been the last fluent speaker. She devoted her life to preserving Aboriginal heritage. In her final years she made wax cylinder recordings of Tasmanian Aboriginal songs and speech, which in 2017 were inducted into the UNESCO Australian Memory of the World Register as the only audio recordings of any of Tasmania's indigenous languages.

There are so many other women I want to write about. The great **Louise Mack** (*see* 10 October) who, in 1914, became the first female war correspondent reporting from the front line for the English papers. **Catherine Helen Spence** who, in 1897, became Australia's first female political candidate after standing (unsuccessfully) for the Federal Convention held in Adelaide. **Henrietta Dugdale** who, in May 1884, initiated the first female suffrage society in Australia. And on and on but, fascinated as I am by each and every one of them, I am a little shallow when it comes to Australia. I've been and what I loved most, apart from the wine and the people, was the beaches.

You cannot celebrate Australia without wondering if the surf is up or thinking about swimming. In that regard there are several women who leap from the waves of history. First off, a pair of female friends who, in the early 20th century, rewrote the book on women's swimming – **Mina Wylie** and **Fanny Durack**. Mina and Fanny loved to swim but in their youth females were banned from any competition where males were taking part. That meant any major sporting event like the Olympics was out of bounds. Here is where having the good fortune to have the right father so often plays a part. Mina's dad built the Wylie Baths in Coogee and the public began to see how brilliant the pair of them were. Then the Olympic Committee decided to allow women to swim in the 1912 Olympics in Stockholm. The New South Wales Ladies' Swimming Association didn't think it was a good idea, but the public objected and at last they were allowed to compete.

Durack won a gold medal and Wylie a silver. Wylie would go on to win 115 swimming titles, while from 1910 to 1918 Durack was acknowledged as the world's greatest female swimmer across all distances. They both did so wearing something shocking – a one-piece bathing suit made famous by another Australian water wonder, **Annette Kellermann**.

Annette, too, hailed from New South Wales, where she was born in 1887. Annette's story is one of triumph. She was born with legs so weak that she needed steel braces to walk. Her parents enrolled her in swimming classes at a tidal pool in North Sydney, which did the trick. By the time she was thirteen she could walk normally, and by fifteen she had won her first race. She began giving diving exhibitions, for a while did two shows a day swimming with fish in a glass tank at the Exhibition Aquarium and, my favourite thing of all, performed a mermaid act at Princes Court entertainment centre, which frankly there is not enough of in life.

At the turn of the 20th century women in the water were expected to wear a rather awkward dress and pantaloon combination which cramped anyone's style. Annette became famous and controversially began advocating for the right of women to wear a one-piece bathing suit. She went to America and became a movie star in a series of aquatic-themed adventures in which she did her own stunts, including diving sixty feet into a pool of crocodiles. She was the first movie star to appear nude in a Hollywood picture and, in 1907, she gave the first performance of a water ballet in a glass tank at the New York Hippodrome, which would go on to popularise synchronised swimming.

Despite her fame she was arrested on Revere Beach, Massachusetts, charged with indecency for wearing a one-piece swimsuit. Later in life she owned a health food store in Long Beach, California, advocating vegetarianism and exercise. She died in 1975 knowing that in her youth a Harvard University study of 3,000 women had named her the 'Perfect Woman' because she looked most like the Venus de Milo.

So here is the way to celebrate Australia Day: plan a trip. I'm going to go to Eastwood in New South Wales in October and attend the annual Granny Smith Festival. Then, when I have had enough apple fun, I'm heading for the beach. There are loads of fabulous places. I'm just a tourist but I'll sit there and think about an Aboriginal saying I once heard: 'We are all visitors to this time, this place. We are just passing through. Our purpose here is to observe, to learn, to grow, to love … and then we return home.'

27 January 1836
Begum Samru dies

Born around 1753, Samru began life as a nautch, an Indian dancing girl. She became ruler of Sardhana in Uttar Pradesh. She was just four foot eight but she led a professionally trained mercenary army of 3,000 including at least 100 European mercenaries. Said to be a brilliant leader, she wore a turban, smoked a hookah and called herself Joanna, after Joan of Arc. When she died she left a fortune equivalent to an almost unimaginable 40 billion dollars in today's currency.

28 January 1881
Hetty Reckless dies

Reckless, born in 1776, was a runaway slave who campaigned against slavery and was part of the Underground Railroad, operating a safe house in Philadelphia. She ran a women's shelter aiming to free women from sexual exploitation, and taught prostitutes skills that might gain them employment. She lived to be 105 and deserves an entire book to herself.

29 January 1902
Lyubov Orlova born

First recognised star of Soviet cinema, theatre actress and singer. She starred in *Volga-Volga*, which was Joseph Stalin's favourite film. She was a superstar and, in 1950, she was proclaimed a People's Artist of the USSR. Her somewhat bizarre 1936 film *Circus* is available on YouTube with subtitles.

30 January 1961
Maud Wagner dies

Born in 1877, Wagner was the first known female tattoo artist in the US. Before that she was a circus aerialist and contortionist. In 1904 she met Gus Wagner, a tattoo artist, at the World's Fair in St Louis and exchanged her first tattoo lessons from him for a date. Eventually they married. They were among the last tattooists to work by hand using the 'stick-and-poke' method and not machine.

31 January 1889
Ella C. Deloria born

Deloria was also known as Aŋpétu Wašté Wiŋ, which translates as Beautiful Day Woman. Anthropologist, ethnographer, linguist and novelist, who recorded Native American oral history and legends and contributed to the study of Native American languages. Ella was born on the Yankton Sioux Reservation as part of a traditional Dakota Sioux family who spoke both the Dakota and Lakota dialects of the Sioux language. Her work focused on kinship, tribal structure and the role of women. The Ella C. Deloria Project at the University of South Dakota continues to preserve the culture of the Dakota people.

FEBRUARY

'There is always in February some one day, at least, when one smells the yet distant, but surely coming, summer.'

– **Gertrude Jekyll**, British horticulturist, born 1843

Cabbage Month

Okay, it's not compulsory to call February 'cabbage month', but it's possibly a more interesting name than the one we usually use. Before the Romans grabbed hold of the month-naming business, the Anglo-Saxons (Germanic people who popped over to the British Isles in the 5th and 6th centuries) used to call this time of year either *Kale-monath* ('cabbage month') or *Solmonath*, which is a less appetising name meaning 'mud month'. I don't know enough about kale to be familiar with when it wants to start growing but I am going to guess it was February.

If you're not taken with the idea of cabbage and kale, there are plenty of other names you could use for this time of year:

February fill-dyke: Old English country phrase for this month. It relates to the rivers overflowing and dykes brimming with water. I'm going to use it whenever possible.

Hornung: Those Germanic folk again – they also called this season *Hornung*, which means bastard. Which is weird until you remember that a 'bastard' traditionally gets less inheritance than any legitimate siblings, and February gets fewer days of the year than any other month so …

Helmikuu: A Finnish word meaning 'month of the pearl'. This is lovely. When snow melts on tree branches you get droplets that freeze again and look like pearls of ice.

Luty or лютий ('lyutiy'): The Polish and Ukrainian month of ice.

Sechko (сечко): Macedonian, meaning 'month of cutting' (wood not remarks).

As February follows January, which is named after a Roman god, it would be reasonable to suppose that this month's name is also a tribute to some deity, in this case the Roman god Februus. But, in fact, February is named after a festival of purification called *Februa* or *Februatio*, which was held on the 15th of the month. This was the last month in the Roman calendar before a new year, so to mark it they had a three-day shindig during which people were ritually washed. Februus the god is in charge of purification but he seems to have been named for the festival and not the festival for him.

Whatever you call it, the good news is that this seems to be an excellent month for eating. In the US, where people love a holiday celebration that no one else has thought of, this month includes Ice Cream for Breakfast Day (the first Saturday in February), National Frozen Yogurt Day (the 6th) and Open That Bottle Night (29th), when you make sure wine isn't just stored but actually drunk.

PANCAKES!

February is also the time, in Europe at least, for pancakes. The oldest known natural human mummy is of a man called Ötzi the Iceman, who was discovered in 1991 in the Ötztal Alps on the border between Austria and Italy. He lived nearly five and a half thousand years ago and, because the poor fellow has been relentlessly examined, measured and x-rayed, I can tell you that his last meal included some kind of Neolithic bacon and something very close to pancakes. Bacon and pancakes! What's not to love?

No one knows for sure but it's possible the Stone Age people 30,000 years ago were greasing up a rock, heating it and frying these delicious pieces of batter. Ancient Greek poets Cratinus and Magnes wrote about pancakes, and Shakespeare mentions them in both *All's Well That Ends Well* and *As You Like It*.

For more than a thousand years the traditional day to eat pancakes has been Shrove Tuesday which, in 2021, falls on the 16th of February. Shrove is the past tense of the old verb 'to shrive', meaning to confess, be assigned penance and be absolved of one's sins. The whole thing is supposed to have some religious significance but really it was a cooking wheeze to use up leftover fatty and rich foods before Lent began the following day, Ash Wednesday.

Other names for pancake-like foodstuff

Indian cakes, Welsh crampog, hoe cakes, Irish boxty, johnny-cakes, Indian poori, Hungarian *palacsinta*, journey cakes, Russian blini, buckwheat cakes, crepes, griddle cakes, flapjacks, potato latkes and Dutch *pannenkoeken*.

The Olney Pancake Race

The oldest pancake race in the world takes place in Olney in Buckinghamshire in England. The women of the town have been running an annual pancake race since the 15th century. Dressed as 'traditional' housewives (by which I think they mean headscarves and aprons), and holding pancakes in cast-iron pans, twenty-five women (no men allowed) run 415 yards from the marketplace to the parish church. The legend is that it all began in 1445 when one woman was late for church and ran out of the house still carrying her pan and pancake. We'll never know. I do know that entrants have to have lived in the town for at least three months and be over eighteen, so if you're not local and want to take part then you need to move there in plenty of time.

If you can't get to England then the town of Liberal in Kansas, USA, holds the exact same race on the same day. That's been going since 1950 although the difference in approaches says something about the two cultures. The Brits have the longest history but the Americans have supersized theirs. They've turned their event into a four-day festival with all manner of contests and, of course, a parade.

Largest pancake ever made

Rochdale, UK, in 1994: 15.01m (49ft 3in) in diameter, 2.5cm (1in) thick, weighing 3 tonnes (6,614lb).

POEM OF THE MONTH

Snow Flakes by Emily Dickinson

I counted till they danced so
Their slippers leaped the town –
And then I took a pencil
To note the rebels down –
And then they grew so jolly
I did resign the prig –
And ten of my once stately toes
Are marshalled for a jig!

This seemed an appropriate poem for the month but it's not my favourite of Emily's work. 'Snow Flakes' is rather jolly and I think I prefer the more introspective work. Emily was born in one of my favourite towns, Amherst, Massachusetts. It's a quiet New England place with a wonderful bookshop and a large green where you can sit and read. Emily was prolific, writing almost 1,800 poems, but she never sought fame. In fact, she only saw ten of her pieces published in her lifetime.

She became quite reclusive in her later years and sat writing in her bedroom. I've been and stood in that room. I like the fact that she used to lower a basket with sweets in it for the local children who called up to her. Her style is unique, often short and sharp but full. My favourite begins, 'I am Nobody! Who are you?' It's about the pointlessness of fame, which would have been an odd choice for this book, I guess, as I am trying to bring all these women to the fore.

1 February
St Brigid's Day

The month begins with the feast day of Brigid of Kildare who Wikipedia describes as 'Virgin, abbess, inspirer', and who among us doesn't wish for a similar report of our lives? I'd like to tell you she was born about 451 in Ireland and died about 525, still in Ireland, but it's hard to say whether an abbess depicted with a shepherd's staff and flames over her head was a real person. Real or not, she's one of Ireland's patron saints and the only girl, which is maybe why she got a list of responsibilities which requires serious multi-tasking.

She's saint of 'County Kildare; babies; blacksmiths; boatmen; brewers; cattle; chicken farmers; children whose parents are not married; children with abusive fathers; children born into abusive unions; Clan Douglas; dairymaids; dairy workers; Florida; fugitives; infants; Ireland; Leinster; Mac Brádaigh family; mariners; midwives; milkmaids; nuns; poets; poor; poultry farmers; poultry raisers; printing presses; sailors; scholars; travellers and watermen'.

Her feast day used to be a pagan festival called *Imbolc*, which I like. It meant 'in the belly', which seems a great way to mark the beginning of spring, of new growth. My real interest in her lies in a story of a curious female friendship.

Another feast day on the same day celebrates the saint **Dar Lugdach**, which is nice because she was Brigid's best friend. I know even less about her except that she succeeded Brigid as abbess of Kildare, also made it to sainthood and is recorded to have died exactly one year after her pal, which I think is carrying friendship too far.

Here's what I know. There was a monk called Ultan who was a hermit for a while so he had time to write a biog of Brigid or Brigit. In it he explained that Dar Lugdach and Brigid were close. So close that they shared a bed but Dar had fallen in love with a young man. Mindful that this would not get her that sainthood, Dar decided to put a stop to it. On a night when she was supposed to have met her beau, she got out of bed and did the obvious thing to stem the tide of love. She put burning embers from the fire into her shoes and put them on.

Then she went back to bed. Whether she was still wearing the shoes I am not sure. Ultan was not a stickler for detail. Brigid was no fool. She knew what was happening but just pretended to be asleep. The next day Dar confessed. I wouldn't have thought she needed to – I mean, the smell of singed flesh, the ruined shoes …

Brigid said it was fine. That Dar was now safe from 'the fire of passion' in this life and fiery hell later on, and then she did what any friend who had the power ought to do, she healed her feet. It's a nice story but I think a therapist would have a field day.

1 February 1966
Hedda Hopper dies

Hopper, born in 1885, was an American actress and gossip columnist. At the height of her fame in the 1940s, she was read by 35 million people and feared by Hollywood. She had a syndicated column in the *Los Angeles Times* from 1938 until her death. She could ruin careers and called herself 'the bitch of the world'. Her real name was Elda Furry. She married actor DeWolf Hopper and changed her name to Hedda, apparently because he had had previous wives called Helen, Ida, Edna and

Nella and got confused. He and Hedda eventually divorced. She
kept the name and he married a woman called Lillian.

2 February
Groundhog Day
The date on which, by American tradition, the groundhog
emerges from hibernation. If she sees her shadow, she returns
to her burrow for six more weeks of winter. If she doesn't see
her shadow, spring is on its way. Thanks to the 1993 film star-
ring Bill Murray, Groundhog Day has become an expression
referring to the unwelcome repetition of a series of tedious
events that occur in exactly the same way each time.

2 February
Groundhog Day
The date on which, by American tradition, the groundhog
emerges from hibernation. If she sees her shadow, she returns
to her burrow for six more weeks of winter. If she doesn't see
her shadow, spring is on its way. Thanks to the 1993 film star-
ring Bill Murray, Groundhog Day has become an expression
referring to the unwelcome repetition of a series of tedious
events that occur in exactly the same way each time.

3 February 1995
Eileen Collins becomes the first woman to pilot and command
the Space Shuttle
Collins, born in 1956, is a US Air Force colonel, former military instructor and test pilot. She decided to be an astronaut
when she was about nine but didn't tell anyone in case they said
she couldn't do it. She joined the USAF as one of the first four
women out of 450 pilots to be allowed to train. Colonel Collins
has logged 38 days 8 hours and 20 minutes in outer space.

— *First week of February* —

National Girls and Women in Sports Day (US)

Founded in 1987 in memory of Olympic volleyball player **Flo Hyman** and her work on behalf of female equality in sport Women's exclusion from sport has a long history. The first Olympics were held in 776 BC in ancient Greece. Women weren't allowed to take part and married women weren't even allowed to watch. Indeed, the Greeks were so anxious that no married woman should attend that all male trainers and the athletes had to take all their clothes off before entering the stadium to prove their masculinity. For some reason the Greeks made an exception with horse and chariot racing and girls were allowed to enter as owners of horses. They were not supposed to actually race but then no one had reckoned with a Spartan princess named **Kyniska** (born *c*.440 BC). She seems to have been dared to enter and she won the four-horse chariot race in 396 BC and again in 392 BC. In the sanctuary of Olympia, an inscription was written declaring Kyniska the only female to win the wreath in the chariot events at the Olympic Games. She was, however, not allowed to collect her prize in person.

Even more than 2,000 years later, having just one day where women and girls could strut about in ill-fitting sportswear seemed impossible back in the early 1920s. The International Olympic Committee had refused to include women's events in the forthcoming 1924 Olympic Games. Pierre de Coubertin, founder of the modern Olympics, said that the inclusion of women would be 'impractical, uninteresting, unaesthetic, and incorrect'. Up until then women had only been allowed to pop in for a tiny bit of archery or croquet. It was for their own good. In 1874 Dr Edward Clarke had written down his concerns about the newfangled desire for women to seek improvement of themselves in his book *Sex in Education; or, A Fair Chance for Girls*. He stated categorically that 'both muscular and brain labor must be reduced at the onset of menstruation'. So true. Once a month when I was young I could hardly hold a pen.

So in the summer of 1922, the women athletes decided to go it alone and they gathered at the Pershing Stadium in Paris to celebrate their skills in the first track and field competitions for women. The games were organised by the Fédération Sportive Féminine Internationale and included seventy-seven participants from five nations – Czechoslovakia, France, Great Britain, Switzerland and the USA – taking part in eleven events. In front of 20,000 spectators, they kicked off with an Olympic-style ceremony and then got to work proving their worth by setting eighteen world records in a single day.

Personally I've never been sporty. For myself I can't see the point of it. I'm not tribal. I don't like to pick teams so for me it's just that somebody wins, somebody loses, everyone's armpits honk. Having said that, though, I can see what an extraordinary battleground for equality the sporting field has been. There are so many women who have not only had physical prowess but the determination to be allowed to show it. None more so than the French rower **Alice Milliat**. She was the driving force behind that sporting day in Paris.

Alice had form for this kind of endeavour. In 1920 she assembled a soccer team of Parisian women which toured the UK and played the celebrated Dick, Kerr's Ladies Football Club in the world's first internationally recognised women's football tournament. Anyway, Alice Milliat's alternative Olympic event had the right effect. It pushed the boys along and she did finally get her way with women gradually being allowed to hop, skip and jump more although, to this day, the Olympics does not offer an equal slate of men's and women's sports.

In the world of shooting it was, for example, hard to beat the Chinese woman with a gun, **Zhang Shan**, born 1968. The Olympic Skeet Shooting event used to be mixed, open to both men and women. In the 1992 Summer Olympics in Barcelona, Zhang won the gold medal. After that the International Shooting Union barred women from shooting against men, and Zhang retired.

There are sports that are seen as traditionally male, like fishing and, to some extent, golf. Yet it was a woman, **Dame Juliana Berners**, who, in about 1450, wrote the first book on angling, *A treatyse of fysshynge wyth an Angle*. In which she proved she couldn't spell but she could describe how to make a rod and flies, tell you when to fish, and how many different kinds of fishing there were.

Mary, Queen of Scots, born 1542, was a keen golfer who came up with the splendid idea that someone else ought to carry the heavy bag when she invented the 'caddy' for the game. Scotland sees itself as the home of golf and in the town of St Andrews you can find the club, the Royal and Ancient, which sets golf's rules. How ironic that Mary, the queen of Scotland, would not have been allowed to be a member as women were not permitted until 2014. A decade before that milestone Prince Andrew had been captain of the R & A. He got the job because he is second son to the queen, so he was captain of a club that the queen herself would not have been allowed to join.

Every sport has marvellous women worth reading about. The 'Cockney Championess', **Elizabeth Wilkinson**, beat **Martha Jones** in the first ever female boxing match in 1722. **Hessie Donahue** used to make people laugh by pretending to fight legendary heavyweight champion John L. Sullivan. One night in 1892 when he accidentally hit her during the act she knocked him out. Sullivan was out cold for over a minute.

I long to have seen **Maria Speltarini** who, in the 1870s, crossed Niagara Falls on a tightrope with peach baskets on her feet. I have no idea why she chose peach baskets. There is a marvellous black and white picture of her doing it, which defies any sense but good on her for thinking of it. How I should like to have applauded **Vera Komarkova** and **Irene Miller** who, in 1978, became the first women and the first Americans to reach the top of Annapurna, one of the world's most dangerous mountains. They raised the money for the trip by selling T-shirts with the slogan: 'A Woman's Place Is On Top'. And who wouldn't have wanted to cheer on **Althea Gibson** who, in 1950, became the first African American to play in the US Open tennis competition. She was the first black person of either sex to win at Wimbledon.

These amazing females got to some of the boys. In the world of baseball it was hard to find a better pitcher than **'Jackie' Mitchell**, born in 1912. She joined a side called the Chattanooga Lookouts in 1931 as the only woman on a professional men's team. When the Lookouts played an exhibition match against the world-famous New York Yankees, Jackie struck out their two most famous players – Babe Ruth and Lou Gehrig. The commissioner of baseball, Kenesaw Mountain Landis, heard about it and was furious. He banned women from baseball because it was 'too strenuous' for them. They continued to be banned from 1931 to 1992.

Some female sporting achievements have been crazy. In 1901 **Annie Taylor** became the first person to go over Niagara Falls in a barrel and live. She was sixty-three and couldn't swim. When she was taken out of the barrel after her fall she said, 'Nobody ever ought to do that again.' My favourite ever mad Olympic athlete was an American swimmer called **Eleanor G. Holm**. She was due to be in the 1936 Berlin Olympics but got chucked out for what these days I suppose is called doping, except that her drug use was spectacular. Obviously drug-taking is bad but you have to admire that her drug of choice was champagne. She was apparently on her way to the Olympics on board the SS *Manhattan* and popped to a cocktail party. There are those who say the team doctor found her in a state approaching a coma. Years later she defended herself: 'This chaperone came up to me and told me it was time to go to bed. God, it was about 9 o'clock, and who wanted to go down in that basement to sleep anyway? So I said to her: "Oh, is it really bedtime? Did you make the Olympic team or did I?" I had had a few glasses of Champagne. So she went and complained that I was setting a bad example for the team, and they got together and told me the next morning that I was fired. I was heartbroken.'

You don't need to worry about Eleanor. She went on to become quite the celebrity socialite and interior designer, even appearing in a couple of movies. She also married well and lived to be ninety still enjoying a drink.

Are things better today? In May 2020 the US women's soccer team lost their court case for equal pay. There is work to do. Almost a hundred years since she made a stand, Alice Milliat would be appalled to know how little progress has been made.

4 February 1921
Betty Friedan born (she also died on this date in 2006 which is a rubbish birthday)
Friedan was an American author, feminist and co-founder of the National Organization for Women (NOW). Her book *The*

Feminine Mystique, published in 1963, is often credited with sparking the second wave of American feminism in the 20th century. She began writing it after a class reunion in the late 1950s of old female college pals showed her how unhappy most of her friends were as suburban housewives.

4 February 1703
Wife of Onodera Junai commits *seppuku*
This is a complex story which needs some cultural context. Ritual suicide (which we Westerners sometimes call *hara-kiri* but which is, more properly, *seppuku*) has a long history in Japan. It was about honour and it was also about class. Only members of the samurai class were allowed to commit *seppuku*. It was important, so young boys were taught early on how they might disembowel themselves with a knife should the need arise. Japanese noblewomen too were taught how to perform this act at a very young age in case they married a man who committed *seppuku* or who brought dishonour to himself, as his dishonour meant her own. Women needed to choose their husbands well because it was his behaviour, not hers, that was critical.

So here is the story, which took place at the turn of the 18th century. In 1702 Lord Asano Naganori of Ako was pro-voked by a court official called Kira Yoshinaka. So provoked that he drew his sword in the shōgun's palace. This was a terrible thing, for which he was forced to take his own life by perform-ing *seppuku*. Lord Asano was the *daimyō* (feudal lord) of a group of forty-seven samurai. Samurai who are left leaderless are called *rōnin* and these men were now all without a boss. They decided to wait a year and then kill Kira to avenge their master's death.

At the end of the year the men finally attacked Kira, killed sixteen of his men and wounded twenty-two. They chopped Kira's head off and took it to place on Asano's grave. The group sent one of their number, Terasaka Kichiemon, to say what they had done. Having committed murder the remaining *rōnin* now had to commit *seppuku* themselves, and they did so on 4 February 1703. Except that one of them, Onodera Junai, did not. He returned alive, and was eventually pardoned by the shōgun (some say on account of his youth). Which meant his wife had to commit *seppuku* instead for the sake of the family's honour.

It's a long complicated story which to the outsider seems, well ... not a great story for women ... or anyone. It is worth seeking out more details on this tale, which includes far more deaths than I have space to include here. The British Museum has the most wonderful woodblock print of Mrs Onodera Junai seated, hiding a knife inside her sleeve.

5 February 1848
Belle Starr, aka Bandit Queen, born

Notorious American outlaw born Myra Maybelle Shirley. Associated with the James–Younger Gang, she used to ride side-saddle dressed in black velvet wearing a plumed hat. She spent time in prison for stealing horses. Died of gunshot wounds just before her forty-first birthday. No one was ever charged with her murder.

5 February 1908
Daisy and Violet Hilton born
'I'm not a machine; I'm a woman. I should have the right to live like one.' (Daisy Hilton)

There's a place in North Carolina called Charlotte. Make a cursory check of its history and you can read how the indigenous Catawba Native Americans were wiped out by smallpox brought in by Europeans. You can discover that it was named for Queen Charlotte of Britain (who, like so many British royals, was actually German) and how this city was the origin of America's first gold rush when a seventeen-pound rock used for years as a doorstep turned out to be almost solid gold. What you won't find, but should, is any mention of Daisy and Violet Hilton, who are buried in the Forest Lawn Cemetery in the town. Daisy and Violet were born on this day in Brighton, England. They arrived joined at the hip as conjoined twins and the medical men predicted a short life. Their mother was an unmarried barmaid called Kate Skinner and perhaps she couldn't cope for she sold them to her boss, a pub landlady called Mary Hilton. Mary saw money in the girls. She taught them to sing, dance and play instruments so that she could put them in music hall.

By the time they were only three she took them on tour through Britain, and later exhibited them in freak sideshows in Europe and America. They were talented and a huge success on the 1920s vaudeville circuit, appearing alongside such familiar names as Charlie Chaplin and Bob Hope. Mary died and her daughter Edith Meyers took control of the girls' lives. She seems to have been mean, even abusive, and the girls kept making money for Edith, but not for themselves. It wasn't until 1931, when they were twenty-three, that Daisy and Violet were freed by becoming legally emancipated from the Meyers family.

They carried on working but it was tough. Violet fell in love with a musician but twenty-one different US states rejected their marriage application for being 'immoral and indecent'. They both 'married' gay men for publicity and starred in two movies – one a loose biographical picture called *Chained for Life* and one with the horrible title *Freaks*. Vaudeville died and so did their work. In 1961 they went on the road for the last time in a tour of drive-in movie theatres. It was after their final show in Charlotte, North Carolina, that their tour manager abandoned them. They were destitute and delighted when Charles Reid, the owner of the local Park-N-Shop grocery store on Wilkinson Blvd, offered them a job. For the next eight years they saw out their days packing groceries and working the till. In 1969 they died of the Hong Kong flu, Daisy first and Violet two or three days later. They had no money so they share their gravesite with Troy Thompson, a young man who died in Vietnam. In 2010 a public bus in Brighton was named in their honour.

So much more interesting than certain other sisters called Hilton.

6 February 1694
Dandara commits suicide

Dandara was an Afro-Brazilian warrior, one of the leaders in Quilombo dos Palmares, a fugitive community of several thousand escaped slaves in colonial Brazil. She fought many battles to defend Palmares. She and her husband Zumbi dos Palmares, the last king of the Quilombo dos Palmares, had three children. When captured, she chose suicide over a return to slavery.

7 February 1970
Tawakkul Karmān born

Yemeni women's rights activist who received the Nobel Peace Prize in 2011 for her role in leading a pro-democracy protest movement as part of the Arab Spring. Shared prize with **Ellen Johnson Sirleaf** (*see* 16 January) and **Leymah Gbowee**, also recognised for leading non-violent campaigns for women's rights and democratic freedoms.

8 February 1876
Paula Modersohn-Becker born
German painter. One of the most important representatives of early expressionism. First known female artist to paint nude self-portraits. She also painted herself pregnant. Her bold portraits of women and children in particular are splendid and avoided the depictions of idealised femininity which were traditional at the time. I love *Old Peasant Woman*, painted in 1905. Paula died, aged thirty-one, from postpartum embolism just twenty days after the birth of a daughter.

9 February 1979
Zhang Ziyi born
Chinese actress internationally famous for her performance in the martial arts drama *Wò hǔ cáng lóng* (*Crouching Tiger, Hidden Dragon*) and *Memoirs of a Geisha*. For her performance in *The Grandmaster* she won twelve different Best Actress awards, making her the most awarded Chinese actress for a single film.

10 February 1891
Sofya Kovalevskaya dies
(Name in Russian: Софья Васильевна Ковалевская) Born in 1850, Kovalevskaya became a Russian mathematics pioneer for women. She was the first woman to get a maths doctorate, first to be appointed to a full professorship in northern Europe and one of the first to work for a scientific journal as an editor. Sofya was not allowed to attend higher education in Russia. In order to study abroad she needed the permission of her father or husband, so she made an arranged marriage and left to study in Germany.

10 February 1592
Catalina de Erauso, the Lieutenant Nun, born

Catalina was born in San Sebastián, Spain – possibly not on this date, records are unclear. Her dad was in the army. I have no idea about her mum but when Catalina was four she was taken with her sisters to live in her mother's cousin's convent.

The youngster did not take to the cloistered life. She got in constant trouble for fighting and, that thing I've had trouble with, not being pious enough. Eventually she did the only sensible thing – she ran away, cut her hair and disguised herself as a boy. Apparently she claimed to have 'dried her breasts' with a secret ointment. Heaven knows what that might be.

The rest of the tale is a marvellous fugitive adventure. Catalina got a mule driver to take her to Valladolid, where for a while she worked as a male page in the court of King Philip III under the name Francisco de Loyola. Then her dad came looking for her, so she hit the road again. It's a long fascinating story. She got arrested, got another job for a posh bloke, etc. Eventually she went home, saw her relatives and even went to mass at the convent without anyone recognising her. The next logical step was to become a cabin boy and go to the Americas where she fought and defeated pirates.

She worked in Panama, was the only crew member to survive a shipwreck, took part in a duel, nearly had to marry a woman just to maintain her disguise, spent some more time in jail before working as a llama driver and then serving as a soldier. She fought in the Arauco War in Chile, becoming a second lieutenant and at one point taking command to win a battle.

I can't say Catalina was very nice. She killed people she shouldn't have, wasn't above being a vandal and took part in mass killings of the Indians in Chuncos. She kept getting away with murder until she finally revealed to a bishop in Peru that she was a woman and was sent back to Spain. There she petitioned the Spanish Crown to pay her for her services as a soldier. She died running a mule business. We don't really know how. She wrote an autobiography which in English is called *The Nun Ensign*, which you can download for £2.35. Seems cheap for such a life.

11 February 1925
Virginia E. Johnson born

American sex researcher and therapist. She is famous as one half of the Masters and Johnson Institute, which conducted pioneering research on human sexuality. From 1957 until the 1990s, she and William H. Masters diagnosed and treated sexual dysfunctions and disorders and led the way in examining the nature of human sexual response. Her first career was as a country singer called Virginia Gibson. Her first marriage lasted two days. Her subsequent marriage to Masters seems to have been more of a research project than a love match.

12 February 1915
Dr Olivia Hooker born

Sailor, psychologist and Fordham University professor. First African American woman to enter the US Coast Guard, in February 1945. She helped found the American Psychological Association's Division 33, dealing with people with developmental and intellectual disabilities. One of the last known survivors of the infamous 1921 Tulsa race massacre carried out

by the Ku Klux Klan in Oklahoma, which left hundreds dead
and thousands homeless. She was one of the plaintiffs in a
federal lawsuit filed against the state of Oklahoma and the city
of Tulsa in 2003 seeking compensation due to the local government's involvement in the massacre. The US Supreme Court
dismissed the case without comment.

 — 13 February —

International Condom Day
February is a traditional time of fertility rites, so it makes sense
that it is the month that contains International Condom Day.

During the 2020 lockdown I think we all read and watched
more news than usual. Well, you had to fill the days and it meant
I often came across matters that hadn't occurred to me might
be of interest. In my daily paper I read that one effect of self-
isolation was that the bottom has fallen out of the condom
market which is ... well, I don't know ... certainly an odd sentence. I'll be honest, condoms don't play much part in my life and
no algorithm in the world might have guessed I'd be interested
and, to be fair, until I read about the current state of the market,
I hadn't given them much thought but it makes sense. Social dis-
tancing is hell for the condom maker. Couldn't be worse.

The history of the condom is interesting. I don't want to go
into detail but if you have the time, do read about Lazzaro Spall-
anzani, whose studies of sperm in the 1760s involved dressing
frogs in tiny pairs of pants made from pig's bladder and taffeta.
Not surprisingly the frogs didn't take to it. Instead of trying to
mate they kept trying to get the pants off, which suggests frogs
have more sense than I gave them credit for.

Sex is a funny subject and I have been thinking about its

general impact on how women are viewed in history. In this *Almanac* I try to associate the people I talk about with particular dates in history, but I realise it leaves out so many fabulous women whose specific entry and departure from the world no one ever bothered to record. I have a long list of these women and I find, particularly when it comes to those from the ancient world who were sufficiently notable to be written about at all, somewhere, someone will have claimed they were a prostitute.

Take **Aspasia of Miletus**, who was born sometime around 470 BC, so about 2,500 years ago. Next to Sappho and Cleopatra she is the most celebrated woman of the ancient Mediterranean, yet much of what we know about her amounts simply to scandalous gossip. We know so little about ancient Greek women but Aspasia is a good starting point. Madeleine Henry, in her book *Prisoner of History*, says that, 'To ask questions about Aspasia's life is to ask questions about half of humanity.'

We know that Aspasia was born in the Ionian Greek city of Miletus. No one is certain how she first came to Athens. Her family must have had money because she was well educated. As a non-Athenian, the law prevented her from marrying a local citizen, which would have been the usual way for a woman to achieve status, yet Aspasia would go on to be admired throughout the city, establishing a school for girls and running a house that became a magnet for intellectual and political conversation. When you name her contemporaries who thought her amazing it's like a who's who of top old Greeks – the philosopher Socrates and his followers, Plato, Cicero, writers like Athenaeus, the historian Xenophon, and not forgetting the statesman and general Pericles, who fell for her in bed as well. Socrates is quoted as saying about her, 'Once made equal to man, woman becomes his superior.'

Sadly, we have nothing of her own written work. There is

only what is penned about her and every word was written by men, each of whom seems to have had a different axe to grind. There are those who said she was the one who penned the great speeches given by Pericles, including his famous funeral oration at the end of the first year of the Peloponnesian War upon which so many other great speeches have been modelled. That she taught Socrates the stratagems of argument, that everyone loved her quick wit and she was a stupendous teacher of rhetoric. Yet you cannot read a word about her without the descriptions 'prostitute' or 'courtesan' or, as the Greeks called it, a 'hetaera' appearing beside her name or the question being raised that her house was less of an intellectual salon and more of a brothel.

We'll never know. I can't find certainty in my books but I hate that it is gossip, the equivalent of tabloid journalism in history, which continues to dog Aspasia's reputation. Writing hundreds of years after her death, the Greek writer Plutarch couldn't quite give her fulsome praise. He declared that friends of Socrates did bring their wives to hear Aspasia talk but that this was in spite of her immoral life.

What I do know is that she and Pericles had a son but Pericles died of the plague. Aspasia went on to live with Lysicles, another Athenian general and leader. She had another son but he was executed after a battle. What happened to her? No one knows for certain. All that is clear is that everyone who writes about her declares her a rare woman in history, and that even the suggestion that she spoke out and did so brilliantly has to be tempered with what must have been her sexual allure.

There is a very interesting book which I have had for so long that the cover has faded on my shelf. It's called *The Alphabet Versus the Goddess* and it was written by Leonard Shlain. It proposes that perhaps the very writing down of things has affected how women are viewed. I don't agree with all of it, but it is interesting how the writing of history often includes the denigration of women like Aspasia because she can't possibly have been as amazing as her contemporaries claimed. Women who stand out from the ancient past have to have had skills in the bedroom as well. Courtesans and condoms rather than brains and banter.

Either that or they were witches like **Aglaonice**, a Greek astronomer of the 2nd or 1st century BC. She is written about as being a sorceress who could make the moon disappear from the sky. Most likely she'd just worked out when a lunar eclipse would occur. And don't start me on the fabulous women whose names make me long to hear their story but who history now dismisses as myths because they're too good to be true and we lack sufficient evidence. If it's not written down it can't be fact.

Think me mad but all this brings me to the fairies, Maria and Lolita, who live on one of my shelves. For my birthday last year my sister Jeni made me a 'fairy house' out of five old books. It has a door and two windows. Inside you can see tiny furniture illuminated by miniature lights. For reasons I can't recall, we decided two tiny Spanish seamstresses lived in there. They are clearly clever women as they've chosen to live inside a dictionary. Later Jeni gave me an outdoor table and some beer for them. I'm sure this is not a good sign. My worry is that they've turned the fairy house into a place of ill repute. I mean, I'd be appalled but not at all surprised. Oh dear, I do hope that's not how they are remembered. Is it too much to suggest they borrow some taffeta pants from the frogs?

14 February 1911
Emma Smith DeVoe founds the National Council of Women Voters

DeVoe, born 1848, was an American suffragist known as the 'Mother of Women's Suffrage'. Thanks to DeVoe's campaigning, women in Idaho received the right to vote in 1896, while it took until 1920 for women to be permitted to vote in all states of the United States.

15 February 1879
President Rutherford B. Hayes signs a new law admitting women as attorneys who could now submit and argue cases before the US Supreme Court

Belva Ann Lockwood, born 1830, was an American attorney, politician and author who, in 1884, ran for president before women could vote. She petitioned Congress to be allowed to practise before the US Supreme Court. In November 1876, Chief Justice Morrison Waite had replied to Lockwood's request to be admitted to the Supreme Court bar, saying, 'By the uniform practice of the Court from its organization to the present time, and by the fair construction of its rules, none but men are permitted to practice before it as attorneys and counselors ...' The Chief Justice added the court wouldn't change its mind unless 'required by statute'. On this date, the president finally signed that statute. The following year Lockwood became the first woman attorney to speak before the court in the case *Kaiser v. Stickney.*

16 February 1997
Chien-Shiung Wu dies

Chinese-born American physicist, born 1912. She made significant contributions to nuclear physics, and worked on the

Manhattan Project. Her male colleagues Tsung-Dao Lee and Chen-Ning Yang had a theory about parity but couldn't prove it. Wu proved it. I admit I don't understand it, but proving the theory was a fundamental discovery about how the world works. The men got the Nobel Prize in Physics in 1957 and she was left out. Surprise.

17 February 647
Queen Seondeok of Silla dies
The first Queen of Silla, one of the Three Kingdoms of Korea, born between 595 and 610. Described as 'generous, benevolent, wise, and smart'. Led a renaissance in thought, literature and the arts. Check out the incredible Cheomseongdae astronomical observatory in Gyeongju, South Korea, which she had built in 633.

18 February 1934
Audre Lorde born
American poet, essayist, passionate writer on lesbian feminism and racial issues. She was an early writer on the intersections of race, class and gender. She and fellow writer **Barbara Smith** founded Kitchen Table: Women of Color Press in 1981 to further the writings of black feminists.

19 February 1953
Cristina Fernández de Kirchner born
Argentine lawyer and politician who was the first female elected president of Argentina between 2007 and 2015. In July 2010 she signed legislation that made Argentina the first country in Latin America to allow same-sex marriage.

20 February 1778
Laura Maria Caterina Bassi dies
Italian physicist and academic, born 1711. In May 1732 she earned a doctoral degree in philosophy from the University of Bologna. The first woman to earn a professorship in physics at a university. The first woman in the world to be appointed a university chair in a scientific field of studies. Huge contributions to science.

21 February 1846
Sarah G. Bagley becomes America's first female telegrapher
On this day Sarah took charge at the newly opened New York and Boston Magnetic Telegraph Company office in Lowell, Massachusetts. This was cutting-edge technology, as Samuel Morse's first successful demonstration of the electric telegraph had happened only two years before. She was appalled to discover she was paid 75 per cent of the salary of a man in the same job. She was a significant labour activist, campaigning tirelessly for a ten-hour maximum day in factories. She helped found and became the first president of the Lowell Female Labor Reform Association. She also found time to be a writer.

22 February 1680
Catherine Montvoisin dies
French fortune-teller, sorceress and poisoner, born around 1640. Also known as La Voisin. Who doesn't want to read about her? Head of a network of fortune-tellers said to have murdered up to 2,500 people. Charged with witchcraft in the 'Affair of the Poisons'. Executed by burning.

23 February 1931
Dame Nellie Melba dies
World-famous Australian coloratura soprano, born 1861. Both Melba toast and peach Melba are named after her. She got married when she was twenty-one and lived in Queensland. She said her husband and the incessant rain on the tin roof caused her to quit marriage for showbiz, which is a marvellous reason. She had a brilliant career but she was not always easy. It is said she sometimes used to sing the same part from the wings if she wanted to undermine a singer she didn't like.

24 February 1948
Jayalalitha Jayaram born
Indian film actress and politician. Known as the 'Queen of Tamil Cinema', she starred in 140 films between 1964 and 1980. Elected to the Indian parliament in 1984, she served three terms as chief minister of Tamil Nadu. Her political career was controversial, and she was imprisoned for corruption in the 1990s.

25 February 1971
Nova Maree Peris OAM born
Indigenous Australian athlete and former politician. First Aboriginal Australian to win an Olympic gold medal. One of very few athletes to represent their country in two different sports at separate Olympics (hockey and track and field). In 2012, she became the first indigenous Australian elected to parliament.

26 February 1616
Galileo Galilei formally banned by Roman Catholic Church from teaching or defending view that the earth orbits the sun
Spare a thought for **Marina Gamba** of Venice, born around 1570, the mother of Galileo's three illegitimate children for

whom this cannot have been an easy day. Galileo put the two daughters in a convent (to avoid paying dowries) and kept the son. Clever guy but not Dad of the Year.

27 February 1939
Nadezhda Krupskaya dies
Born in 1869, Nadezhda was Soviet Deputy Minister of Education between 1929 and 1939. Married Vladimir Lenin in 1898 after spending time in exile together. She played a central role in the Bolshevik (later Communist) Party. She has a chocolate bar named after her.

28 February 1813
Pōmare IV born
Queen of Tahiti between 1827 and 1877, she was also known as 'Aimata', or 'eye-eater', because of an old tradition that the ruler would eat the eye of a defeated enemy. I doubt she did. She succeeded her brother at the age of thirteen and reigned for fifty years. Three of her kids became monarchs in their own right.

MARCH

'March was an unpredictable month, when it was never clear what might happen. Warm days raised hopes until ice and grey skies shut over the town again.'

– **Tracy Chevalier**, American author, born 1962

Length Month

Yes it's *Lenet-monath*, which is where we get the term 'Lent' from. It's Anglo-Saxon for 'length month', which works as soon the spring equinox will be at hand as the days grow longer and the sun higher.

It's spring! Hurrah! This is the time of year when I feel I ought to rush up into some hills like Julie Andrews in *The Sound of Music* and listen to babbling brooks while cavorting among the first spring flowers. At last we can begin to look forward to a mild evening where we might stroll to see a friend unencumbered by our winter coats. It is a time of renewal and fresh hope. Why, there'll be lambs and violets, nest-building and daisies and, hopefully, little rain. You know the old saying – 'A dry March never begs its bread.'

What?

It's to do with sowing and planting and I admit it may have lost a slight sense of relevance these days to some of us. The Slovenians seem to have understood the sentiment, though, as their traditional name for March is *sušec*, which means the month when the earth becomes dry enough to be cultivated (I'm summarising).

Climate caveat

All of these joys of spring and renewal work from my desk in London but not necessarily in Canada where it can still be freezing in March, or Lake Baikal in Russia where the average maximum temperature is about 0.5°C (32.9°F). Nevertheless, the Baikal folk seem an optimistic people, declaring, 'If you enjoy looking at a blue sky and like sunbathing then this month is a great period to visit Lake Baikal.' Sunbathing? 0.5°C.

March is ... Women's History Month

So, strictly speaking, I should have contained all the women in the entire *Almanac* into this one month but I had a fit of the vapours and just carried on writing.

But March had other names, right?

I suspect you are beginning to get the hang of this.

Finnish: *Maaliskuu*, meaning something like 'the land is at hand'. Maybe to do with the earth emerging from the winter snow.

Ukrainian: *Berezen* (or березень, if you prefer), meaning birch tree.

Anglo-Saxon: *Hyld-monath*, meaning 'loud or stormy month', which presumably is less good for planting. I feel I am getting the hang of the whole farming thing.

'A peck of March dust is worth a king's ransom!'

Yep, I'm on an agricultural roll.

The Saxons: Apart from *Lenet-monath* they also called this month *Rhed-monath* or *Hreth-monath* after the goddess Rheda.

HOLY RITUALS

Time for a goddess

In Anglo-Saxon paganism, Rheda (meaning 'the famous' or 'the victorious') was a goddess connected with this month. Don't worry about the name Hreth or Hretha. That's just everyone anglicising things when they fancied. It's basically the same goddess. That scribbling monk, the Venerable Bede, wrote about Hretha in his work *De temporum ratione* and said March is the time for all pagans to sacrifice to her. Writing a book is a hard labour and every writer takes short cuts so old VB doesn't say what sacrifice was appropriate or how or what would happen if you didn't do it, which is annoying.

Maybe Hretha was a bit like the Roman god of war Mars from whom we get March, the current fashionable name for this time of year. Hretha means 'victorious', which seems war related, but she was a girl so she lost out when it came to month names.

Time for a god

Mars was the ancient Roman god of war but also had some oversight of farming, which works well with everything else we know. Mars seems to have been a nice guy who liked the army to keep peace rather than make war. He was regarded as a father to the Roman people and I love the rituals dedicated to him because, despite being a humanist, I am mad for an energetic bit of worship. I'd much rather be there when the whirling dervishes of the Sufi do their meditation through energetic dance than listen to a Church of England priest give the parish notices. If you lived in Roman times then this month marked some fabulous holy rites led by the Salii, the leaping priests of Mars. Who doesn't want to see that?

King Numa Pompilius, born 753, was the second king of Rome. You remember, he was the one who brought in the month of January. He was said to be very wise but he must also have been a laugh because he gets the credit for the idea of the 'leaping priests' of Mars. Numa had the good fortune to have a shield fall from heaven in front of him, a shield so divine that anyone who had it could take charge of the earth. This is what every boy wants and he didn't want anyone to steal it, so Numa had eleven copies made which apparently was enough to befuddle anyone trying to pinch it. These shields were called the *ancilia* and they were kept in the Temple of Mars where they were looked after by the Salii.

The Salii consisted of twelve young men (obviously from 'good' families) who every March would dress up as old-fashioned warriors. Thousands of years ago that consisted of a *paludamentum* (military cloak or cape fastened at one shoulder) over an embroidered tunic, a breastplate, a sword, a kind of cap with a pointy bit of wood sticking out of it called an *apex* and, of course, the precious shields. From the first of March, and possibly for the next twenty-four days, the Salii made a procession around the city, dancing and singing something called the *Carmen Saliare*, a piece which may not have stood the test of time. Even the Roman poet Ovid thought it was outdated 2,000 years ago. Then it all ended with a bang-up feast. Twenty-four days! Bring on the leaping priests.

Holidays you might consider celebrating in March

Noche de Brujas (Night of the Witches), Catemaco, Mexico
Catemaco is Mexico's witchcraft capital. On the first Friday in March, a cavalcade of shamans, witches and healers gather to cleanse themselves of the previous year's negative energies.

Purim Street Party, Tel Aviv
Purim is celebrated annually on the fourteenth day of the Hebrew month of Adar (and on Adar II in Hebrew leap years,

which happen every two or three years). Let's just say, it's usually sometime in March. A holiday straight out of the Book of Esther – commemorating an unsuccessful plot to massacre the Jews of Persia. Celebrated around the world but quite the rave in Tel Aviv.

Holi, India and Nepal
Hindu festival of love that lasts for a night and a day, starting on the evening of the Purnima (full moon day) falling in the Hindu calendar month of Phalguna – which is roughly equivalent to the middle of March in the Gregorian calendar. Just look for the explosions of colour as street revellers cover themselves in coloured powders to mark the god Vishnu's defeat of the demoness Holika – the triumph of good over evil.

Las Fallas (The Fires), Valencia
Five-day festival, 15–19 March, celebrating St Joseph, patron saint of carpenters, dating from the Middle Ages. Craftsmen create *ninots* – larger-than-life papier-mâché puppets in a competition to make the best. At midnight on 19 March, all the *ninots* are set on fire except the winner which, since 1937, has gone in the Fallas Museum.

Starkbierzeit (Strong Beer Festival), Munich
Held on 13 March, this is like Oktoberfest but stronger.

St Patrick's Day, Ireland
On 17 March, find any Irish person anywhere and celebrate.

⤞ POEM OF THE MONTH ⤝

A Birthday by Christina Rossetti

My heart is like a singing bird
Whose nest is in a water'd shoot;
My heart is like an apple-tree
Whose boughs are bent with thickset fruit;
My heart is like a rainbow shell
That paddles in a halcyon sea;
My heart is gladder than all these
Because my love is come to me.

Raise me a dais of silk and down;
Hang it with vair and purple dyes;
Carve it in doves and pomegranates,
And peacocks with a hundred eyes;
Work it in gold and silver grapes,
In leaves and silver fleurs-de-lys;
Because the birthday of my life
Is come, my love is come to me.

Christina was born in London in 1830. There is a commemorative plaque to her at 30 Torrington Square in Bloomsbury, but in fact she was born in what is now Hallam Street near the BBC's Broadcasting House. Like many women of her time she was educated at home. Her dad was a poet and political exile from Abruzzo, Italy, and the house was filled with expat intellectuals. Her sister and one brother became writers, while the other boy in the family was Dante Gabriel, who became a significant artist and poet. It must have been quite a household. She achieved fame and popularity in her lifetime. I expect many have forgotten that she wrote the words to the Christmas carol 'In the Bleak Midwinter'.

1 March 1781
Javiera Carrera born
Known as the 'Mother of Chile', she was an important leader in the early struggle for independence during the period known as the Patria Vieja (Old Republic). Credited with sewing the first national Chilean flag. A symbol of a Chilean woman standing up to authority.

2 March 1949
Sarojini Naidu dies
Political activist, born 1879. Known as the 'Nightingale of India' for her poetry. Important in India's struggle for independence, the civil rights and women's emancipation movements. Jailed for her efforts. First woman governor in India. President of Indian National Congress in 1925. Spoke for universal suffrage to the British parliament in 1917.

3 March 1678
Madeleine de Verchères born
Known as the Canadian Joan of Arc, she was credited with repelling a raid by Iroquois on Fort Verchères in Quebec when she was fourteen years old. Her parents were away getting supplies and she had been left in charge with one old man and two soldiers. Among other things she fired cannons and muskets to make the noise of more soldiers and saved the fort. Her mother had commanded a similar defence two years earlier.

4 March 1815
Frances 'Fanny' Abington dies
Famous British actress, born 1737, also noted for her avant-garde fashion sense. Started as a flower girl. She was clever and witty but, as is so often the case, rumoured to have been a prostitute for a while. Sigh.

5 March 1897
Soong Mei-ling born
Also known as Madame Chiang Kai-shek. First Lady of China. She undertook several tours of the US to gain support during the Sino-Japanese War. Crowds of 30,000 heard her speak. In 1943 she became the first Chinese national to address both houses of the US Congress.

6 March 1937
Valentina Tereshkova born
Politician, engineer and former cosmonaut. The first and youngest woman to have flown in space. Embarked on a solo mission on the Vostok in June 1963, and is still the only woman to have been on a solo space mission. Current member of the national State Duma.

7 March 1938
Janet Guthrie born
'You can go back to antiquity to find women doing extraordinary things, but their history is forgotten. Or denied to have ever existed. So women keep reinventing the wheel. Women have always done these things, and they always will.'
Professional race-car driver, and, in 1977, Guthrie became the first woman to compete in the Indianapolis 500 and Daytona 500.

— *7 March 1897* —

Harriet Jacobs dies

'The war of my life had begun; and though one of God's most power-less creatures, I resolved never to be conquered.'

Incidents in the Life of a Slave Girl, published in 1861, was written by Harriet Jacobs, a former slave born in Edenton, North Carolina. It is an American classic and yet I doubt many Europeans know the story. We know about Anne Frank, the Jewish girl who hid in a loft from the Germans, but not Harri-et's suffering in a tiny space in the attic of her grandmother's house to escape the sexual harassment of her master. It was a space so small that Harriet couldn't even stand yet she was to live there for seven years. Here is an outline of this incredible life which I hope moves you to read Harriet's own account.

Harriet Jacobs was born in 1813. Her mother Delilah Horn-iblow was a slave of the Horniblow family who owned a local tavern, and under the law that made Harriet a possession of the Horniblows as soon as she was born. When she was six Delilah died and Harriet came into the care of a female member of the Horniblow clan who, most unusually, taught her young charge to read and write, something that became illegal in North Caro-lina in 1830. When she was twelve Harriet's 'owner' died and she came into the charge of a local doctor, Dr James Norcom, who began to sexually harass her.

Harriet sought protection in a relationship with Samuel Sawyer, a white lawyer, by whom she had two children by the time she was about twenty. Norcom still owned her and threatened to sell her kids. In June 1835, aged twenty-two, she decided to escape. It was then that she moved into her grand-mother's garret, which measured 9ft (2.7m) by 7ft (2.1m) and 3ft (0.91m) at its highest point. Here she would live with just some boreholes in the roof to let in fresh air and light by which she could read. Norcom did sell her kids but Sam Sawyer was in on it and saw to it that they went to live with their great-grand-mother, Molly Horniblow. From high above them Harriet would sometimes watch her children play.

At last, in 1842, anti-slavery activists of the Philadelphia Vigilant Committee helped Harriet escape by boat to Philadelphia and then on to New York City, where she got a job as a nanny for the children of a successful author of the time, Nathaniel Parker Willis. It is a long, complicated story of heartache and distress. Norcom went after her to force her back to slavery, which was entirely within his legal rights as she was still his 'chattel' and once more she had to escape. Her brother John began to become involved in the anti-slavery movement, giving lectures and helping to run the Anti-Slavery Office and Reading Room in Rochester, New York. In the same building Frederick Douglass, the most influential African American of his century, was running *The North Star* newspaper and Harriet began to spend time with radical activists.

The attempts to reclaim Harriet as a slave went on after Dr Norcom died. In February 1852, Norcom's daughter followed Harriet to New York intent on claiming 'her property'. It was Nathaniel Parker Willis's second wife Cornelia who would eventually buy Harriet's freedom for $300. It was a traumatic moment. Happiness and gratitude but also, as she wrote, bitterness at the thought that 'a human being [was] sold in the free city of New York'.

Encouraged by others, Harriet sat down to write her life story but she felt unable. Then in June 1853 she happened to read an article in an old newspaper written by Julia Tyler, wife of former president John Tyler, in which Tyler claimed that household slaves were 'well clothed and happy'. Harriet sat down and wrote a reply which the *New York Tribune* published and Harriet's writing career began. It took four or more years to write her book and more to find anyone who would publish it. It was when Lydia Maria Child agreed to write the preface that at last her work came to print in January 1861. That same year her brother John would also write his own memoir, entitled *A True Tale of Slavery.*

There is so much more to Harriet's story. It really isn't mine to tell but please, please go find it for yourself. Read about her work as an activist, a humanitarian and a teacher. It is a story of today. I don't care how you came to hear this tale. Slavery still needs our attention. It's still going on. The best guess is that about 40 million people in the world live in such conditions.

8 March
International Women's Day
Yeah!!! Fireworks!!! We got a whole day!!! The ideal time to celebrate a woman without a specific date attached to her name ...

Christine de Pizan or Pisan, the Venetian-born poet, author and prominent political thinker at the court of King Charles VI of France. Born in 1364, she was the first professional woman of letters in Europe. She began writing to support her kids when she was widowed and is best remembered for defending women in *The Book of the City of Ladies*, in which she creates a literary city of famous females from history. Excellent idea.

9 March 1986
Hannah Kudjoe dies
Born in 1918, Kudjoe was a prominent activist for Ghanaian independence in the 1940s and 1950s, including the Positive Action campaign of mass civil disobedience that eventually led to the end of colonial rule. Also an active philanthropist who worked to improve women's lives.

10 March 1881
Kate Leigh born
Leigh was a notorious Australian underworld figure known for illegal trade in alcohol and cocaine in Sydney, turf 'razor' wars and, by contrast, fantastic philanthropy and patriotism during the Second World War. Check out her twenty-year feud with Tilly Devine, a Sydney madam.

11 March 1702
Elizabeth Mallet publishes *The Daily Courant*, England's first national daily newspaper
Mallet, born 1672, declared she would publish only facts about foreign news and no comments of her own. She felt that her readers had 'sense enough to make reflections for themselves'.

12 March 1959
Kundeling Kusang, aka Pamo Kunsang, initiates the Tibetan women's movement for independence
Mother of six. Leader of Tibetan women's movement united against Chinese occupation of Tibet. This was the spark that initiated the Tibetan women's movement for independence. On this date thousands of Tibetan women gathered in front of the Potala Palace in Lhasa. She and other Tibetan women activists were tortured and later executed by China. Also remember her

fellow activists: **Galing Shar Choe-la, Pekong Penpa Dolma, Tavu Tsang Dolkar, Demo Chime, Tson Khang Meme, Kukar Shar Kelsang, Rizur Yangchen, Tson Khang Tsamla, Ghalingshar Choe-la.**

13 March 1900
Sālote Tupou III born

First queen regnant of Tonga and longest-reigning Tongan monarch, with a forty-eight-year reign. She had a difficult childhood, being shunned because her mother had not been part of Tonga's upper class. Her mother died and, when her father remarried, Sālote was sent away to boarding school in New Zealand. She became queen when her father died in the Spanish flu pandemic of 1918. She proved very successful and popular.

14 March 1977
Fannie Lou Hamer dies

American voting and women's rights activist, a leader in the civil rights movement. Born in 1917, she became physically disabled due to polio and a severe beating in a Mississippi jail. In 1961, while having surgery to remove a uterine tumour, she was given a hysterectomy by a white doctor without her consent. The forced sterilisation of black women to reduce the black population was so widespread it was known as a 'Mississippi appendectomy'. Please read her story. She is a legend.

15 March 1933
Ruth Bader Ginsburg born

American lawyer, Supreme Court justice. I have socks with her picture on, because she is a hero of mine. She spent her life fighting gender discrimination. At Harvard she was one of nine women in a class of 500 and was chastised by the authorities for taking a man's place.

16 March 1822
Rosa Bonheur born
French artist, painter and sculptor. Probably the most famous female painter of the 19th century. Most noted for her lifelike depiction of animals. Check out *The Horse Fair* from 1853. In 1865 she was the first woman to be awarded the Grand Cross of the Legion of Honour.

17 March 1923
Olive May becomes the first ever telephonist for the BBC
She lost her job when she got engaged, as married women were not allowed to work for the BBC. Let's not forget all the Olives in the world who no one noticed and who were keeping everything running.

18 March 1634
Madame de La Fayette baptised
French author of France's first historical novel and one of the earliest novels in literature, *La Princesse de Montpensier*, which was published anonymously in 1662. Her later work *La Princesse de Clèves* (1678) is regarded as a prototype of the psychological novel. Like her earlier novel, it too used historical fact as a basis for fiction.

19 March 1919
Emma Bell Miles dies
American artist, naturalist and author. Born in 1879 and lived in poverty. Please, please read about her life in the Appalachian wilderness in her journal *Once I Too Had Wings*. She was one of the early settlers of Signal Mountain in Tennessee and documented her

life on Walden's Ridge through watercolour painting and writing. She could have made a living from her writing but it would have meant living in the city of Chattanooga and her husband refused.

20 March 1281
Empress Chabi dies
Wife of Kublai Khan who conquered all of China in the 1270s. Born around 1225, she was patron of the arts and Kublai Khan's unofficial adviser. Today she and Khan would have been considered a power couple. She seems to have been a big help to a young Venetian traveller called Marco Polo. It is said that Khan suffered great depression after her death, from which he never recovered.

20 March 2021
Best place to watch the sun set today: Chichen Itza, Mexico
Chichen Itza is a spectacular Mayan ruin. Watch from late afternoon on the spring equinox – where day and night are equal length – as sun and shadow on the pyramid of Kukulcan, the Yucatec Maya feathered serpent deity, give the illusion of a snake creeping down the main staircase.

21 March 1838
Wilma Neruda born
Also known as Lady Hallé, Neruda was a Moravian virtuoso violinist, chamber musician, wunderkind and teacher. Her parents wanted her to play piano but she secretly played her brother's violin and was clearly talented. She performed publicly for the first time when she was six. She became the first woman violinist considered good enough to rank with the greatest male performers and so led the way for female violinists to have a solo career.

22 March 1913
Sabiha Gökçen born (she also died on this day in 2001)
Turkish aviator, flight instructor and the world's first female
fighter pilot. She was one of thirteen children adopted by
Mustafa Atatürk, founder of the Republic of Turkey. He gave
her the surname Gökçen, which means 'belonging to or relating to the sky', before she showed any interest in flying. Atatürk
introduced her to flying but women were not allowed to train
so he arranged lessons just for her. Sabiha Gökçen International
Airport in Istanbul is named after her.

23 March 1614
Jahanara Begum born
(Name in Persian: جهاں آرا بیگم) Mughal princess and Padshah
Begum (First Lady) of the Mughal empire between 1631 and
1681. This made her the most powerful woman in the Persian
empire at the time. She was a true renaissance figure, an author;
architect, businesswoman and Sufi scholar. Daughter of
Emperor Shah Jahan and **Mumtaz Mahal** (*see* 17 June) of Taj
Mahal fame.

24 March 1968
Alice Guy-Blaché dies
Pioneering French filmmaker, director, screenwriter, producer
and actress. Born in 1873, she became the first woman to direct
a film. One of the very first to make a narrative fiction film in
1896, *La Fée aux Choux* (*The Cabbage Fairy*). In the period 1896 to
1906 she was probably the only female filmmaker in the world.
She directed and produced or supervised almost 600 silent films
and 150 synchronised sound films. Her 1906 film *The Life of
Christ* featured 300 extras.

25 March

The Tichborne Dole Festival, England

Fancy some flour? Well, if you live in Tichborne near Winchester, England, today is the day. It's Lady Day, or Feast of the Annunciation if you want to be posh, and this Hampshire village has a curious way of celebrating. An open-air service is held outside the church, after which two tons of flour is given out to the burghers in whatever they want to carry it home. I'd use a pillowcase myself. Before it is given out, the flour is blessed and sprinkled with holy water. May I say, I spent some years working on a television baking show, and I can tell you that making flour wet is not an ideal thing to do to it if you plan to store it but I'm not in charge on Lady Day.

The origin of this act of charity is a really weird story. Sometime in the 12th century (possibly around 1150) a woman called Lady Mabella Tichborne lay dying. Of what I'm not sure. All I've read is 'wasting disease', which is the sort of diagnosis that would lead you to seek a second opinion. Apparently, she was what used to be known as a 'good egg', a person of kindness who cared about the poor. She asked her husband to donate some farm produce in her name to the less well-off in the village. Sir Roger Tichborne does not seem to have been a good egg because he immediately reached for a burning stick from the fire and told his fading wife that he would give away the produce from as much land as Lady T could crawl around with a lit torch. I mean, he must have been drinking. She was, however, a game girl and the twenty-three acres she crawled around are still known locally as The Crawls.

Some marriages really do need the help of a counsellor.

— *25 March 1931* —

Ida B. Wells dies

'The way to right wrongs is to turn the light of truth upon them.'
So many exceptional stories about amazing women of colour have gone unwritten, which is why we need to know about people like Ida B. Wells. It's a common thing today to talk about having a portfolio career. Well, she had that. She was a fighter for women's rights, an investigative journalist and newspaper editor, teacher, and one of the early leaders of the US civil rights movement. During her life she was probably the most famous black woman in America as she campaigned tirelessly against lynching and fearlessly exposed violence against the black community.

Ida was born into slavery in 1862 in Holly Springs, Mississippi. I have searched my shelves to find anything about her. I have many, many books on American history but she gets no mention. Nor does the *Encyclopedia Britannica* – not my father's volumes from 1929 or the more up-to-date ones I have – find her worth a mention, yet she was one of the founders of the National Association for the Advancement of Colored People and spent a lifetime fighting for equality for African Americans, especially women.

In 1884, aged just twenty-two, and seventy years before **Rosa Parks** refused to give up her seat on the bus, Ida refused to give up her seat on a train and it took three men to drag her from the carriage. In 1892 she became part-owner of *The Memphis Free Speech* newspaper in Memphis, Tennessee. It was a radical publication in which she printed an article denouncing the lynching of three of her friends. She wrote: 'Somebody must show that the Afro-American race is more sinned against than sinning, and it seems to have fallen upon me to do so.'

The offices of the paper were destroyed by an angry mob and she was forced out of town. She spent the rest of her life fighting the good fight. She spoke across the United States and abroad about women's suffrage and about the emancipation of African Americans. She came to Britain twice to solicit support for her campaigns and spoke to thousands of people. She wrote about her journey for a Chicago newspaper, becoming the first African American woman to be a paid correspondent for a mainstream white newspaper. Ida always spoke her mind, to the extent that even some of her fellow activists found her too radical. Many of the press were unkind. The *New York Times* called her 'slanderous and nasty-minded'. That's often what people say when a woman is right.

It would not be until 8 March 2018, eighty-seven years after her death, that the *New York Times* finally published a belated obituary for Ida B. Wells. It was part of a series entitled 'Overlooked' which tried to make up for the fact that, in 167 years of the paper's existence, its obituary pages have been dominated by white men, while fabulous women like Ida were overlooked.

26 March 1994

Dame Whina Cooper dies

Born Hōhepine Te Wake in 1895 in New Zealand. Schoolteacher, historian, activist, respected *kuia* (Māori elder). Her work for Māori rights, especially for women, led to her being given the title Te Whaea o te Motu (Mother of the Nation). She campaigned for land rights and social justice. Became the first president of the Māori Women's Welfare League. In 1975, despite needing a cane, she walked the length of North Island at the head of the month-long Māori Land Reform March.

Terrible Victorian terms for no reason except in March you sometimes need to find things to talk about while you wait for the weather to improve

Mutton-Shunter: Policeman who tells prostitutes to move on.

Ringer House: Brothel belonging to a central office where women (often just girls) were registered according to age, looks, measurements and years of experience.

Muffin-Walloper: An old or unmarried woman who likes to meet friends for tea, cakes and gossip.

 — 27 March —

World Theatre Day

> '*I think a play the best divertisement that wise men have.*'
> – **Aphra Behn**

This day is celebrated in theatres all over the world but for some isolationist reason Britain doesn't take part, which is a shame. Although if you're interested in gender equality then there is not much to celebrate in the UK. The National Theatre was started in 1963 and it wasn't until forty-five years later that a play by a living female playwright was performed on the main stage. Research in 2012 by Elizabeth Freestone, then artistic director of Pentabus theatre, revealed that women were vastly underrepresented in pretty much every aspect of British theatre.

Later research suggested that, far from improving, the situation had got worse for women in theatre. At the Royal Shakespeare Company, one of the best-funded institutions in the UK, they had gone from nearly a third of new plays being written by women in 2012 to none at all between December 2018 and September 2019.

When you look at the history of theatre this absence of the female voice seems astonishing. As it happens the very person of either sex since antiquity to start writing drama in the West at all was a woman called **Hrotsvitha of Gandersheim**. She's quite the nun. She was the first German writer and the first female historian as well. Being a nun was a great way for a woman to be left alone at her desk. **Katherine of Sutton** was the first English playwright of a female persuasion, crafting her theatre more than 650 years ago. In 1358 she became abbess of Barking nunnery, which is a very pleasing name as it sounds like a convent full of lunatics. She seems to have made what these days is known as immersive theatre. Everyone got involved, including all the nuns and priests. She would have been in full swing this time of year as Easter was her top inspiration for a spot of theatre. Her aim apparently was to liven up church services to stop the congregation drifting off, which clearly was an ongoing problem. Nothing dampens the ardour of a sermon more than the sound of snoring.

There are a number of Katherine's mystery plays which we know about, including one where she and a couple of priests pretended to be in limbo while they waited for Christ to open the gates of hell. This was a promenade performance that involved everyone wandering about the abbey opening a lot of gates and carrying lit candles. Actually, the last time I went to a church service I'm not sure they'd cracked the whole keeping everyone awake thing. Surely it's time for a revival of Katherine's best work?

If anyone knows the name of a female playwright at all it is possibly that of **Aphra Behn**, who was born in 1640. Aphra is a Hebrew name that means 'dust', although originally in this country it was a name for a woman from Africa. I'm not sure why Aphra Behn's parents chose it. They were called Johnson and came from Canterbury although they did travel. Facts about Aphra are hard to come by. The story goes that sometime in the 1660s her dad got the job of Lieutenant-General of Surinam, which has never even occurred to me as a career aspiration. Off the whole family went to the Guianas. Sadly Mr Johnson died on the way, which rather spoiled the excitement of the trip. It was a long way, so Mrs Johnson and the kids stayed in Surinam for a bit before returning to London, where she became the wife of a Mr Behn about whom we know very little except he was perhaps Dutch or German. It says something about how brilliant Aphra was that he has faded so much into the background.

Anyway, she must have been quite the thing because she came to the attention of the royal court of Charles II. The best thing for any writer of drama is to have had some in their own life and Aphra's was far from dull. The king clearly thought her capable because before long she was given the code name Astrea and sent to Antwerp as a spy. Chambers says: '… she succeeded so well as to obtain information of the design of the Dutch to sail up the Thames and burn the English ships in their harbours, and at once communicated her information to the English Court'.

Sadly, the king failed to pay for her services so when she got back she began clearing her debts by writing for two theatre companies – the King's Company and the Duke's Company. The theatres had been closed for eighteen years thanks to the English Civil War. I don't know whether it was Aphra's influence but both companies would eventually include the very first actresses on the English public stage, most notably, perhaps,

Nell Gwyn. Her first play, *The Forc'd Marriage; or, The Jealous Bridegroom*, was about a young woman who was made to marry someone she didn't want and who was then unfaithful to her husband. Seventeenth-century women were not supposed to even know such goings-on existed. The play was immoral and far too daring which, of course, made it a huge hit.

I think Aphra would have disliked modern media where everyone is allowed to be a critic. She spent her professional life battling those who constantly had a go at her, criticising her very existence, her right to put pen to paper at all, and inventing scandalous stories about her private life. The *Daily Mail* did not invent the shaming of a woman who dared to live in a man's world. Did Aphra have affairs as everyone at the time suggested? I do hope so. One of her most famous quotes suggests it when she wrote, 'Love ceases to be a pleasure, when it ceases to be a secret.'

Aphra's nineteen plays made her one of the most prolific playwrights of the time, second only to the Poet Laureate John Dryden. I wish I knew more about her. Hers is a story with more holes in it than a lace collar. She was the first woman to earn a living as a professional writer in this country and I love that she decided to do that when no one else had ever even thought it was possible. Writing was clearly a passion for her. In the last years of her life she was unwell but nevertheless kept putting her pen to paper.

Despite all the stories and scandals she must still have been well thought of because when she died in 1689 she was buried in Westminster Abbey. While we wander through the abbey's glories to pay our respects to Aphra, it is worth noting other dramas that lurk here. For example, hidden away and hard to find in the chapel of St John the Baptist lies a fascinating plaque dedicated to **Mary Kendall** and her companion **Lady Catherine Jones**, who died in 1740. Lady Catherine was an amazing English philanthropist who focused her attention on women's rights and education. Her ashes were mingled with those of Mary Kendall, with whom she had shared her life. There is an inscription which expresses the women's desire that 'even their ashes, after death, might not be divided'. Were they a couple? Is there a play in it?

Aphra herself lies in the east cloister, near the steps up into the church. A plain black marble slab covers her grave and on it is the following inscription:

> *'Here lies a proof that wit can never be*
> *Defence enough against mortality.'*

I like that.

---

27 March 1883

Marie Under born

One of the greatest Estonian poets. Nominated for the Nobel Prize in Literature eight times. Considered the 'Estonian Goethe'. She wrote first in German but was persuaded to translate her work into Estonian. During the Soviet occupation of 1940–41 she wrote political work. She fled to Sweden with her family when the Soviets reoccupied Estonia in 1944. She is translated worldwide.

28 March 1760
Peg Woffington dies
British actress, socialite, philanthropist of the Georgian era. Born in 1720, she got her start as an apprentice to Madame Violante, a famous 'tumbler and tightrope dancer' (said to have been able to dance on a tightrope with a basket on each ankle containing an infant). In 1749 Peg became the first female member of the Beefsteak Club, the all-male dining club.

29 March 1929
Sheila Kitzinger born
Childbirth campaigner, author, feminist and activist. Campaigned for women to be able to make informed choices about childbirth and to prevent it becoming medicalised. She fought for the mother's wishes to be listened to and for her not to just be dictated to by the medical profession. Well-known advocate for breastfeeding. She was influenced by her own mother who worked in an early family planning clinic.

30 March 1842
Élisabeth Vigée Le Brun dies
Prominent French portrait painter of the late 18th century, born in 1755. Member of the Académie de St-Luc and the French Academy, she was taught by her painter father. Queen Marie Antoinette was a big fan. She caused a small scandal in 1787 when her painting *Self-Portrait with Her Daughter Julie* showed her smiling and revealing her teeth. This was considered shocking at the time. *Mémoires secrets* was a sort of newsletter of the time. It declared, 'An affectation which artists, art lovers, and persons of taste have been united in condemning, and which finds no precedent among the ancients, is that in smiling, [Mme. Vigée Le Brun] shows her teeth … This affectation is particularly out of place in a mother.'

31 March 1865
Anandibai (Anandi) Gopalrao Joshi born
First Indian female physician. First Indian woman to graduate abroad when she became an MD at the Women's Medical College of Pennsylvania (1886) with the topic of her thesis being 'Obstetrics among the Aryan Hindoos'. She became a doctor after she gave birth aged just fourteen to a child who died due to lack of medical care. Her husband, Gopalrao Joshi, was very unusual in his passionate support of her desire for education and deserves credit. She died of tuberculosis, aged twenty-one. She never did practise medicine, but she inspired millions of Indian women.

APRIL

'En avril, ne te découvre pas d'un fil.'

*(Roughly – don't put away your winter clothes in
April, it might still get cold.)*

– French proverb

Ēastre Month

Ēastre was a goddess of spring and fertility so this Anglo-Saxon month is known as *eastre-monath*. It's almost certainly where we get 'Easter' from. A Christian festival named for a pagan woman. April itself has nothing to do with gods. Blame the Romans. It's from the Latin *Aprilis*, but why? Maybe from *aperire*, 'to open', as now is the time when trees and flowers tend to do that. This month was sacred to the goddess Venus. Maybe it was her month. For the Romans she was the goddess of victory, fertility and prostitution. Maybe the boys just wanted her to be open.

The Greeks called her Aphrodite. You often see her depicted as naked, rising from the sea in a clam. It's an interesting image but a horrible story. According to Hesiod's *Theogony* poem, Aphrodite was born after her dad Cronus (Saturn to the Romans) deposed his own father Ouranus (Uranus) by castrating him. Ouranus' blood fell to the sea and Venus appeared out of the foam. We all have a family tale that doesn't reflect well on us but that one takes some beating.

Other names for April

Finnish: *Huhtikuu*, which seems to mean it's time to slash-and-burn in the fields.

Slovenian: *Mali traven*, 'small grass' – in other words, the month when plants start growing.

Ancient Greek: *Aphro*, short for Aphrodite.

Saxon: *Ostermonath* – probably to do with eastern winds and who hasn't had those?

APRIL FOOL'S DAY

Why?

Well, 'fool' from the Latin *follis* meaning 'bellows' or 'windbag', referring to an empty-headed person. April is the time when the sharp spring winds, known as 'the assinines', blow across Europe, and it was believed that the draught could get in anyone's head and empty them of reason. As it could happen to anyone, a day was set aside to celebrate all foolishness. Believe me? You shouldn't. I totally made it up. Fooled you. The truth is we don't know exactly why April 1st is the big day for gagsters so I won't waste your time.

A heavenly gag on the BBC

British astronomer and broadcaster Sir Patrick Moore was a very reliable man. If he said there was cheese on the moon, we all asked, 'What kind?' But even he was not averse to a light-hearted leg-pull. On 1 April 1976 he gave a broadcast on BBC Radio 2 about what he called 'The Jovian–Plutonian gravitational effect'. He declared that the unique alignment on that day of the two planets Jupiter and Pluto would exert a stronger tidal force than usual. This would momentarily counteract Earth's own gravity and make people weigh less and indeed pull them skywards. We all like precision from science and he announced that this would occur at exactly 9.47am that day. Sir Patrick's advice was for anyone listening to jump in the air at that time, which would result in them experiencing 'a strange floating sensation'.

At the appointed moment, Moore proclaimed, 'Jump now!' The marvellous thing is, it worked. The BBC switchboard lit up with dozens of listeners phoning in to say the experiment was a triumph. One woman declared she and a large group of friends and the table they were sitting at were wafted aloft and orbited gently around the room. Of course, there is always a grumpy participant. One man rang furious because he had risen upward so rapidly that he had hit his head on the ceiling.

It was a marvellous joke that merely underlined how little most of us know about science. Pluto is what's known as a dwarf planet. It's so small that it could align with Jupiter till the cows come home and never have any effect on that giant whatsoever.

More April Fools

1698
Honest Ichabod
From 1696 to 1716 a London printer called Ichabod Dawks, known as 'Honest Ichabod', produced a newsletter three times a week. The 2 April 1698 edition of his News-Letter reported that, 'Yesterday being the first of April, several persons were sent to see the Lions washed at the Tower of London.'

1996
Taco Bell
The fast-food chain Taco Bell announced they had purchased that iconic symbol of American independence, the Liberty Bell, which would be rebranded as the Taco Liberty Bell.

⇥ POEM OF THE MONTH ⇤

The Duchess to Her Readers
by Duchess of Newcastle Margaret Cavendish

A Poet am I neither born nor bred,
But to a witty poet married:
Whose brain is fresh and pleasant as the Spring,
Where Fancies grow and where the Muses sing.
There oft I lean my head, and listening, hark,
To catch his words and all his fancies mark:
And from that garden show of beauties take
Whereof a posy I in verse may make.
Thus I, that have no gardens of my own,
There gather flowers that are newly blown.

I give a lot of talks about women's history and I have spoken often about Margaret Cavendish. She was an English aristocrat and I am not a big fan of titles, yet I am slightly in love with her. This is not a relationship that is going to go anywhere as she died in 1673. I don't know where to begin in telling you about her. She was a poet, as you've seen, but so much more. A philosopher, a scientist, a playwright, one of the very first writers of science fiction, and a woman who in the 17th century dared to publish under her own name. She was a groundbreaking woman in so many respects and the very first to attend a meeting at the Royal Society of London. There, in 1667, she was not afraid to criticise and engage with the members. She also openly said she wanted to be famous, so I am doing my bit to please her by spreading the word.

1 April 1940
Dr Wangarĩ Muta Maathai born
First African woman to win the Nobel Prize, for Peace, in 2004.
Renowned Kenyan social, environmental and political activist.
The first female professor in Kenya. She founded the Green Belt
Movement, an environmental non-governmental organisation
focused on the planting of trees, environmental conservation
and women's rights.

2 April 2012
Elizabeth Catlett dies
American-born Mexican sculptor and printmaker, born 1915.
The granddaughter of slaves, she was refused entry to the Carnegie Institute of Technology because she was black. Renowned
for her intensely political art. Left-wing activist. Investigated by
the US House Un-American Activities Committee during the
1950s. Continued to work well into her nineties.

3 April 1980
Megan Rohrer born
American pastor and activist. First openly transgender minister
ordained by the Evangelical Lutheran Church in America. In
2017, hired by the San Francisco Police Department as their first
chaplain from the LGBTQ community.

4 April 1802
Dorothea Lynde Dix born
Dix was a teacher, writer and mental health advocate who
helped create the first US mental asylums, founding or expand-
ing more than thirty hospitals for the mentally ill. She was
Superintendent of Army Nurses for the Union army during the
Civil War, helping the wounded no matter which side they were

on. Dix campaigned to have the mentally ill in prisons treated more humanely.

5 April 1908
Bette Davis born
Davis was an American actress with a sixty-year career, and the first woman to receive a Lifetime Achievement Award from the American Film Institute. She became the first female president of the Academy of Motion Picture Arts and Sciences. Winner of two Academy Awards, and the first actress to gain ten Oscar nominations. If you haven't seen *What Ever Happened to Baby Jane?* (1962) I think there may be a big hole in your life.

6 April 2010
Wilma Mankiller dies
Born in 1945, Mankiller became the first woman elected as Principal Chief of the Cherokee Nation. Activist, social worker, community organiser. Took part in the nineteen-month-long occupation of Alcatraz Island in 1969 to reclaim it for Native Americans.

6 April
Beginning of UK tax year
Another chance to ask, why? Why not the beginning of the year? Why not 1 January? It's the old pesky change from Julius's calendar to Gregory's. The official start of the year on the Julian calendar used to be Lady Day (25 March), and this was also the official start of the tax year. When the new calendar began, in 1752, eleven days were lost. No government wants to lose eleven days of tax revenue so, in 1753, the start of the tax year was changed to 5 April.

Then in 1800 they added one more day because this would have been a leap year in the Julian calendar but not in the new Gregorian calendar. The tax year was extended once more and the date changed to 6 April. After that no one could be bothered to do it again.

7 April 1938
Suzanne Valadon dies
Fabulous and bold French painter, born 1865. First woman admitted to the Société Nationale des Beaux-Arts. Taught herself to draw from observing artists when she worked as a model. See her in Renoir's *Dance at Bougival* and Toulouse-Lautrec's portrait of her from 1885.

 — April: National Garden Month —

'The love of gardening is a seed that once sown never dies.'

– **Gertrude Jekyll**, British horticulturist, born 1843

Fooling the world in April reminds me of the French botanist **Jeanne Baret**, who would never have been able to collect a single sample if she hadn't first duped everyone. There is a long history of women in the world of botany despite the fact that for years they were not allowed to join the scientific societies set up for such study. Jeanne had to dress up as a man just to take part.

The bougainvillea is one of the most popular flowering vines in the world and the story behind it is as spectacular as its magnificent flowers, which burst out in white, red, mauve, purple-red or orange. The plant takes its name from the 1766–69 expedition of the French explorer Louis Antoine de Bougainville. On board, unbeknown to Louis and indeed his crew, was a woman who would become the first female in history to circumnavigate the globe. Jeanne sailed as a man named Jean Baret, valet and assistant to the expedition's naturalist, Philibert Commerçon. It seems Commerçon was complicit and her lover, which was probably intended to make the voyage more fun. The fact is that Baret was an accomplished botanist herself. She had been brought up in a rural area with no formal education. Almost certainly taught by her mother, she had become known as a 'herb woman' who knew about medicinal plants. In Brazil she and Commerçon collected specimens of a flowering vine, which we would come to know as bougainvillea.

It was said to be Tahitian natives who spotted Jeanne's true gender and this made things dangerous for her. She seems to have been attacked by fellow crewmen on a beach. She wanted to gather shells; they wanted to see for themselves that she was a woman. When the expedition stopped at the island of Mauritius in the Indian Ocean to restock supplies, Baret and Commerçon did not sail on. Jean became Jeanne again and cared for Commerçon until his death in 1773. Eventually, Jeanne returned to France where she lived out her days. Her achievements were long overlooked but her work collecting exotic plants still provides important information today. We do not have her notes but Commerçon was careful to record that she should be honoured for her records on the specimens she collected.

Taking care of detail so that the rest of us may learn is key to a brilliant career as a naturalist. I love that someone can be bothered, which brings me to **Maria Merian** and her somewhat obsessive attitude to caterpillars. Maria was born in 1647 in Frankfurt, Germany. Naturally no one thought to educate a mere girl, but her stepfather was a painter and, as there was paint in the house and no TV, she took to doing drawings. Maria is a lesson to all of us that you can never predict how your kids are going to turn out, for she also took to insects. As an adolescent she began collecting them, which beats any occupation of the modern teens I know. One thing led to another and before you knew it Maria was raising silkworms.

By the time she was in her thirties she had published not one but two books on caterpillars, providing her own exquisitely detailed drawings on their life cycles. She documented evidence on the process of metamorphosis which is so impressive. It took me till my fifties to be able to spell the word. We owe much of what we know about insects to Maria and yet I expect few folk outside the Attenborough clan have heard of her.

Maria made a living by teaching drawing to posh girls. This meant she had access to the gardens of the wealthy. There is nothing bugs like more than a well-stocked flower or vegetable bed and she was able to carry on collecting and documenting insects. This was the amateur science of naturalism, which was popular in her day but only for men. She was extraordinary.

She moved on to learning Latin so she could read scientific books, and the less attractive hobby of collecting frogs in order to dissect them. Her status as a scientist grew and, in 1699, she got permission to travel to Surinam in South America, along with one of her daughters. To finance the journey she sold 255 of her own paintings so that she might spend two years studying the insects of Surinam. She was mocked by the Europeans who had gone there simply to grow sugar and she in turn was appalled by their treatment of slaves and said so. She concluded her life in the Netherlands, where she opened a shop selling specimens she had collected and engravings of the plant and animal life she had seen.

From her endeavours, the wonder of metamorphosis became clear. Her work detailing the study of entire species of insects, their life cycle and habitat, set a new standard for entomology. Hard to believe but until she published her studies many people believed that insects were spontaneously generated. Metamorphosis is astonishing. Take the simple ladybird. They undergo an epic metamorphosis, starting as tiny yellow eggs which hatch into black worm-like larvae then turn into blob-like yellow pupae and, finally, the immaculate little black and red insects that we see in the garden. Once you know that, it makes you look at them with renewed wonder.

Maria Merian and Jeanne Baret both lacked formal schooling. The thing to remember about home education, though, is that for women in the past it was often the only way to learn anything. Another name in this mix ought to be **Jane Colden**, the first female botanist of the United States. She was born in 1724 and is probably most famous for her descriptions and drawings of the fauna of New York. She had her mum to thank for her education. In the *American Journal of Botany* Mama Colden was described as 'the capable instructress of her children'. It also helped that her father was interested in botany. Indeed, he was the first person to apply the Linnaeus system of botanical classification to American plants. (Random Scandinavian fact – it was Swedish botanist Carl Linnaeus who developed this system.)

There was no school for Jane, so her dad spent his time getting books and plant samples for his daughter in order that she might learn as much about the botanical sciences as possible. Between 1753 and 1758 she catalogued more than 400 species of plant from New York's lower Hudson River Valley. It was an amazing achievement. In 1756 Colden discovered the gardenia. In spite of all her work, she was never formally recognised during her lifetime by having a plant named after her. There was one named after her father. Her great manuscript is, for reasons I can't fathom, in the British Museum. The only other thing I can discover about her is that she made excellent cheese. How nice to have sat in a garden with any of these women and wondered at the world.

8 April 1893
Tiny Broadwick born
American pioneering parachutist. Invented the ripcord. First person to jump free-fall. Married at twelve, and became a parent at thirteen. Reinvented her life performing skydives and aerial stunts. Aged fifteen she jumped from a hot-air balloon at the 1908 North Carolina State Fair. Describing the moment, she declared, 'I tell you, honey, it was the most wonderful sensation in the world!' She made about a thousand jumps, once landing on top of a train and once getting tangled in a windmill.

9 April 1860
Emily Hobhouse born

British welfare campaigner, feminist and pacifist. At her own expense, she gathered information pressuring the British government to acknowledge the terrible deprived conditions inside British concentration camps in South Africa during the Second Boer War. Her outspoken criticism forced the British government to send a group of women, under Dame Millicent Fawcett, to examine the situation, which led to reform. Her ashes are spread at the Women's Monument in Bloemfontein.

10 April 1979
Rachel Corrie born

American activist, diarist and pro-Palestinian, who was crushed to death by an Israeli Defense Forces armoured bulldozer in the Gaza Strip under contested circumstances during the second Palestinian intifada. She was just twenty-three. You don't have to agree with her to admire her passion.

11 April 1492
Margaret of Angoulême born

Queen of Navarre. Author, poet, patron of humanists and reformers, one of the most outstanding figures of the French Renaissance. Her brother, Francis I, was King of France and together they gathered the country's most intellectual and cultural people to the court. It made her the most influential woman in the country. Sidebar – Leonardo da Vinci died while staying with her. (She had nothing to do with it. I mean, it wasn't her cooking or anything, just bad manners on the part of a house guest.)

12 April 1912
Clara Barton dies
Born 1821, Barton was a self-taught American Civil War nurse, teacher, humanitarian, women's and civil rights activist, founder and first president of the American Red Cross. During the war she risked her life to bring supplies and support to soldiers on the battlefields. At one point a bullet went through the sleeve of her dress and killed the man she was helping.

13 April 1828
Josephine Butler born
English feminist and social reformer. Campaigned for women's suffrage, better education for women, the retainment of women's legal rights when married, the abolition of child prostitution, and an end to human trafficking into prostitution. A champion.

14 April 1935
Emmy Noether dies
German mathematical genius, born 1882. Brilliant at abstract algebra and theoretical physics. Noether's theorem unites two pillars of physics: symmetry in nature and the universal laws of conservation. It doesn't matter if I understand it. I know it's important. Some say Noether's theorem is as important as Einstein's theory of relativity but hardly anyone knows about her.

She often published groundbreaking work under a male pseudonym. She had to leave Germany for the US because she was Jewish. Let's take a minute for Emmy.

April: A big month for saints and horse racing

Festival of Cerealia

Ancient Roman weeklong celebration for the grain goddess Ceres. There was horse racing and theatre but some of it sounds unpleasant. Lit torches blazing with fire were tied to the tails of live foxes who were then released into the Circus Maximus. Nobody really knows why. Lit torches were quite the thing, though. There was also the *Ludi Ceriales*, or 'Games of Ceres', in the same Circus Maximus, where women clothed in white ran about with lighted torches pretending to be Ceres searching for her lost daughter Proserpina.

23 April
St George's Day

Patron saint of England who was actually from Turkey, died in Palestine and never set foot on English soil. Very busy guy. Also patron saint of Venice, Genoa, Portugal, Ethiopia, Catalonia; agricultural workers, farmers, field workers; soldiers; archers; armourers; equestrians, cavalry, saddle makers; chivalry; skin diseases, lepers and leprosy, syphilis; sheep and shepherds.

24 April
St Mark's Eve

A superstitious night. Ideally one should spend it sitting silently on the local church porch between 11pm and 1am, then you'll see the ghosts of anyone who is going to die during the year pass into the church.

— 15 April 1764 —

Madame de Pompadour dies

Mistresses have a long history of influence in the world but there is no day to commemorate them so let's choose the day Madame de Pompadour, one of the most famous mistresses in history, left the world stage. She is remembered as the lover of the French king Louis XV, indeed his 'official' lover, but there is so much more to her. She was beautiful and the king adored her, but simply calling her his mistress suggests it was all about sex. The upshot is that any other aspect of her being is often disregarded.

She was born Jeanne Antoinette Poisson, which obviously means 'fish' in French and may not be an ideal start. She was said to be witty and charming and, aged nineteen, she married a rich man called Charles. They seem to have loved each other. She openly declared she would never leave M. Poisson unless the king was interested, which is a marriage caveat that has never occurred to me. Jeanne started hanging about in the places rich people do and soon the king *was* interested and she became his mistress. It was Louis who gave her the title of the Marquise de Pompadour, which is how she is recalled.

Louis XV was the last generation of royals before the French Revolution, during which so many lost their heads. His reign can't have gone well as it is said to have sown many of the seeds for the great revolution. Because of that Jeanne Antoinette may have been more unkindly recalled in history than she deserves. She had a lot of influence over the king and has been portrayed as a power-grabbing wench who used sex to gain influence. The fact that it was a time when everyone in court was doing whatever it took to gain power and influence seems to be overlooked.

The real woman was a great patron of the arts and quite the artist herself. Her etchings are lovely, she learned to cut gems, played music and both curated and commissioned artists in a range of mediums including porcelain and tapestry. This was the intellectual and scholarly time known as the French Enlightenment and Madame was an invaluable patron. She knew and supported great writers like Voltaire, as well as the work of the first French encyclopedia. I should have liked to see her extensive book collection, some printed with her own printing press.

Mistresses and printing your own books reminded me of **Teresia Constantia Phillips**. I know about her because I have an original pamphlet which she self-published in 1750. History most often describes her as a British 'courtesan', which is a posh word for a mistress or even prostitute. It's not how I think of her. I think of Teresia as a survivor and an exceptional writer.

She was born in 1709 and led a troubled childhood. Early in life she found herself parentless in London trying to make a living while caring for her younger sister. She did her best to earn money through needlework, but she was plunged into a very different life when she was raped aged twelve or thirteen by a man with a title but no manners. It was a terrible event which would lead her to a life still belittled down the years by those who write about her. A life most often described as notorious.

Aged just thirteen she married a bigamist because in those days marriage meant the man assumed responsibility for a woman's debts and she was in terrible financial trouble. Less than two years later she married a rich merchant called Henry Muilman in the same church. The marriage didn't last long. No one knows why but perhaps Muilman discovered her past because he refused to pay her any money. As she wrote herself: 'I am conscious my misconduct has not arisen from Ignorance, so much as a thousand concurring unhappy Circumstances that have attended me.'

She went on to have a bewildering succession of affairs, some more successful than others. Luring men became easy for she was one of the most beautiful women of her day. From the 1720s to the 1740s she was the talk of London as she graced the theatres, pleasure gardens and even the court bedecked in jewels and finery. She had many a liaison with prominent men of the day but age is not always a woman's friend and, by the late 1740s, she was running out of money. She even served two years in a debtors' prison.

Desperate for money she wrote a series of memoirs, pamphlets really, in part to raise funds and, perhaps, also to blackmail one of her paramours, the Earl of Chesterfield, into paying her an annuity. These she sold from her home in White Hart Street, a small dead-end road in Kennington in south London, and I am lucky enough to have one. Written 270 years ago it still has the capacity to break my heart when I read it.

She expresses so painfully how the sexual double standard of society allowed women to be treated so badly both by the law and life in general. How young women were used and discarded by great men like pocket handkerchiefs. She writes about 'the disadvantages we labour under from being born women' and says, 'they are such that for my own part, were beauty as lasting as our date of life, to change my sex I would be contented to be as deformed and ugly as Aesop'.

She would go on to have five marriages and concluded her life in Jamaica with her lover, a wealthy plantation owner. Reading about her journey is marvellous, as she braves a near shipwreck and even performs surgery on deck for seamen wounded while defending the ship against pirates. In Jamaica the governor made her the only woman to be given an official government post. She was appointed Mistress of the Revels, whose office oversaw all official celebrations and entertainments in the colony, which sounds like fun. But the saddest sentence I read about her is that she was said to have died without mourners.

Historically I don't think mistresses have ever had an entirely good time but their impact has often been long-lasting. It was on 15 April 1452 that the great Leonardo da Vinci was born. Even after all these years those who discuss him are keen to tell you that he was the illegitimate son of a Florentine notary called Messer Piero Fruosino di Antonio da Vinci, which is a mouthful, and a peasant woman whom history has recorded simply as **Caterina**. There have been attempts to find out more about her. The historian Martin Kemp – emeritus professor, not the one in the band Spandau Ballet – has searched long and hard for detail about Caterina. He thinks her full name may have been Caterina di Meo Lippi, which I read about in an article with the marvellous headline 'Renaissance Mom', which made her sound like someone who would make an inspirational supporter of the kids' soccer team.

Leonardo's surname da Vinci simply meant he came from Vinci, which is near Florence. According to Kemp, Leonardo's father also came from the same town. He was due to get married but he met poor Caterina and before you knew it the greatest polymath the world has ever known was on his way. Eventually Caterina seems to have lost out and her brilliant boy was brought up by his father and stepmother. It does not sound a happy story. Like so many mistresses, Caterina was sidelined.

What happened historically is that women like Caterina, Teresia, Madame de Pompadour and others were denigrated because they were burdened with a reputation for immorality which the men, the other half of their affairs, were not. The differences in how society deals with men and women generally continue to be stark.

Anyway, if you are a mistress and you're not being treated well, remember the power of the memoir. At least the rest of us will enjoy it.

15 April 1558
Hurrem Sultan dies

Also known as Roxelana. Believed to have been born around 1502, she was chief consort and legal wife of Ottoman sultan Suleiman the Magnificent. Kidnapped aged about fifteen and given to Suleiman as a gift, she became his favourite concubine then wife and state adviser. One of the most powerful and influential women in Ottoman history. She has inspired paintings, opera, plays, novels, ballet and music, including Haydn's Symphony No. 63.

16 April 1850
Marie Tussaud dies

French artist known for her wax sculptures of famous figures. Born in 1761, she founded Madame Tussaud's wax museum in London. She made death-masks of prominent victims of the French Revolution, including Louis XVI, Marie Antoinette, Marat and Robespierre.

17 April 1885
Karen Blixen born

Also known by her pen name, Isak Dinesen. Danish author writing in Danish and English. Work includes *Out of Africa*,

Seven Gothic Tales, Shadows on the Grass, Babette's Feast. In 1913, she and her husband Baron Bror Blixen-Finecke went to Kenya to start a coffee farm. He left it to her to run and she began having to speak English daily. It was tough but she wrote, 'Here at long last one was in a position not to give a damn for all conventions, here was a new kind of freedom which until then one had only found in dreams!'

18 April 1692
Abigail Hobbs arrested for witchcraft in Salem, Massachusetts
Abigail was between fourteen and sixteen years old when she was accused of being a witch in the notorious Salem witchcraft trials. She confessed and accused others. During the trials more than 200 people were accused of witchcraft and nineteen were executed (fourteen women and five men). At least five others died in jail. It is a famous case of mass hysteria. Abigail was sentenced to be executed but reprieved.

19 April 1997
Maria Wittek dies
Born in 1899, Wittek became the first Polish woman promoted to brigadier-general, having first joined the Polish army in 1919. After the Nazi invasion of Poland in 1939, she joined the underground ZWZ, which later became the Home Army. She fought in the Warsaw Uprising. She was arrested by the communist authorities in 1949 and spent time in prison. After her release she worked in a newspaper kiosk. Following the collapse of communism, President Lech Wałęsa appointed her brigadier-general in 1991.

20 April 1534
Elizabeth Barton executed for treason
Barton was known as 'The Holy Maid of Kent' or 'The Mad Maid of Kent', depending who you believe. She was an English Catholic nun, born in 1506 and executed as a result of her prophecies against the marriage of King Henry VIII of England to Anne Boleyn. Hanged at Tyburn for treason aged twenty-eight. She is the only woman in history to have her head put on a spike on London Bridge. Probably not a goal for anyone.

21 April 1879
Raden Adjeng Kartini born
Indonesian national hero. Pioneer of girls' education and women's rights. A symbol of women's empowerment. This date is celebrated in Indonesia as Kartini Day. *Selamat Hari Kartini* (Happy Kartini Day).

The Lyrids meteor shower
16–26 April each year
The Lyrids are among the oldest known meteor shower. There are records of its occurrence from about 2,700 years ago. What's a meteor? Space rubble, really. These come from the comet Thatcher. No matter where you are on the planet, the best place and time to watch the meteor shower is in the countryside between midnight and dawn. The shower takes its name from the constellation Lyra the Harp, near the brilliant star Vega, which the meteors appear to come from (although in reality they are light years from Vega).

22 April 1909
Rita Levi-Montalcini born
Italian Nobel Laureate in Physiology or Medicine. Neuro-biologist. In 1938 a law barred Jews from university positions. In 1943 she and her family fled to Florence following the German invasion. They took false identities and were protected by some non-Jewish friends. She set up a lab in her bedroom where she studied the growth of nerve fibres in chicken embryos. Her work on cell division has been invaluable in fields such as senile dementia, delayed wound healing and tumour diseases.

23 April 2007
Barbara Hillary becomes the first black woman to reach the North Pole
Born in 1931, Hillary was an American nurse and publisher. At seventy-five she became the first black woman to reach the North Pole and, at seventy-nine, she reached the South Pole. She did it because she learned it hadn't been done. She became an inspirational speaker, giving lectures on climate change. The year she died she travelled to Mongolia to highlight the threat of global warming.

24 April 1947
Willa Cather dies
American writer, teacher, journalist, born 1873. Pulitzer Prize winner. Her novels, focused on frontier life in the Great Plains, include *O Pioneers!*, *The Song of the Lark* and *My Ántonia*. She lived for her last thirty-nine years with the editor Edith Lewis.

25 April 1926

Premiere of *Turandot* by Puccini at La Scala, Milan

Turandot contains possibly the most famous tenor aria in all of opera, 'Nessun Dorma' ('None Shall Sleep'). Even the person who can't bear opera would most likely recognise this piece of music. It swells with excitement and, because it is in Italian, we can all overlook the story behind the tune. Let me set the scene. A cold-hearted princess named Turandot (Persian for 'daughter of Turan') is refusing to get married. One of her suitors, whose name she does not know, challenges her to guess what he is called. It is an odd bet. If she guesses correctly she may execute him but if she can't, she must marry him. I'm not sure this would set the scene for a happy marriage. The princess is clearly a sociopath for she decides that 'None shall sleep' in the entire kingdom until the name is discovered. If none of her subjects is able to guess then she will have ALL OF THEM executed. This is clearly a bad idea as she will end up with no one there to make the tea, but the suitor, Calef (tricky name to guess), is confident and sings his song.

It's not the most politically correct opera. Set in China, there are characters in it called Ping, Pong and Pang. Anyway, it all works out in the end. Love wins. Everyone keeps their heads. The trouble is, the story is based on a much more interesting character than depicted in the opera.

Princess Khutulun, born around 1260, was a Mongol noblewoman, but if she is remembered at all, it is because she was a wrestler. We know this isn't legend as both the Italian writer Marco Polo and the Persian Rashid al-Din Hamadani wrote accounts about her. She was the daughter of Kaidu, who was a cousin of Kublai Khan. Old Kublai was very powerful. He ruled the Mongol empire, which pretty much stretched from the Pacific Ocean to the Black Sea and from Siberia to what is now Afghanistan. Kaidu, too, was powerful and he and Kublai used to go to war all the time.

When he was warring Kaidu liked to take his daughter with him. It turns out she loved it and started serving as a warrior in loads of battles. Dad was thrilled and wanted her to run the business when he died, but the other men were not keen on this. Maybe Kaidu also wanted her to get married because Khutulun made a deal. She would marry any man who could defeat her in wrestling. If a man tried and lost he had to give her 100 horses. She is said to have ended up with a herd of 10,000. She did fall in love in the end but everyone seems to have lost interest in her private life by then.

25 April 1920
Sofia Ionescu-Ogrezeanu born

Romanian neurosurgeon, and one of the first female neurosurgeons in the world. Became a doctor after a school friend died due to infection after brain surgery. During the bombing of Bucharest in 1944, she was forced to perform emergency brain surgery on an injured boy due to lack of medical staff. Her career as a neurosurgeon spanned forty-seven years.

Fishy festivals

Herring Festival
Hvide Sande, Denmark
Time to head to my homeland of Denmark and what else would you attend but a herring festival!

I don't know how herring know that it is April but, every year at this time, schools of them swim into the Ringkobing Fjord to spawn in its sheltered waters. Party time for the people! Unless you are Danish you cannot know just how many ways there are of serving herring – pickled with dill, curried, filleted, fried, baked and on and on. Heaven.

While we're on fish, don't miss:

The Interstate Mullet Toss (NB fish not bad haircut)
Perdido Key, Florida
Basically a huge beach party at the Flora-Bama Lounge, Package and Oyster Bar. Spend the weekend attempting to 'throw a dead mullet from a 10-foot circle in Florida across the state line into Alabama'.

Mullet Toss rules:
- The mullet must be whole (approx. 1lb).
- No gloves or sand on mullet are allowed.
- Mullet must be thrown from a 10-foot circle down a designated alley.
- No stepping out of the circle during your throw and follow-through (obvs).
- Only one attempt.

26 April 1889
Anita Loos born
American screenwriter, playwright and author. In 1912 she became the first ever female staff scriptwriter in Hollywood. Check out comic novel *Gentlemen Prefer Blondes*, and the Broadway adaptation of Colette's novella *Gigi*. Loos lived an extraordinary life. She claimed to be furious with women's

liberation saying, 'They keep getting up on soapboxes and pro-claiming that women are brighter than men. That's true, but it should be kept very quiet or it ruins the whole racket.'

27 April 1906
Alice Dunnigan born

Journalist, teacher, civil rights activist and author. In 1947 she became the first black female member of the Senate and House of Representatives press galleries, and in 1948 she was the first African American female correspondent to receive White House credentials. She became one of the first black journalists to accompany a president while travelling (Harry S. Truman in 1948), and paid her own way to do it. Sadly, she was treated appallingly during her career.

28 April 1761
Marie Harel born

Harel was the French cheesemaker credited with inventing Camembert, unless you want to fight and say some guy must have done it, which lots of cheese folk have done over the years.

29 April 1659
Sophia Brenner born

Swedish writer, poet, feminist, salon hostess, polyglot (six languages), mother of fifteen children. Just going to say that again. Mother of fifteen children. Brenner was the first pub-lished woman poet in Swedish, and was the first woman to be granted a state pension for writers. She rather boldly believed women were as clever as men. She was famous in her lifetime. Fifteen children!

30 April 1972
Clara Campoamor dies
Spanish politician, teacher, typist, lawyer, feminist. Born in
1888, she fought for women's rights and suffrage during the
writing of the Spanish constitution of 1931. She insisted that
the language guaranteed gender equality. Fled during Spanish
Civil War, and died in exile in Switzerland.

30 April 1793
The Law to Rid the Armies of Useless Women
passes the National Convention in France
This law banned all women from the armies,
including female soldiers. Only *vivandières* (cooks) and *blan-
chisseuses* (laundresses) were allowed to stay.

Vivandière or cantinière
French name for women who cooked for military regiments.
They started as *vivandières*, women who sold wine, but you
know how you just need a little something to eat when you've
had a drink and, by 1793, they were also called *cantinières*. You
would find *vivandières* serving the French army up until the
beginning of the First World War.

When the French Revolution came along the men were keen
on *Liberté, Égalité, Fraternité* but only for themselves. Frenchwomen needed to be put in their place. There had been too
many taking liberties, like **Rose-Alexandrine Barreau**, born in
1773 and also known as 'Liberté' Barreau. Rose got married, and
then dressed as a man and signed up with her new husband and
then for the 2nd Battalion of the Tarn in the army of the French
First Republic. She is particularly noted in a battle against a
Spanish empire incursion into France at Biriatou in July 1793.

She witnessed the death of her brother and the wounding of her husband before running towards enemy fire, shooting until she ran out of bullets and then charging with her sabre. After fourteen months' service she left the army because she was six months pregnant.

The National Convention gave her money for her service and she was written about as a national hero. Now, however, the new men in charge wanted to change the law. Being in the army might mean you'd want citizenship rights and that was not a good idea for women, so the National Convention brought in a series of laws.

The idea of *vivandières*, and even the name, spread to armies around the world. There were *vivandières* in Spain, Italy, Germany, Switzerland, parts of South America and on both sides of the American Civil War. These included **Annie Etheridge**, born in 1839. In April 1861 Annie joined nineteen other women to enlist as nurses and *vivandières* with the Union's 2nd Michigan Volunteer Regiment. She served with the regiment during all its fighting, including both famous battles at Bull Run. She was wounded in the hand when an officer tried to hide behind her. He died. She survived.

Kady Brownell, born 1842, was a Union army *vivandière* who fought in battle and saved the lives of many injured. At the First Battle of Bull Run, she carried the flag during the fighting. She was the only woman to receive discharge papers from the Union army. Her husband also served. He got a pension of $24 a month. She got $8 per month.

MAY

'I thought that spring must last forevermore; For I was young and loved, and it was May.'

— **Vera Brittain**, English nurse, writer, feminist, pacifist, born 1893

Month of Three Milkings

May seemed like a time of plenty to the Anglo-Saxons. They called it *Thrimilce*, or 'the month of three milkings'. It was a time of bounty, when livestock were so happily full on fresh spring grass that they could be milked three times a day. This sounds a happier tale than the story of the Greek goddess Maia for whom May is most likely named. Maia was the eldest of seven nymphs known as the Pleiades. They were the daughters of the Titan Atlas and the sea-nymph Pleione. Maia seems to have been shy, which is not ideal if you're going to end up as a star. She lived alone in a cave near the peaks of Mount Cyllene where she was born. Sadly, Zeus took advantage of her and this resulted in her giving birth to the messenger god Hermes. Frankly, Maia's story is quite the soap opera. She also raised a boy called Arcas because his mother, Callisto, had been turned into a bear by Zeus' jealous wife, Hera. Don't you hate when that happens?

Maia's dad Atlas was eventually forced to carry the heavens on his shoulders. This meant he couldn't protect his girls. When the giant huntsman Orion began to pursue all seven of the Pleiades, Zeus at last thought he ought to behave better and look out for them. First he turned them into doves, and then into stars. The Pleiades are a famous constellation in the night sky where the constellation of Orion is said to still pursue them because why let the poor women have a break?

Of course it is also possible I have mentioned all that for no reason. The name May might come from the Latin *maiores*, meaning 'ancestors' or 'elders'.

Other names for May

Cherokee: *Anaagvti*, 'month of the planting moon'.

Finnish: *Toukokuu*, meaning seed and planting time.

Irish (Gaelic): *Bealtaine*, Old May Day.

Korean: *Owol*.

Lithuanian: *Gegužė*, the cuckoo.

MAY DAY

Aka Walpurgis Night, or Sankt Walpurgisnacht if you want to be German.

I hope I'm not too late with this. Strictly speaking, this celebration has to begin the night of 30 April and then go on into 1 May. It's a slightly weird thing. The evening celebration is for **Saint Walpurga**, an 8th-century abbess in Francia, but the next-day part is when her relics (bones) were moved on 1 May 870, which is creepy. She'd already been dead for years.

Anyway, I love a good saint and this one is a cracker. She was famous for dealing with 'pest, rabies and whooping cough, as well as against witchcraft'. Which sounds like the ultimate call-out service. There are those who still hope to ward off evil spirits by lighting bonfires on Saint Walpurga's Eve. Good news for England – she was English! From Devon, where she was born in AD 710. She was quite the girl in her day because she studied medicine. She was obviously keen as you often see her depicted carrying bandages. Her tomb is in Eichstätt, Bavaria (great castle), where the nuns will give you Saint Walpurga's oil to heal sickness. She's a very popular saint. Walpurgis Night is a huge celebration in Finland, up there with Christmas and New Year's Eve.

The Padstow 'Obby 'Oss May Day Festival

Celebrated in Padstow, Cornwall, this is possibly the oldest dance festival in Britain. The 'Obby 'Oss may be a relic of ancient Celtic horse worship. It's fun. There's a maypole and lots of greenery. People dance and sing led by a dancer dressed as a horse before heading for the 'stables', or pub as we usually call it.

⤞ POEM OF THE MONTH ⤝

Extract from *The Pillow Book* by Sei Shōnagon (translated by Meredith McKinney)

Things that just keep passing by
A boat with its sail up.
People's age.
Spring. Summer. Autumn. Winter.

Sei Shonagon is a Japanese author and poet who was born somewhere around 966. I am being vague because I don't think Sei Shōnagon is even her real name. I do know that she served in the court of the Empress Teishi and that her name probably derives from the job held by one of her husbands. She married three men or maybe not. She did write *The Pillow Book*, which is a contemporary account of life in the court. It's not written as a book but more as lists and notes and ideas mixed with some poetry. She wrote for her own enjoyment but it's a fantastic account of noble life at the time. I read that she had a rivalry with her contemporary writer and court lady Murasaki Shikibu, author of *The Tale of Genji*. I hate that gossip has such long life. I have no idea what happened to Shōnagon later in life because no one wrote it down.

1 May 1751
Judith Sargent Murray born

Murray was an early American advocate for women's rights and the concept of gender equality. An essay writer, playwright, poet and letter writer, she believed women had the ability to achieve economic independence. Her essay 'On the Equality of the Sexes' was an important foundation for later feminist writing. She sometimes wrote under a male pen name 'Mr. Vigilius' or 'The Gleaner', because she thought readers would be more likely to listen to her ideas if presented by a man.

2 May 1872
Ichiyō Higuchi born

Ichiyō Higuchi is the pen name of Japanese author Natsu Higuchi, considered the first prominent Japanese female author of modern times. She specialised in short stories and began to write to support her family. Her focus on the use of classical Japanese rather than Western influence set her apart. She died of tuberculosis aged twenty-four. Her image is on the 5,000-yen banknote.

3 May 1937
Esther Boise Van Deman dies

American archaeologist, born 1862. She was the first woman to specialise in Roman field archaeology and, in 1898, became the first woman to gain a PhD in Latin from the University of Chicago. She established a methodology for the dating of ancient constructions which is the standard procedure in Roman archaeology to this day.

4 May 1902
Dr Sidnie Manton born
British zoologist regarded as one of the most outstanding of the 20th century. Manton worked on the structure, physiology and evolution of the arthropods. She became the first woman to be awarded an ScD from Cambridge University, and was elected as one of the first female fellows of the Royal Society (as was her sister, **Irene Manton**, who studied ferns and algae). There is a Sidnie Manton Award for early career ecologists.

5 May 1864
Nellie Bly born
Nellie Bly is the pen name of Elizabeth Cochrane, an American journalist whose around-the-world race against the fictional eighty-day record of Phileas Fogg brought her world renown. She began her career when her angry letter to the *Pittsburgh Dispatch* newspaper about an article entitled 'What Girls Are Good For' got her a job.

6 May 1980
María Luisa Bombal Anthes dies
Chilean author, born 1910. One of the few Latin American female authors to receive worldwide acclaim. She led a pretty interesting life. She married a homosexual painter and shot her lover, but was acquitted because he said he didn't blame her. Afterwards she moved to the US and married a count. She produced fascinating writing about gender, which is probably not surprising. Hans Christian Andersen was an early influence.

7 May 1919
Eva Perón born
Wife of Argentine president Juan Perón, and a powerful unofficial political leader herself. Adored by the masses, especially the poor – *los descamisados* (the shirtless ones). Largely responsible for the passage of the Argentinian women's suffrage law in 1947. Formed the Peronist Women's Party to help women stand as political candidates.

 — *Revolutionary women* —

> *'A woman has the right to mount the scaffold. She must possess equally the right to mount the speaker's platform.'*

> – **Olympe de Gouges**, born 1748

May Day is celebrated round the world. It's often seen as a day to celebrate labourers and the working classes. In 1889 the Marxist International Socialist Congress in Paris chose 1 May as the day to demonstrate in support of working-class demands for the eight-hour day. For many years it was a day of revolution in Russia.

But as far as I can make out, there has never been even one revolution for equality in history where women were better off afterwards. The sad truth is that there is not a single country in the world where women have achieved equality.

So far, all democratic experiments, all revolutions throughout history, all demands for equality have stopped short of sexual equality.

Let's gallop through some of the top revolutions.

The Russian Revolution, 1917

The great revolutionary Vladimir Lenin himself spoke of his admiration for women, how social equality for women was a principle needing no discussion for communists. Nearly a hundred years on and Russian women hardly hold any positions of political leadership. It is not a good country for domestic violence statistics. As far as I can ascertain from the records, two thirds of all murders are committed in a family setting. Feminist political protest is dealt with harshly. The protest group **Pussy Riot**, founded in August 2011, have been at various times both imprisoned and assaulted for their work.

The Chinese Revolution, 1949

Chairman Mao famously talked about the importance of women, who hold up half the sky. He was a feminist, saying there was nothing men could do that women couldn't, yet his pronouncements seem to have done women no good. He liked women so much he married four of them. Today, just over half of Chinese women complete secondary education compared to 70 per cent of men. Women hold about 20 per cent of seats in the national parliament and the idea of feminist protest is out of the question. In March 2015 **Zheng Churan**, a Chinese women's rights activist, and four other women were detained because they planned to distribute stickers on buses to raise awareness of sexual harassment on public transportation. They were charged with 'picking quarrels and provoking trouble'. It's hard to escape the irony that they were taken away on International Women's Day. There is a phrase in China for women who are interested in women's rights and it's 'women's rights bitch'.

The Arab Spring, 2010–12

The breathtaking and thrilling sight of the crowds in Tahrir Square in Cairo were broadcast worldwide. About half of the crowd was female. Women, with and without veils, participated in the defence of the square, set up barricades, led debates, shouted slogans and, together with the men, risked their lives. Some participated in the protests, were present in news clips and on Facebook forums, and were part of the revolution's leadership during the Egyptian revolution. As a group, women had been proportionally underrepresented in parliament and other civic offices. During the final years of Hosni Mubarak's leadership, women held just 12 per cent of parliamentary seats. After the revolution that ousted Mubarak, what happened? The number of women in office decreased to 7 per cent. The turmoil gave rise to an epidemic of sexual violence. The United Nations Entity for Gender Equality and the Empowerment of Women reported that 99.3 per cent of Egyptian women had experienced some form of harassment.

The French Revolution, 1789–99

This is the one that should surely do what it says on the tin. Women had no political rights in pre-revolutionary France; they were considered 'passive' citizens; forced to rely on men to determine what was best for them. The late 1780s was a time of great poverty and much of the population, apart from the very top echelon, got caught up in revolutionary fervour. So caught up that, for a brief moment, the women of Paris thought the battle for equality meant them too. On 1 January 1789 a document was addressed to the king entitled, 'Petition des femmes du Tiers Etat au roi', which stated that women wanted equal opportunities.

Among the things women were seeking were:

1. Legal equality in marriage
2. Educational opportunities for girls, including vocational training
3. Public instruction, licensing, and support for midwives (so reproductive rights)
4. Guarantees for women's rights to employment
5. An end to the exclusion of women from certain professions
6. Some even dared to argue equality of sexes

Any of it sound familiar? It's 1789, people! The Storming of the Bastille that year, in which women played a major part, led to the publication of the Declaration of the Rights of Man and the Citizen – this is considered historically as one of the great milestones in human rights history, even though women are not really mentioned.

In October one of the earliest and most significant events of the French Revolution occurred – the Women's March on Versailles. It began among women in the marketplaces of Paris who, on the morning of 5 October 1789, were near rioting over the high price and scarcity of bread. Their demonstrations quickly became intertwined with the activities of revolutionaries and signified the change of power and reforms about to overtake France.

But it wasn't long before the women were being sidelined. In 1791 a French playwright called **Olympe de Gouges** wrote the *Declaration of the Rights of Woman and of the Female Citizen* in which she challenged the practice of male authority and the notion of male–female inequality. The following year the Tuileries Palace was stormed by men and women including one of my heroines, **Claire Lacombe.** She was an actress. She was shot through the arm but kept fighting on, earning herself the lifelong sobriquet, 'Heroine of August 10th'. Together with **Pauline Léon**, a chocolate maker, they founded the Society of Revolutionary Republican Women. Other women's clubs flourished, producing pamphlets and supporting the revolution.

There were four years of women marching, being shot at, beaten, and making the revolution happen. Were they feted and applauded? No. On 30 October 1793, the president of the new government, Pierre Chaumete, banned all women's political associations, declaring that he had a right to expect his wife to attend to the running of his home while he attended political meetings. The leaders of the women's clubs were arrested.

Olympe de Gouges, author of the *Declaration of the Rights of Woman and of the Female Citizen*? She was executed by guillotine during the Reign of Terror for attacking the regime of the revolutionary government. Her death was used as a warning to other women who wanted to be involved in politics. A decade later and the Napoleonic Code confirmed and perpetuated women's second-class status.

So much for *Liberté, Égalité, Fraternité*.

What does all this teach us? That the fight for equality is doomed? That we should all just pick up our knitting needles and forget about it? Not at all. The great suffragette **Emmeline Pankhurst** was arrested on numerous occasions and suffered violent force-feeding. There is a picture of her in Holloway prison. She is knitting. What we learn is that in the midst of adversity women still manage to be both productive and creative. It also teaches us that the battle is so very far from over.

8 May 1932
Ellen Churchill Semple dies
American geographer, born 1863, who believed the physical environment determines human history and culture. Studied at Vassar College in New York, and the University of Leipzig, but was not allowed to matriculate at Leipzig 'cos of that pesky girl thing. In 1921 Semple became the first woman president of the Association of American Geographers.

9 May 1951
Joy Harjo born
American poet, musician, playwright, author. Member of the Muscogee Nation. First Native American US Poet Laureate. She has voiced strong support for women's rights and equality. 'I feel strongly that I have a responsibility to all the sources that I am: to all past and future ancestors, to my home country, to all places that I touch down on and that are myself, to all voices, all women, all of my tribe, all people, all earth, and beyond that to all beginnings and endings.'

10 May 1958
Ellen Ochoa born
American engineer and astronaut. In 1993 she was the first Hispanic woman to travel into space on board the Space Shuttle *Discovery*. She made four space flights, logging 1,000 hours in space. She was in Mission Control during the Space Shuttle *Columbia* disaster of 2003, and later became director of NASA's Johnson Space Center.

11 May 1849
Madame de Récamier dies
French hostess and celebrated beauty. Born in 1777, she ran a fascinating political and literary salon in early 19th-century

Paris. Aged fifteen she married a man thirty years older who was rumoured to be her natural father. He was said to want to ensure she inherited his wealth. The marriage was never consummated. She was forced into exile by Napoleon. She apparently liked to lie on a type of chaise longue which was named the *récamier* in her honour.

12 May 1910
Dorothy Hodgkin born
An English chemist who was awarded the Nobel Prize in Chemistry in 1964. Hodgkin solved the structure of penicillin and vitamin B12. She used x-ray crystallography in a way that had not been done before and which became an essential tool in structural biology. She devoted her last years to helping scientists in developing countries. She taught Margaret Thatcher chemistry, and Thatcher had a picture of Hodgkin in her office at Number 10 when she was PM. Dorothy supported the Labour Party.

RIP

12 May 1996
Momia Juanita arrives in Washington, DC
She'd been dead more than 500 years.
Momia Juanita is Spanish for Mummy Juanita, 'mummy' in this instance meaning not a parent, but someone who was well preserved. In fact she was a young Inca girl, about twelve to fifteen years old, who was discovered on Mount Ampato in southern Peru in 1995. She had been sacrificed as an offering to the Inca gods sometime in the mid-15th century. Her perfectly preserved frozen body was hailed as a breathtaking discovery. The anthropologist who discovered her did so by chance, and then brought her body down from the

mountain tied to his rucksack. From there Momia Juanita was transported first on a burro, and then a public bus, to a freezer in the Catholic University at Arequipa.

The Inca empire was the largest in pre-Columbian America and existed for almost a hundred years from 1438. It was customary to choose a child at birth to be brought up as an offering for the gods, so perhaps Juanita always knew what the future held for her. The practice was called *capacocha*, or 'solemn sacrifice'. It was clearly an honour. Juanita was dressed in the finest of clothes and wearing jewellery. She would have been accompanied up the high mountain by priests and hangers-on carrying very alcoholic beer called *chica* and food. We know that she was killed by a sharp blow to the back of her head which caused a massive haemorrhage. The beer was strong. Perhaps she knew nothing about the blow. It is believed that the Inca did not want the sacrifice victim to go into the world of the gods 'hungry or crying'. Then she was buried with funeral offerings including pottery, figurines made of gold, silver and shell, and even miniature llamas in clay.

Mostly these days you can find her residing in a glass case in the Museo Santuarios Andinos (Museum of Andean Sanctuaries) in Arequipa, Peru. Her hands are folded and her knees bent as if she is trying to sit up. The degree of preservation was extraordinary. She has hair. You can see her teeth, her fingernails and even small muscles on her arms. In 1996 she came to America for a CT scan. She travelled from Peru via American Airlines with a Miami stopover, entombed in a special container kept in dry ice.

After her scan she was put on exhibition in the National Geographic Society's Explorers Hall. The attitude to her was mostly reverential, although one company 'involved in human fertilization inquired about obtaining one of Juanita's eggs and fertilizing it with a dose of 20th-century sperm'.

We've learned a lot from Juanita. From the scan scientists gathered much about her background and the origins of the first people to populate the Americas. She was seen to be in perfect health, an impeccable gift for the gods. We know that she ate a meal of vegetables before she died and that she was dressed in sacred Inca textiles.

Juanita is a messenger from another time. So many girls and women exist silently in the past. At least she spoke to us.

13 May 1888
Inge Lehmann born
Danish seismologist and geophysicist whose main discovery, in 1936, was that Earth has a solid inner core within a molten outer core. She lived to be 104. An annual Inge Lehmann Medal is awarded by the American Geophysical Union to honour 'outstanding contributions to the understanding of the structure, composition, and dynamics of the Earth's mantle and core'.

14 May 1979
Jean Rhys dies
Pen name of Caribbean-born novelist Ella Williams, born 1890. She is best known for the novel *Wide Sargasso Sea*, written as a prequel to Charlotte Brontë's *Jane Eyre*. Rhys worked for a while as a chorus girl in England. During the First World War she volunteered in a soldiers' canteen. It was the writer Ford Madox Ford who persuaded her to change her name. Struggling with poverty for much of her life, she became famous in her later years and said, 'It has come too late.'

15 May 1759
Maria Theresia von Paradis born
Austrian musician and composer who lost her sight at an early age. By sixteen she was performing as a singer and pianist, having learned over sixty concertos by heart. She toured Europe, receiving great reviews. In 1785 she helped to establish the Institution Nationale des Jeunes Aveugles in Paris, the first school for the blind. Also a composer and teacher.

16 May 1975
Junko Tabei becomes the first woman to reach the top of Everest
'Technique and ability alone do not get you to the top; it is the will-power that is most important.'
    Japanese climber, born 1939. As well as climbing Everest, Tabei was the first woman to ascend the Seven Summits, climbing the highest peak on every continent. Some male mountaineers refused to climb with her, others thought she only climbed to find a husband, so she founded the Joshi-Tohan Club (Women's Mountaineering Club) in 1969. The club's slogan was 'Let's go on an overseas expedition by our-selves'. In 1970 the club completed the first female and first Japanese ascent of Annapurna III in Nepal. To fund the climb for Everest, Junko taught piano and tutored kids in music and English. The club members made their gloves out of old car seats and sewed their own sleeping bags.

17 May 1912
Mary Kenner born
Kenner was an American florist and inventor who, in 1956, developed a sanitary belt which was adjustable, with a built-in, moisture-proof napkin pocket. The Sonn-Nap-Pack Company wanted to buy it but changed their minds when they found she

was African American. Her patent expired and others took her idea. She held five patents for inventions. Owned four flower shops. Fostered five boys.

18 May 1803
Catherine Flon sews the first Haitian flag
We have no birthdate for Flon, a Haitian seamstress, patriot and national heroine. The Haitian Revolution was the only successful slave revolt in the world and Catherine is a heroine of it. Admired by woman-led Haitian activist movements of today.

19 May 1474
Isabella d'Este born
Marchioness of Mantua, known as the 'First Lady of the Italian Renaissance'. A well-educated humanitarian, prolific letter writer, fashion leader and mother of eight children. Regent of Mantua during husband's absence. Official ruler of Solarolo in Romagna. A great patron of the arts, she commissioned painters including Mantegna, Titian and da Vinci.

20 May 1882
Sigrid Undset born
Norwegian novelist whose best-known work, *Kristin Lavransdatter*, was a trilogy about medieval Norwegian life seen through the life of one woman. She was awarded the Nobel Prize in Literature in 1928.

21 May 1810
Chevalier d'Éon dies
Born Charles-Geneviève-Louis-Auguste-André-Timothée d'Éon deBeaumont in 1728, d'Éon was a French diplomat, spy and soldier who, for thirty-three years from 1777 to 1810,

lived as a woman. The term 'eonism' is named for the Chevalier d'Éon, who claimed to have been female at birth but raised male for inheritance purposes. The chevalier is now thought to have been intersex.

22 May 1896
Amelia Elizabeth Dyer pleads guilty to murder
Dyer was born in 1836 and hanged on 10 June 1896. She was a nurse and one of the most prolific serial killers in history. Dyer murdered many infants in her care over a thirty-year period, possibly more than 400. On this day she pleaded guilty to one murder, that of four-month-old Doris Marmon, for which she was sentenced to death. Her case led to stricter laws on adoption. She was known as the 'Ogress of Reading' which, just to be clear, is the town in Berkshire and not what happens when you spend too long with books.

23 May 1793
Dortchen Wild born
German storyteller who married Wilhelm Grimm of *Grimm's Fairy Tales*. She was the source of about a quarter of the stories but received no credit. **Jeannette, Marie and Amelie Hassenpflug** also provided tales, as did **Jenny von Droste-Hülstoff** and **Dorothea Viehmann**.

24 May 1883
The Brooklyn Bridge is opened, thanks to **Emily Warren Roebling**
Emily's husband, Washington Roebling, was chief engineer of the bridge but he became ill. Emily, born 1843, took over and for a decade project-managed the whole thing. At the opening ceremony, Abram Stevens Hewitt, Mayor of NYC, said the bridge was: '... an everlasting monument to the sacrificing devotion

of a woman and of her capacity for that higher education from which she has been too long disbarred'.

25 May 1925
Rosario Castellanos born

Novelist, short story writer, poet, essayist, diplomat and probably the most important Mexican woman writer of the 20th century. Castellanos wrote about cultural and gender oppression and became a symbol of Latin American feminism. She was appointed Mexico's ambassador to Israel from 1971 to 1974 and died in Tel Aviv when she was accidentally electrocuted in her home.

26 May 1702
Zeb-un-Nissa dies

Mughal princess and poet with pen name 'Makhfi' ('Hidden One' in Persian), born 1638. As a child she was a favourite of her father, Emperor Aurangzeb, and received a wide education. She wrote many books of poetry but something went wrong because her beloved father imprisoned her for the last twenty years of her life at Salimgarh Fort, Delhi.

27 May 1907
Rachel Carson born

American marine biologist, author and environmentalist. Her book *Silent Spring*, published in 1962, woke many Americans to conservation concerns, especially around the use of pesticides. The environmental movement owes her a great debt.

— *27 May 1643* —

Women of Courage

> '*Upon the surrender of Warrington, May 27th,*
> *1643, a sum'ons came from Mr Holland, Governor*
> *of Manchester, to the Lady Derby, to subscribe to the*
> *propositions of parliament or yield up Lathom House;*
> *but her ladyship denyed both ...*'

> – Tracts Relating to Military Proceedings in
> Lancashire during the Civil War

The English Civil War was actually a series of wars that lasted from 1642 until 1651. During these wars the Parliamentarians (Roundheads) and Royalists (Cavaliers) fundamentally fought about how England ought to be governed. The lead folk in this debacle were Oliver Cromwell, John Pym and Charles I, who completely lost his head over the matter. It was a terrible conflict in which 7 per cent of the entire population died, and the effect on women must have been terrible. Nevertheless, few female names bubble to the top of the history books in this matter unless you take time to search.

Many of them ought to be remembered. There was **Elizabeth Alkin**, born around 1600, and known as Parliament Joan, who was a publisher, a spy for the Parliamentarian forces and a mother of three who also had time to do some nursing of the wounded. In the 17th century, there were no newspapers but daily news was published in small, eight-page pamphlets known as 'newsbooks'. These were sold on the street, often by women who became known as 'Mercury Women', after the Greek messenger of the gods. Just like today there were publications supporting both sides. Elizabeth became involved in uncovering those behind the publication of newsbooks supporting the Royalist cause. She published several newsbooks with Royalist-sounding names so that she might win the confidence of Royalist sympathisers and get them to reveal the location of illicit printers. By July 1655 we find Elizabeth writing to a parliamentary committee that dealt with the navy requesting money to care for the 'sicke & wounded men' she had been commissioned to look after in the port of Harwich.

Then there is **Mary Crompton**, a renowned Royalist, who is said to have led the defence of Dawley Castle in Shropshire. She wasn't the only one. There was **Lady Mary Bankes**, who defended Corfe Castle against a three-year siege; **Lady Brilliana Harley**'s defence of Brampton Bryan Castle; and **Dorothy Hazard**, who led a group of women to barricade breaches in the walls of Bristol during the Royalist assault in 1643. Who wouldn't have wanted to see **Queen Henrietta Maria** as she marched from Bridlington to Oxford leading a military unit to provide reinforcements and supplies for King Charles at Oxford? She didn't fight but it was so radical a move that she called herself the 'She-Generalissimo'.

There are many more but my favourite is **Charlotte Tremouille**, Countess of Derby. I should love to have met her. Charlotte was a Royalist. She lived in Lathom House, which to me sounds like something mid-terrace but it was actually a fabulous castle. She came to live there from France, where she was born in 1599, so I think for this story you need to imagine that she had an excellent accent. She married the 7th Earl of Derby and moved into his house, which demonstrates the general confusion with titles in this country – he was the Earl of Derby, the castle was in Lancashire. I once met the Duke of Kent. Stuck for conversation I told him how much I liked Kent, to which he replied, 'Yes, I've never really been.'

Anyway, during the war Charlotte's husband was sent off by the king to do Royalist things on the Isle of Man and Charlotte was left at home. In February 1644 Parliamentarian forces turned up at the door (or drawbridge maybe), demanding the castle for themselves. I think the soldiers thought – it's a woman, this will be a pushover.

Back then war had a bit more decorum about it. It was all very politely done. Sir Thomas Fairfax, who was in charge of the besieging Parliamentarians, popped in and asked Charlotte to surrender. She said that surrendering was quite a big ask and she needed a week to think about it, which he apparently thought was so reasonable that he agreed. So he left to do I don't know what, camping with his men I imagine. Meanwhile, Charlotte cracked on. She gathered anyone who was good with a gun and happy to be on her side. There were 2,000 Parliamentarian soldiers outside but she managed to muster a small army of 300. Game girl. I mean, I felt besieged in my house during the coronavirus pandemic and could barely muster a toilet roll.

A week later the soldiers outside got fed up and started firing cannons at her, but Charlotte held on for months until a load of Royalist forces turned up and finally helped her get out. She went off to see her husband on the Isle of Man where she also spent time refusing to surrender. Spoiler alert – I'm afraid her side lost in the end but there are those who say that Charlotte had 'the glory of being the very last person in the three kingdoms – so Scotland, England and Ireland – who submitted to the victorious rebels'.

Hats off to her.

There was a poem written about the siege of Charlotte's castle by a woman called **Letitia Elizabeth Landon**. I don't think she's all that well known these days but other women poets like **Elizabeth Barrett Browning** and **Christina Rossetti** thought she was fab. Letitia was an English poet and novelist born in 1802 in London. If you look for her work you may find she was better known by her initials L.E.L. because, heaven knows, you couldn't really enjoy a poem back then if you knew a woman had thought of it. Anyway, I think her poetry is wonderful and wanted to reproduce a bit from her verse entitled 'Lord and Lady Derby', which commemorates Charlotte Tremouille's tremendous courage. It's a piece which for anyone having to dig deep and find courage is especially poignant. Funny how you can so often find what you are looking for in the past.

> *'Tis in such troubled times, the few*
> *Find they have powers they never knew;*
> *And yonder highborn dame, who stands*
> *With flowerets in her graceful hands,*
> *With broidered robe, and ringlet fair,*
> *Scarce breathed on by the fragrant air,*
> *Dreamed not that she should stand alone*
> *When pikes were raised, and trumpets blown,*
> *And gathered foes around the wall,*
> *And she sole chief in Lathom Hall.*
> *But ere she put aside her fears,*
> *And woman's weakness – woman's tears,*
> *How many a long; and anxious hour*

She must have passed in secret bower,
Till she stept forth, the calm and proud
To meet and animate the crowd.

I love that:

'Tis in such troubled times, the few
Find they have powers they never knew ...

28 May 1981
Mary Lou Williams dies
A jazz great, born 1910. Williams was a musician, composer, arranger, bandleader and mentor. As a child it was said that her playing piano kept racist neighbours at bay. She composed hundreds of pieces and arrangements, including for Duke Ellington and Benny Goodman. She recorded more than 100 records and mentored Charlie Parker, Dizzy Gillespie and Thelonious Monk. In 1975 she performed the first jazz mass at NYC's St Patrick's Cathedral, to a crowd of thousands. All those boys' names so much more familiar than hers.

29 May 1851
Sojourner Truth gives legendary 'Ain't I a Woman?' speech
Born into slavery around 1797, Sojourner Truth was an American abolitionist, women's rights activist and inspirational speaker. There is almost too much to say about this incredible woman who escaped slavery with her daughter in 1826 and

won a court case against a white man in 1828 to recover her son. It was in May 1851 that she gave an ad-libbed speech at the Ohio Women's Rights Convention in Akron, Ohio, which later became known by the title, 'Ain't I a Woman?' Please read about her. I cannot do her justice in this short paragraph.

30 May 1926
Christine Jorgensen born
American transgender woman, soldier, actress, entertainer. First person in the US widely known for having sex reassignment surgery. In 1952 she went to Copenhagen, Denmark, to have a series of operations that were not available elsewhere. On 1 December 1952, the *New York Daily News* ran a front-page story with the headline 'Ex-GI Becomes Blonde Beauty'. They incorrectly stated that Jorgensen had become the recipient of the first 'sex change' (Why not check out **Dorchen Richter** and Danish artist **Lili Elbe**?).

31 May 1978
Hannah Höch dies
German Dada artist and political commentator, born 1889. Höch was best known for her work critiquing the failings of the Weimar government. She was one of the originators of photomontage. See *Cut with the Dada Kitchen Knife Through the Last Weimar Beer-Belly Cultural Epoch of Germany*. It's an extraordinary piece which includes a small map of Europe showing countries where women could vote. Höch believed women should be free to vote, to have sex and be financially independent. The Nazis deemed her works 'degenerate art' because of their political content and because she was a woman. She was the only woman in the Berlin Dada group and her male colleagues never fully accepted her.

31 May

Spring Bank Holiday, United Kingdom

The last Monday in May is a national holiday in the United Kingdom. It's a day of general revelry when morris dancers

 suddenly seem less weird. Time to put on some motley and head off to a traditional event.

Cooper's Hill Cheese-Rolling

Cooper's Hill, Brockworth, Gloucester, England: A 7–9lb, round Double Gloucester cheese is set off down the hill, competitors chase it and whoever catches it gets to keep the cheese. The cheese can reach speeds of up to seventy miles per hour, which is not a sentence you write every day. The hill is steep and uneven and there are usually injuries. There are separate races for men and women.

Hunting of the Earl of Rone

Why not end the month with a manhunt? Okay, this is not some new form of app for single women in search of a fellow. There is a village in the English county of Devon called Combe Martin. It's a very pretty seaside place. Lovely beaches, nice pubs (try the Pack o' Cards) and good fun. They hold the record for the world's longest street party. Every year there is an annual event called the 'Hunting of the Earl of Rone', and in 2021 it is due to happen between Friday 28 May and Monday 31st. Like so much of British life, the festival is based on something that may or may not have happened hundreds of years ago.

The earl in question was Hugh O'Neill, 2nd Earl of Tyrone, who had led an unsuccessful Roman Catholic uprising against English rule in Ireland. It is said that in 1607 he fled Ireland in a boat heading for Spain. Sadly, the vessel came to grief on

Rapparee Cove to the west of the village. It's a beautiful beach. I hope he did land there. I can't find it as a fact anywhere. All I know is his compass was off because, after Devon, he landed eventually in France, rather than Spain, and lived out his life in Italy.

Never mind, it's a jolly event in Devon which features a hobby horse, the hunting of the earl, and music, dancing and a donkey.

JUNE

'A cold in the head in June is an immoral thing.'

– L. M. Montgomery, Canadian author, born 1874

Dry Month

I found two sayings about June and can't decide if they cancel each other out. The first is:

'If June be sunny, harvest comes early.'

Which seems clear enough but then there is:

'June damp and warm does the farmer no harm.'

So I have no idea – sunny or damp, it seems like a good month. The Anglo-Saxons called it *Seramonath*, or 'dry month', which sounds like they preferred the former. I don't really have enough agricultural knowledge to go either way but I did find a Sicilian proverb which goes:

'Prepare the sickles in May, use the sickles in June, and in July carry the sickles to the tool shed.'

Which I'm going to pass on as just generally good sickle advice. Anyway, it's a …

Woman's month!

June is named for the Roman goddess Juno, patroness of marriage and childbirth, which these days don't have to go together. She was married to Jupiter and is basically the queen of the gods. She tends to be depicted armed, wearing a goatskin. Goatskin smells so maybe it was a kind of birth control.

Of course, it could be that the month is nothing to do with her and the name came from either:

1. The Latin *juvenis*, meaning 'young people', or
2. Lucius Junius Brutus, semi-legendary founder of the Roman Republic.

I'm not keen on Lucius as he condemned his own sons to death, and the young get enough attention already, so let's go with the goddess.

Trivia
No other month ever begins on the same day of the week as June. It's basic maths but sounds a great fact on its own.

Sphenopalatine ganglioneuralgia, or cold-stimulus headache, is the scientific term for brain freeze when you eat ice cream too quickly, which you might in June. These two pieces of trivia are not related.

Good news for the Northern Hemisphere:
June is the month with the longest daylight.

Not so good for the Southern Hemisphere:
June has the shortest daylight hours of
the year in the Southern Hemisphere.

Other names for June

Afrikaans: *Junie* (is it just me who thinks that's cute?).

Welsh: *Mis Mehefin*.

Old English: *Sēremōnaþ*, which seems so like *Seramonath* it must mean the same.

Tagalog: *Hunyo*.

Scottish Gaelic: *An t-Ògmhios*.

Quecha: *Kuski*.

Polish: *Czerwiec*.

JUNE FESTIVALS

If you feel like travelling (and it's allowed):

The Dragon Boat Festival

China, Taiwan, Hong Kong, Macao, Malaysia, Singapore Traditional Chinese holiday on the fifth day of the fifth month of the traditional Chinese calendar, so you'll have to work it out but usually June.

Eat: *Zongzi* rice dumplings. Glutinous rice stuffed with different fillings and wrapped in bamboo, lotus or banana leaves.

Drink: *Realgar* wine. Alcoholic rice wine.

Watch: The spectacular Dragon Boat Race, which is 2,500 years old.

National Cereal Festival and Grand Cereal Parade

McCamly Street, Battle Creek, Michigan
The cereal folk Kellogg's have their HQ in Battle Creek so it's not surprising the town hosts the annual festival for cereals, held each second Saturday in June. It sounds like fun – craft stalls, people dressed as cereal characters, and eateries, each one producing 'a unique dish using cereal as one of the ingredients'. What fun. A chance to meet Tony the Tiger while eating something indefinable made with Rice Krispies. The world's longest breakfast table consists of 100 six-foot tables.

(Don't tell anyone but Ajialouna charity in Lebanon had a breakfast table that was longer and strictly speaking they hold the record of 7,165.4ft, but let's not start a fight.)

Cornflakes – made by accident
John Harvey Kellogg was a Michigan doctor. In 1876, he became the superintendent of the Battle Creek Sanitorium, which was a sort of hospital and spa combo for rich people. John's brother Will (W. K. Kellogg) was the sanitorium bookkeeper. They both became keen on the idea of a vegetarian diet and began experimenting with new recipes. Either, one day they were trying to make granola out of wheat when they got called away. On their return the wheat had turned. Waste not want not, so they put the wheat through some rollers and out came thin flakes.

Or, Will spilled some liquified cornmeal on a heating device and flakes resulted.

Either way they served it up to the sanitorium clients and history was made. It's not a great ending. The brothers fell out over sugar. Will wanted to add some and John wasn't having it. In the end Will (bookkeeper, so better at business) went on to make the Kellogg company whose boxes of accidental cereal grace many a table.

Why we should all go to Battle Creek
Never mind breakfast. Go to the Oak Hill Cemetery at South Ave and Hussey St and you can pay your respects at the grave of **Sojourner Truth**, one of the most important women in US history (*see* 29 May).

> *'I will not allow my life's light to be determined by the darkness around me.'*
>
> – Sojourner Truth

⤜ POEM OF THE MONTH ⤛

By Harriet Elizabeth Prescott Spofford

Ah, happy day, refuse to go!
Hang in the heavens forever so!
Forever in midafternoon,
Ah, happy day of happy June!

1 June 1990
Odette Fabius dies
French Resistance fighter, born 1920. She was a survivor of the infamous Ravensbrück concentration camp. Her life was saved by **Dr Anne Spoerry**, who hid Odette for four months in the

camp infirmary. Part of a group of women who affirmed that friendship helped their survival.

2 June 1965
Nannie Doss dies
Also known as the 'Giggling Granny', the 'Lonely Hearts Killer', the 'Black Widow' and 'Lady Blue Beard'. American serial killer, born Nancy Hazel in 1905. She is known to have killed eleven people between the 1920s and 1954. A 'self-made widow' who killed four of her own husbands, one of her kids, two of her grandchildren, her sister, her mother and a mother-in-law. She died of leukaemia in Oklahoma State Penitentiary.

3 June 1906
Josephine Baker born
American-born French entertainer, French Resistance agent and civil rights activist. There is almost too much to say about her. Picasso painted her. Ernest Hemingway said she was 'the most sensational woman anyone ever saw. Or ever will.' Baker was the first African American to star in a major motion picture. After the Second World War she was awarded the Croix de Guerre and the Rosette de la Résistance, and was also made a Chevalier of the Légion d'honneur. She refused to perform for segregated audiences in the US, and helped achieve integration in Las Vegas shows. In 1963 she was the only official female speaker at the March on Washington alongside Martin Luther King Jr. Weirdly, she has, to this day, an agency licensing her image so people are still making money off her.

— 3 June —

World Bicycle Day

'She who succeeds in gaining the mastery of the bicycle will gain the mastery of life.'

— **Susan B. Anthony**, American social reformer
and women's rights activist, born 1820

June marks the birthday of the bicycle, that genius invention which first allowed women to head off up the road without some bloke keeping an eye. At last they could find independence and travel alone. The first such two-wheeled form of human transport was the brainchild of a prolific German inventor, Karl von Drais. It was in June 1817 that Karl first mounted the earliest form of bicycle, the *Laufmaschine* ('running machine') or 'dandy horse', which looked like a bike without pedals. You sat on it and ran your feet along the road to make it move forward. His first outing took him from Mannheim to a coaching inn called the Schwetzinger Relaishaus. I love this. Human beings can finally get somewhere faster and they use it to get to the pub. He covered the 4.3 miles in a dizzying time of just over an hour. Soon everyone wanted to have a go but unfortunately most roads were too rutted from carriage wheels, so daring *Laufmaschine* owners took to the pavement where alarmed pedestrians caused the authorities in Germany, and then Great Britain, the United States and even Calcutta, to ban their use. It would be forty or so years before folks had another go at cycling, this time adding pedals to push the thing along.

The penny farthing bicycle was launched in 1869, with one large front wheel and a smaller back wheel. Pedals were attached to the giant front wheel as there was still no chain between the wheels. The large wheel meant greater distances could be covered but you could also fall off in a nanosecond. Finally, someone in the 1880s thought of having two wheels the same size connected by a chain. They were known as 'safety bicycles'. Why, they were so safe and easy to use that some women began to think they could ride them, which was obviously a shocking notion. A bicycle craze swept across Britain, Europe and the USA and, before you knew it, women began to reconsider their wardrobe in need of something more suitable to pedal in. Bloomers became the dress of the day and soon women were ditching their corsets, emerging from the cocoon of their drawing rooms and discovering an intoxicating freedom (admittedly mostly white, middle- and upper-class women).

Not everyone was thrilled by this development. There was concern that bicycling women might endanger their modesty by revealing their ankles, so **Margaret Corrie** from Woking in Surrey invented an ankle guard which could be attached to the frame of the bike. The problem of hair becoming dishevelled while cycling was solved by **Clara Moore**, who came up with an artificial fringe of curls which could be fixed to a band to disguise anything unkempt.

The press were appalled by these corset-free bicycling ladies and warned that women exerting themselves while not being held in by whalebone and ribbon would produce sickly babies. Of course, the reverse happened. The women were fitter and so were their kids. There were those who felt the whole cycling thing was too sexual. Why, a woman astride a saddle like that might have orgasms in the middle of the street. No female should be permitted the vibrations available from traversing a cobbled street on two wheels. Special saddles were produced to try to prevent women from getting aroused. A rather fearful woman doctor called Arabella Kenealy warned women that exercise of any kind might reduce their ability to be the 'mother of men'. Women were warned about something called 'bicycle face' – a strained expression from all the concentration needed on a bike. This would mar a woman's beauty, as indeed would being out in the sun at all. Go for too long a ride and your face might get stuck in a terrible, bulging stare and all that pedalling might make you bowlegged to boot.

Women on bikes were seen as a menace by some. When male undergraduates at Cambridge University wished to protest against the full admission of female students in 1897 they hung an effigy of a 'New Woman' on a bicycle from a window in Market Square.

Despite all this, women kept pedalling and some did amazing things. On 27 June 1894 a Latvian immigrant to the United States called **Annie Londonderry** set off from Boston, Massachusetts, to cycle around the world on her own. She was twenty-four and wore a long skirt and corset, carrying with her some spare clothes and a pearl-handled revolver. She was married with three kids and, until a few days before she set off, she'd never even ridden a bicycle. Her married name was Annie Kopchovsky but she was sponsored for her trip by the Londonderry Spring Water Company and agreed to use their name while she travelled. The trip took fifteen months and she made her money through lectures and sponsorship. During the course of her trip Annie went from wearing a long skirt to bloomers to a man's suit. She became an inspiration to many women who felt the same as she did when she declared, 'I didn't want to spend my life at home with a baby under my apron every year.'

Even now, men are still more likely to cycle than women. That's true in the UK and it's certainly true in other parts of the world. In Yemen in 2015 a photographer named **Bushra al-Fusail** decided to find an alternative mode of transport for women in a country where petrol was at a premium. She launched a Yemeni women's bike group and broke conservative taboos in doing so. There are other places where a bicycle represents an important tool for justice and social change. It can enable a woman to go to school, to the doctor's, and keep her safe away from harassment on public transportation. When the Indian Ocean tsunami of 2004 brought devastation to thousands, bicycles helped many rebuild their lives. In the refugee camps of the world, a woman on a bicycle can reach food distribution points that may be miles away. During the Covid-19 pandemic many turned to bicycles for essential transport. In places like Pakistan, many women found freedom in quarantine through cycling.

Hopefully the upsurge in cycling that happened in 2020 will continue. Women have often cited safety as the reason for not making as many bicycle trips as men. Now infrastructure changes may start to make cities such as London as safe for the cyclist as, say, Copenhagen, where women make up more than half of all bike riders.

> *'The bicycle is the most civilized conveyance known to man. Other forms of transport grow daily more nightmarish. Only the bicycle remains pure in heart.'*
>
> – **Iris Murdoch**, Irish-British novelist and philosopher, born 1919

4 June 1873
The war between the Native American Modoc tribe and the US Army comes to an end

Toby 'Winema' Riddle, born in 1848, served as an interpreter in the negotiations that ended the war. 'Winema' means 'woman chief'. She saved the life of peace commissioner Alfred B. Meacham when a Modoc attack took place. In 1891 she became one of the few Native American women ever to be awarded a military pension.

5 June 1893
Mary Ann Shadd dies

Born in 1823, Shadd was the first black female newspaper publisher in North America. She founded the *Provincial Freeman* in Canada in 1853 to publicise the successes of black persons living in freedom in Canada. In 1883 she became one of the first black women to complete a law degree.

6 June 1841
Eliza Orzeszkowa born
A Polish novelist, Orzeszkowa wrote thirty novels plus dramas and other writings dealing with the social conditions of occupied Poland. In 1905 she was nominated for the Nobel Prize in Literature.

7 June 1968
Ford sewing machinists' strike begins
Rose Boland, Eileen Pullen, Vera Sime, Gwen Davis and Sheila Douglass led the strike at the Ford factory in Essex demanding equal pay to men as 'skilled workers'. The strike, which ended after three weeks, helped pave the way for the Equal Pay Act of 1970, but the women would have to strike again in 1984 to achieve the same wages as male workers. It was joining the EU in 1973 that caused the law to make it mandatory for men and women to receive equal pay for equal work, but in 2019 the gender pay gap for all UK employees was 17.3 per cent.

8 June 1956
Marie Laurencin dies
French painter and printmaker, born 1883. Laurencin was one of the few female Cubist painters, and an important figure in the Parisian avant-garde of the early 20th century. She was part of **Natalie Clifford Barney**'s salon. There was once a museum dedicated to her in Tokyo but it seems to have closed.

9 June 1843
Bertha von Suttner born
Austrian-Bohemian pacifist and novelist, von Suttner was the second female Nobel Laureate, and the first woman to be awarded the Nobel Peace Prize. Her pacifist novel, *Die Waffen*

nieder! (Lay Down Your Arms!), published in 1889, was an international hit, which made her a leading figure in the peace movement. She campaigned for the establishment of an International Court of Justice and took part in the First Hague Convention in 1899. She also wrote on gender.

10 June 1876
Calamity Jane gets famously drunk

Martha Jane Cannary, born 1852, and better known as Calamity Jane, was an explorer, performer, dance-hall girl, ox-team driver, nurse, frontierswoman, cross-dresser and sharpshooter. She liked a drink. On 10 June 1876, she celebrated her acquittal for grand larceny by drinking at the Tivoli Saloon in Cheyenne. The only woman to do so, as she was dressed like a man. She then rented a horse and buggy to travel the short distance to Fort Russell, but was so drunk she ended up about ninety miles away at Fort Laramie.

11 June 1880
Jeannette Rankin born

In 1917 she became the first woman member of the US Congress, serving two terms. Rankin was a feminist, pacifist and activist for social and electoral reform. She introduced the first bill that would have allowed women citizenship independent of their husbands. She was the only member of Congress to vote against the declaration of war on Japan after the raid on Pearl Harbor.

12 June 918
Æthelflæd dies

Lady of the Mercians, born around 870, she ruled Mercia in the English Midlands between 911 and 918. A female ruler in early medieval history is astonishing. She was the daughter of King Alfred the Great. In the 890s she played an important role in driving out the Danes, which is not all that pleasing to this Dane. She ruled at first with her husband Æthelred, but when he died in 911 she became *Myrcna hlædige* ('Lady of the Mercians') and carried on by herself. There is a statue of her outside Tamworth railway station in Staffordshire. She helped rebuild the town after the Danes had a go at it, so they like her there.

13 June 1660

Katherine Ferrers dies on or around this date

Ferrers, born 1634, was an English gentlewoman, heiress and, according to legend, highwaywoman. She was said to have become the 'Wicked Lady', causing mayhem in the English county of Hertfordshire by trying to shore up her dwindling fortune with highway robbery. She is rumoured to have died, aged twenty-six, of gunshot wounds sustained during a robbery.

14 June 1926

Mary Cassatt dies

American painter and printmaker, born 1844. Leading artist of the Impressionist movement. Edgar Degas said of her painting *La Toilette*, 'I don't believe a woman could draw that well. Did you really do this?' I was eighteen when I discovered her work, and so furious no one had ever mentioned her to me when I was taught about art. She began her studies in 1859 at the Pennsylvania Academy of the Fine Arts in Philadelphia, where female students were not allowed to use live models. She often painted children and domestic scenes, which sidelined her reputation as a great artist.

15 June 1952
Krystyna Skarbek dies
Skarbek, born 1908, was a Polish agent of the British Special Operations Executive (SOE) during the Second World War. Reported to be Churchill's favourite spy. She was described as 'very brave, very attractive, but a loner and a law unto herself'. Skarbek was the first female agent of the British to serve in the field, and the longest-serving of all Britain's wartime women agents. She was stabbed to death by a spurned suitor in London.

16 June 1569
Brita Olofsdotter's family receives her military salary
Brita Olofsdotter was a Finnish soldier of the Swedish cavalry, and probably the first confirmed female soldier in Sweden. Widowed, she dressed as a man and enlisted. She served in the Livonian War and was killed in battle in 1569. On 16 June 1569, John III of Sweden ordered her remaining salary be paid to her family.

17 June 1631
Mumtaz Mahal dies
Born in 1593, she became empress consort of the Mughal empire under Mughal emperor Shah Jahan. He commissioned the Taj Mahal in Agra as her tomb and a monument to his love. She died giving birth to her fourteenth child.

18 June 1873
Susan B. Anthony tried for attempting to vote
Susan B. Anthony, born 1820, was an American social reformer, abolitionist and heroic women's rights activist. She attempted to vote in the 1872 election in Rochester, New York. Her speech in the subsequent trial is magnificent. She was found guilty and fined $100, which she refused to pay. The authorities did not pursue the

matter as they did not want it to go to the Supreme Court. In 1979 she became the first female citizen to be depicted on US coins.

Here's how human beings work

Sunday 18 June 1815: Battle of Waterloo

Monday 19 June 1815: Scavengers begin looting corpses left at the battle scene for their teeth to sell to dentists. The dentists would take the teeth, boil them, cut off the roots, stick them on ivory base plates and sell them on.

---

19 June 1603
Merga Bien arrested for witchcraft
Merga Bien was a German woman, born in 1560, who was convicted of witchcraft during the infamous Fulda witch trials, held between 1603 and 1605. Over 200 people were executed as a result of the trials. Merga was arrested on 19 June 1603, and forced to confess that she was pregnant due to sex with the devil. She was burnt at the stake.

20 June 1914
Muazzez İlmiye Çığ born
Turkish Sumerologist, scientist and historian. Her research into the history of the headscarf revealed it to be not of Muslim origin, but worn 5,000 years ago by Sumerian priestesses who initiated young men into sex. She argued that, with this historical context, the wearing of a headscarf should not indicate a woman's morality today. Aged ninety-two, she was charged with inciting religious hatred but was acquitted.

21 June 1953
Benazir Bhutto born
Pakistani politician, and twice prime minister of Pakistan (1988 to 1990, and 1993 to 1996). Bhutto was the first woman to lead a democratic government in a Muslim majority nation. She attempted to advance women's rights. A controversial figure, she was assassinated in 2007.

22 June 1664
Katherine Philips dies
Born around 1631, she was also known as 'The Matchless Orinda'. Philips was an Anglo-Welsh Royalist poet, translator and woman of letters, highly regarded by many 17th-century writers including John Dryden and John Keats. She is best known for her poems on female friendship.

23–29 June
La Batalla del Vino de Haro, Haro, Spain
The Batalla is a weeklong wine festival that concludes with a massive wine fight, and who doesn't want to go to one of those? Apparently, the festival dates back to the 6th century. The whole shindig begins with the Bonfires of San Juan, a fire and fireworks celebration on the 23rd. This is followed by Amanecer del Chocolate (Dawn of Chocolate), where chocolate is given out. Then on the 29th a lot of people dress in red and white; the mayor leads them out of town to the Hermitage of San Felices. There is a short mass and then everyone throws wine at each other. There are several suggestions as to how this started but no one really cares.

23 June 1879
Huda Sha'arawi born
In 1923, Sha'arawi was the founder of the Egyptian Feminist Union. She was a pioneering feminist leader and nationalist. She spent her childhood and early adulthood secluded in an upper-class Egyptian harem and was married to her cousin when she was thirteen. She took part in the Egyptian Revolution of 1919, a women-led protest seeking Egyptian independence from Britain. Removed her face veil in 1922, considered to be a very significant moment for Egyptian women.

24 June 1519
Lucrezia Borgia dies
Italian noblewoman, born 1480. The daughter of Pope Alexander VI and his mistress Vannozza dei Catanei, she was a key figure in the infamous Borgia family of the Italian Renaissance. It's a complicated family, with rumours of murder, incest and much unpleasantness. Borgia reigned as the governor of Spoleto in her own right, and died aged thirty-nine after the birth of her tenth child. Like so many women, she may well have been maligned by history.

25 June 1878
Marie-Elisabeth Lüders born
A German politician, social worker and women's rights activist. In 1908, Lüders was one of the first women to enrol at Berlin's Friedrich Wilhelm University, where she earned a doctorate in political science. Her political work was focused on the rights of women, workers and children. She was imprisoned by the Gestapo in 1937. After the war she was elected to the German Bundestag, where she served as *Alterspräsidentin* in 1953 and 1957 – sort of Mother of the House.

— Last week of June —

World Immunisation Week

'I give myself sometimes admirable advice, but I am incapable of taking it.'

– Lady Mary Wortley Montagu,
writer, poet, adventurer, born 1689

Lady Mary was born the eldest child of a duke. She was extremely beautiful and no doubt her parents saw a future for her in a well-arranged and hopefully profitable marriage, but Mary had other plans. She wrote in her diary, 'I am going to write a history so uncommon.' And so she did, for Mary would grow up to become a celebrated writer, an advocate for women's rights and the person who introduced smallpox inoculation to England.

From her diaries we get the most wonderful images of this free-spirited child who loved to run across a meadow trying to catch the setting sun. Sadly, her mother died and Mary was left to the care of an ill-equipped governess. Escaping this dreaded person, Mary said she stole her education from her father's library. Fortunately, her dad had one of the largest private libraries in England, no doubt helped by owning a large part of the country to keep it in. Mary read and wrote and taught herself Greek and Latin before, in 1712, ignoring her father's wishes and eloping with a young man called Edward Wortley Montagu.

Edward became an MP and Lady Mary became the toast of London. She was witty and she was gay, which in those days had a slightly different ring to it. She became friends with the glitterati including the Prince and Princess of Wales, but sadly she contracted smallpox which left her great beauty scarred with pitted skin. In 1716 her husband was appointed ambassador to Turkey and Mary shocked the world by deciding to go with him. It was a scandalous decision. Imagine! A refined lady volunteering to go to the barbarous East. Mary loved it. Far from being a brutal society she found Turkish women had more freedom than English ones. She learned the language, made friends and, most importantly, allowed her two children to be 'engrafted' with smallpox by a Turkish medicine woman. This was a kind of inoculation and it worked.

Lady M was soon telling everyone about it. People in London were not keen on the idea of inoculation, partly because Mary was a woman and so what would she know and because the procedure was, well, Turkish. Because she was well-connected, on her return to Britain she managed to get Caroline, Princess of Wales, to help promote the idea. This worked a treat, as there is nothing like a patronising royal to get things done. Without Mary's keenness on the subject, Edward Jenner's later, pioneering smallpox vaccine might never have been accepted.

Mary carried on travelling, spending more than twenty years in different European countries with a succession of lovers. She wrote about her journeys, encouraging other women that such a life might even be possible. Her Turkish letters remain fascinating. She was one of the first Westerners to publish an account of women's lives in the Orient. One of the things I love most about her is that she didn't care what anyone thought of her. Far from being distressed by her pock-marked skin, when she was sixty-nine she confessed she had not looked in a mirror for eleven years. There is a marvellous story of her going to the opera and being told that her hands were dirty, to which she replied, 'You should see my feet.' Her dying words are supposed to have been, 'It has all been most interesting.'

Of course, the name I am missing from all this information on inoculation is the anonymous Turkish woman who taught Mary about it in the first place.

A tribute to a cow

It was in 1796 that the English physician Edward Jenner conclusively established the important principles of vaccination. Jenner had a theory that a person infected with a virus called cowpox might be immune to the similar but very contagious and much worse disease called smallpox. He tested this theory by scraping cowpox blisters off the hands of a milkmaid called Sarah Nelmes, who had caught cowpox from a cow called Blossom. He then injected this stuff into the eight-year-old son of his gardener. I feel this is taking liberties with domestic staff and the gardener should have been furious. Fortunately, the boy survived and the history of medicine was changed. We should thank the child, the gardener and Jenner, but hardly anyone mentions Blossom the cow. It is from her that we get the word 'vaccination', a word that has lately obsessed the world. It comes from the Latin *'vacca'* meaning 'cow'. Poor Blossom eventually died (of what history does not say) and her hide apparently now hangs on the wall of the St George's medical school library in south London, which is the most fame anyone can hope for.

26 June 1861
Jeanne Louise Antonini dies
Antonini, born 1771 in Corsica, served ten years in the French navy and then a further fifteen years in the French army, disguised as a man during the revolutionary period and the Napoleonic Wars. She was wounded nine times and reached the rank of sergeant.

27 June 1880
Helen Keller born
American author, political activist and lecturer. As a toddler she became deaf and blind after suffering from what is thought to have been either scarlet fever or meningitis. The story of Keller and her teacher, **Anne Sullivan** (*see* 20 October), is rightly famous. Sullivan helped Keller to communicate. Keller became the first deaf-blind person to earn a BA degree. She was a member of the Socialist Party of America and campaigned for women's suffrage, labour rights and socialism.

Random words for women if you have time
According to the online *Historical Thesaurus of English* there have been 124 basic words for 'woman' in English, over the past 1,000 years. These include: *cwen, frowe, meowle, stot, minikin, pigsy, ware, mumps* and, from the 17th century, my least favourite – *murrey-kersey*, which basically means 'dark red narrow cloth'.
Trust me, it wasn't a compliment.

28 June 548
Theodora dies
Theodora, born around 500, was Eastern Roman empress by marriage to Emperor Justinian, and one of his chief advisers. He called her his 'partner in my deliberations'. She was very powerful so (obviously) was accused of both prostitution and acting in her early years. She became the first Eastern Roman empress consort to have coins struck in her name. Saved the throne for Justinian during the Nika riots. Justinian and Theodora rebuilt Constantinople, commissioning amazing buildings including the Hagia Sophia, one of the architectural wonders of the world. She closed brothels and made pimping a criminal offence.

29 June 2017
Mother Mushroom sentenced to ten years in jail for publishing propaganda against the Vietnamese state
Mother Mushroom, born 1979, is the pen name of Vietnamese blogger and dissident, Nguyễn Ngọc Như Quỳnh. She criticised the Vietnamese government over human rights violations and corruption. Arrested in 2009 for blogging about government land confiscations in relation to a Chinese-backed bauxite mine. When she was arrested again in 2016, for trying to visit an imprisoned political activist, it caused an international outcry. On this day in 2017 she was sentenced to ten years in jail for publishing propaganda against the state, but she was released in 2018 and exiled to the United States.

30 June 1943
Jetsunma Tenzin Palmo born
Born Diane Perry in Hertfordshire, England, Tenzin Palmo is one of the very few Western yoginis (female master practitioner of yoga) trained in the East. She was the only woman on

her first training programme, and spent twelve years living in a remote cave in the Himalayas. Read *Cave in the Snow: A Western Woman's Quest for Enlightenment*. Tenzin Palmo works to revive the extinct Togdenma lineage, 'a long-forgotten spiritual elite' of women.

'I have made a vow to attain Enlightenment in the female form – no matter how many lifetimes it takes.'

Dolma Ling Nunnery

In June of 2019 Buddhism leapt into the world of equality when two Tibetan Buddhist nuns with geshema degrees were hired to teach Buddhist philosophy at Dolma Ling Nunnery and Institute in India. A geshema degree is the equivalent of a doctorate in Buddhist philosophy and the women hired were **Geshema Tenzin Kunsel** and **Geshema Delek Wangmo**. Historically, the Dolma Ling Nunnery and Institute had only had male teachers, even though it was only women they were teaching. I like the sound of this place. They have a seventeen-year curriculum in Buddhist philosophy and debate but you also get to do butter sculptures and create sand mandalas, although presumably not on the same day as that would be messy.

JULY

'Married in July with flowers ablaze,
Bittersweet memories on after days.'

– Traditional, if not exactly comforting rhyme.
Maybe don't get married this month.

Haymaking Month or the Flowering of the Meadows

This month's name also has Roman origins, being an homage to Julius Caesar, who was born on 12 July 100 BC. The Latin name for the month used to be *Quinctilis* (from *quinctus*, 'fifth') but when Caesar was murdered in 44 BC the Roman Senate renamed the month *Iulius* in his memory.

Interestingly, July was once pronounced to rhyme with 'duly' and 'truly', but it was changed in the 18th century to make it sound less like June.

The Anglo-Saxons called it *Heymonath*, 'haymaking month', or *Maedmonath*, 'month of the flowering of the meadows'.

Quick Caesar trivia

1. He wasn't born by caesarean section.
The procedure existed but it was only used if a pregnant woman was dead or dying. Julius's mum, Aurelia, lived for almost fifty years after his birth.

2. He was kidnapped by pirates.
His ship was hijacked off the southwestern coast of Asia Minor when he was in his mid-twenties travelling from Rome to the Aegean island of Rhodes. When the pirates set a ransom for his release he thought it was too low and demanded they up the price. The ransom was paid. He returned and executed the buccaneers.

Other names for July

Māori: *Hōngoingoi*, meaning to crouch in front of a fire because for them it's midwinter.

Lithuanian: *Liepa*, meaning 'the linden tree', which flowers during this month.

Albanian: *Korrik* – from *korr*, 'harvest'.

Korean: *Chilweol*.

JULY FESTIVALS

These two both take place on the first weekend of the month:

Henley Royal Regatta, Henley-on-Thames, Oxfordshire

Lot of boats. Been going since 1839. Much of the grassy shoreline is taken up by the Stewards' Enclosure. This is reserved for members and their guests. Women are not allowed to wear trousers. Only dresses or skirts with hemlines below the knee are permitted.

CAN THIS REALLY STILL BE A THING? (Sorry for shouting.)
Still, other people's festivals can be worse ...

Wife-Carrying World Championships or Akankanto, Sonkajärvi, Finland

Should I even put this in?

The gist: A male competitor carries a willing female 832 feet along a track while dealing with obstacles like fences and water hazards. According to the official rules, the wife may be 'your own, the neighbour's, or you may have found her further afield'.

The prize: The winning 'wife's' weight in beer.

The history: It began in the good old days when women were stolen from neighbouring villages.

There's also karaoke and a tractor parade (now you're talking). I think I'm speechless.

⤛ POEM OF THE MONTH ⤜

I Asked Myself by Sappho
(translated by Mary Barnard)

I asked myself
What, Sappho, can
you give one who
has everything,
like Aphrodite?

I think this poem may not be working as well as it might on the page because it was written to be accompanied by a lyre which is tricky to organise. Sappho lived about 2,500 years ago on the Greek island of Lesbos. She was clearly good at writing as she was also known as the 'Tenth Muse', which is a huge Greek compliment. We know very little about her except that she was prolific. Sadly, most of her work is missing. She has become a symbol of love and desire between women. In fact, the terms 'sapphic' and 'lesbian' are derived from her name and her home. For a lot of critics over the years that has been all they can think about. To be fair I've had days like that.

1 July 1889
Vera Mukhina born
Mukhina is known as the 'queen of Soviet sculpture', and for her work in Cubist and socialist realism. She also taught and designed clothes, textiles, porcelain, as well as theatrical costumes for Moscow's Vakhtangov Theatre. In 1940 she campaigned to stop the Freedom Monument in Riga, Latvia, being replaced with a statue of Stalin. Creator of world's first welded sculpture.

2 July 1634
Saskia van Uylenburgh marries Rembrandt van Rijn
On this day Saskia, born 1612, married the painter Rembrandt. She was wealthy and educated, while he was wild and the son of a miller. She would listen to no one when she fell for him. Saskia was the model for some of his paintings, drawings and etchings. She died of tuberculosis aged twenty-nine. Rembrandt became so poor he sold Saskia's grave.

3 July 1932
Swarnakumari Devi dies
(Name in Bengali: স্বর্ণকুমারী দবী) Born 1855, Devi was a poet, novelist, musician, science writer and social care activist. She became the first Bengali woman novelist when *Deepnirban* was published in 1876. In 1879 she composed *Basanta Utsav*, possibly the first Bengali opera. She was among the first women to serve in the Indian National Congress, and founded Sakhi Samiti (Society of Friends) to assist orphans and widows.

4 July 1844
Edmonia Lewis born
Good month for sculpture. Lewis was an American sculptor. Her mother was of Mississauga Ojibwe and African American

descent. Her father was Afro-Haitian. Lewis became the first woman of African American and Native American heritage to achieve international fame as a sculptor. As a child she went by her Native American name, Wildfire, and endured racism, prejudice and discrimination during her education. She left the United States and made a new life in Rome, Italy. Her two-ton marble statue *The Death of Cleopatra* is now in the Smithsonian American Art Museum, having been found in a salvage yard in the 1980s. She lived in Hammersmith, London, before her death and is buried in Kensal Green.

 — *Independence and American heroes* —

Trick question: when was the US Declaration of Independence signed?

The US celebrates Independence Day on 4 July but that's not when the document was signed or even when the country declared its independence.

Timeline

2 July 1776: America declares independence.

4 July 1776: The final draft of the declaration is completed and approved by Congress.

2 August 1776: Everyone signs.

I've been thinking about heroes. It's in the air. I don't know how much you know about the American Revolution. It figured large in my life, not because I'm so old but because I grew up in the United States and it was pretty much all the history they had. Even those who know little about it may be familiar with the name Paul Revere, an American silversmith, who in April 1775 took his horse for a midnight dash to alert the colonial militia that the British were coming. His daring was dramatised in Henry Wadsworth Longfellow's poem, 'Paul Revere's Ride'. Someone you may not have heard of, though, is another hero who performed the same feat of courage except rode twice as far, was only sixteen, and a girl.

Her name was **Sybil Ludington** and she was born on 5 April 1761 in Fredericksburg, New York. Her father, Henry, commanded a troop of local militia in Westchester County which, as it happens, is the county where I grew up. News had reached Westchester that a large body of British troops was on its way but Colonel Henry's men had all gone home to plant their fields. This is no way to run an army and Henry needed to rally his troops from every village. It was Sybil who spread the word, riding her horse Star forty miles through the night to raise the alarm.

Great story but there has been a problem in documenting Sybil's bravery. It is a continuous issue with women in history. Sybil's ride was not told in verse by a famous poet but, as so often happens with women, handed down as oral history through her family. It was more than a hundred years after her ride that a local New York historian called Martha Lamb recorded the tale in her book *History of the City of New York*. Lamb was at pains to explain that she had been thorough in checking the facts but for many it was still not enough. In America there is a powerful group known as the Daughters of the American Revolution, women who trace their ancestry to those who fought for American independence. You would think they might embrace Sybil but they have declared that the evidence is not strong enough to support their criteria for a war heroine. Not everyone agreed. Her hometown of Fredericksburg is now called Ludingtonville but this problem of proving the thing affected Sybil herself. When she was seventy-six she tried to claim a war pension through her husband's service but lacked the right papers to prove she had ever been married. She died in poverty the following year never thinking she might have claimed the money in her own right.

When I was a kid I grew up in a small town in New York called Mamaroneck. It was a neat little harbour settlement on the Long Island Sound and the name, I was told, came from a Native American expression meaning 'where the fresh water meets the salt'. That's all the Native American background I have as we weren't taught any more. Even the local historical society seems uninterested. They begin the history of the town on an exact day, 23 September 1661, when a London merchant called John Richbell bought the land where the town now stands from Siwanoy Indians. The fact that the Siwanoy would have had shedloads of history before 23 September goes unremarked. It was never written down, so it didn't exist. What we now know is that the Siwanoy were unlikely to have had the same understanding about the transaction as Mr Richbell. To them, land was simply somewhere that sustained you and not something that you owned.

It's a bit like the myth that the Lenape tribe sold Manhattan for $24 worth of trinkets. This much-repeated nonsense suggests a gullible indigenous population who gave away some of the greatest real estate in the world for a few eye-catching beads. If we want better facts about what happened it's probably useful to look at a later 17th-century deed for the Dutch purchase of Staten Island, also for $24, which lists goods 'to be brought from Holland and delivered' to the Indians, including shirts, socks, cloth, muskets, bars of lead, powder, kettles, axes, awls and knives. This is all sensible stuff. Most likely the Lenape believed they were simply allowing the newcomers to use the land not wipe them out of it.

Time and again the history we learn is dependent entirely on who wrote it down. I've been thinking about heroes and who gets to decide where that mantle of greatness is placed. There are 828 statues of the great and the good registered in the United Kingdom, of which about 10 per cent are named women. Take out the royals and any woman from mythology and you are left with just twenty-seven women who have been thought to have done enough to receive a hero's memorialising in bronze.

One of them is a life-size depiction of the Native American **Pocahontas**, which stands in the grounds of St George's church in Gravesend, Kent. In 1614, aged seventeen, she married the English colonist John Rolfe in Virginia. Pocahontas was the daughter of an important chief of the local Tsenacommacah tribe and the year before she had been held captive for ransom by the English settlers. She had been encouraged to convert to Christianity and change her name to Rebecca. She married John and, two years later, he took her to London to show her off as a 'civilised savage' so that he might encourage investors in the new settlement of Jamestown. I don't know what happened, but she and John had set sail back to Virginia after their trip to the UK when she became ill. The ship docked at Gravesend, where she passed away of unknown causes, aged perhaps twenty or twenty-one.

So much of her life is shrouded in mystery. We don't know the exact date of her birth and it's possible that Pocahontas was not even her real name. Most likely it was a nickname meaning 'playful one'. There is some thought that she concealed her true name because there was some native belief that the English might be able to cause her greater hurt if they knew it.

The movies will have us believe that she saved the life of one John Smith but here fact is muddied by Smith's own tall-tale-telling to big himself up. Most of what has been written about her over the years is, to use a marvellous American expression, hogwash. The fictional depiction of an Indian who admires the white man, and adopts Christianity and the imported European culture, makes white Americans feel better about themselves. The many harms inflicted on the native culture can be overlooked as the story of Pocahontas helps rehabilitate a terrible history.

The true story, if you dig a little deeper, is of a clever and brave young woman, who served as a translator, an ambassador for her own people and a leader in her own right in the face of immense European power. Her people were faced with an interloper who was technologically stronger in every way and she helped negotiate a way forward. Certainly her marriage to John Rolfe helped create peace between the Jamestown colonists and the local tribes. It lasted years and was known as the 'Peace of Pocahontas'.

I should like to have met her. By all accounts she was spunky and forthright. My favourite story about her concerns the time she met the king in the Palace of Whitehall. The story is told that she found King James so unprepossessing that she didn't realise who he was until someone told her afterwards.

5 July 2010
Manuela Sáenz receives full state burial in Venezuela
Sáenz, born in 1797, was an Ecuadorian revolutionary and spy. She was a heroine of South America, and a women's rights activist. Partner of Simón Bolívar, the Venezuelan leader who led much of South America to independence from the Spanish empire. She prevented an 1828 assassination attempt against him and facilitated his escape. He called her 'Libertadora del Libertador' (Liberator of the Liberator). Sáenz ended her life a destitute outcast selling tobacco. On 5 July 2010, she was finally given a full state burial in Venezuela. It was symbolic as she actually lies in a mass grave.

6 July 1937
Bessie Head born
Though born in South Africa, Head is considered to be Botswana's most influential writer. She is the author of novels, short fiction and autobiography. Born to a 'white' woman and a 'non-white' man when such interracial relationships were illegal in South Africa. As an infant she was placed with foster parents who returned her when they realised she was not white. Hers is an extraordinary and complicated story. Her work focused on the micro of everyday life within the macro of African political struggles.

7 July 1861
Nettie Stevens born
American geneticist credited with the discovery of sex chromosomes. Edmund Wilson published his 'discovery' of sex determinism at the same time as Stevens, but he claimed environmental factors affected sex. Stevens thought the determination of sex was only genetic. She was right.

8 July 1593
Artemisia Gentileschi born
Italian Baroque painter, and the first woman member of the
Accademia di Arte del Disegno in Florence. Hugely successful,
she was one of the most accomplished 17th-century artists at a
time when women were not expected to pursue careers in the
arts or anywhere. Simply one of my favourites.

9 July 1774
Anna Morandi Manzolini dies
Italian anatomist and sculptor, born 1714. At first she worked
with her husband but her skill and reputation was recognised
as surpassing his. Manzolini learned anatomy by dissecting
over a thousand cadavers and was renowned for modelling
anatomical models. She was the first person to reproduce tiny
body parts like nerves, and she also lectured on anatomical
design at the University of Bologna. Her fame was such that
she was invited to the court of Catherine II of Russia and
other royals.

More July fun

**The Boryeong Mud Festival, Boryeong,
South Korea**
The Boryeong mud flats lie 200 kilometres south of Seoul. In
1996, mud from these flats was turned into cosmetics which
were said to be full of naturally occurring minerals. The festival basically began to market the cosmetics but now it's a
full-on, filthy festival. Mud races, mud wrestling, mud facials,
Mr Mud competition plus soap making if you fancy a change.

World Bodypainting Festival, Klangenfurt, Austria
Three-day festival where artists from more than fifty countries compete for awards in body- and face-painting, special effects make-up and other ways of using faces and torsos as canvases to create works of art. Lots of workshops, lots of food, masses of naked people with paint on them.

The National Baby Food Festival, Fremont, Michigan
More than 100,000 people overwhelm this small town which proclaims itself 'Baby Food Capital of the World'. Hard to know if that's true but it is home to the Gerber Products Company who make a lot of mushy food. Anyway, it's a three-day event with a parade plus a baby-food-eating contest (obvs), a crawling race and bib decorating.

10 July 1891
Edith Quimby born
American medical researcher and physicist, Quimby was one of the founders of nuclear medicine who helped develop the diagnostic and therapeutic applications of x-rays. The American Association of Physicists in Medicine established a lifetime achievement award in her honour.

11 July 1997
'Eve' DNA analysis reported in the *New York Times*
Scientists in London report DNA analysis of a female Neanderthal skeleton. It supports the 'out of Africa theory' of human evolution and places an 'African Eve', from whom all humans are descended, at 100,000 to 200,000 years ago.

12 July 1780
Juana Azurduy de Padilla born
Bolivian female guerrilla military leader who earned the rank
of lieutenant colonel. De Padilla is remembered for her leadership of the indigenous people of Upper Peru. She organised
the Batallón Leales (Loyal Battalion) which successfully fought
in the Battle of Ayohuma in 1813. During a later battle she left
the fight to give birth. Several of her children died. She lived
out her life in poverty and was buried in a communal grave.
A hundred years later her body was exhumed and moved to a
mausoleum. In July 2015 a 52ft-high statue of her was erected
in Buenos Aires, replacing one of Columbus.

13 July 1934
Kate Sheppard dies
Sheppard was an English-born women's rights activist who was
instrumental in making New Zealand the first country in the
world to grant women the right to vote (1893). She promoted
sensible clothing for women, bicycling and other physical activ-
ity. Also active in US and English suffrage.

14 July 1561
Sayyida al Hurra dies
Her name translates as 'Lady who is free and independent;
the woman sovereign who bows to no superior authority'.
Born Lalla Aicha bint Ali ibn Rashid al-Alami, in 1485. Pirate
queen. Very important woman of the Islamic West, and fluent
in several languages. Became *al Hurra* (queen) of Tétouan
in northern Morocco in 1515 after the death of her husband
and because she was 'the undisputed leader of pirates of the
western Mediterranean'. Ruled for thirty years till overthrown
by her son-in-law. Lived twenty years in retirement.

— 14 July —

Bastille Day and revolutionary women

> *'You can bind my body, tie my hands, govern my*
> *actions: you are the strongest, and society adds to your*
> *power; but with my will, sir, you can do nothing.'*

> – **George Sand**, French writer, born 1804

Time to celebrate all things French. It's Bastille Day, or Fête nationale. It's also known as le 14 juillet, which just means 'the 14th of July' which doesn't really tell the non-French person what a national celebration this commemorates. It is a day that marks the Storming of the Bastille on 14 July 1789, which was quite the turning point in the French Revolution. The Bastille was an old fortress in the centre of Paris. It was a place that French royalty had traditionally used as a state prison. Louis XIV used it to lock up anyone who had annoyed him, including quite a lot of Protestants. Louis XV and XVI carried on the family tradition, using it as a dumping ground for disagreeable people who didn't believe in government censorship. The ancient building became a symbol of authoritarian rule which was not a popular idea during a revolution for equality.

Like most fortresses it was a stout building, so those in charge also liked to keep their guns and ammo there. Early in July 1789, the governor of the Bastille received 250 barrels of valuable gunpowder. By then there were only seven prisoners inside. It's fair to say the combative crowds on the street weren't all that bothered about them, but they were bothered about the ammunition. The fortress became a symbol of the evil the revolutionaries said they were fighting, and it was stormed and taken over. From within the Bastille they produced evidence of vicious 'torture equipment'. In fact, this equipment was some bits of an old printing press and an assortment of leftovers from various suits of armour, but it was enough to cement the place as the very embodiment of what the revolution was designed to defeat. Today the successful vanquishing of the Bastille will bring a tear to any French person's eye and a glass of wine to their lips.

If you want the finest backdrop to Bastille Day then you need to find a view of the Eiffel Tower and watch the fireworks explode around it. If you do go, please raise a glass to **Marie-Sophie Germain**. The tower would not be there without her. Marie was born in Paris in 1776. It was not a time for any girl to grow up to be a mathematician or physicist or philosopher but she became all three. Her father was a wealthy man who seems to have managed to stay on the right side of the revolution. Marie was thirteen when the Bastille was stormed so, as you can imagine, she spent much time confined to her house.

It wasn't a good time to lose your head and go out or, indeed, to go out and lose your head. Fortunately Papa had a wonderful library and, stuck for entertainment, she began to read. Once she'd started, she couldn't stop.

Marie taught herself Latin and Greek. She read the story of Archimedes, the greatest mathematician of his age, and determined to learn maths. Her parents thought it was bad for her so they tried to make it too cold in her room for her to study, but she just wrapped herself in a quilt and carried on. After a while her mother, Marie-Madeleine, secretly helped her and her father would support his daughter financially for her whole life as she never married. Marie's determination was marvellous. No woman was allowed to attend the local college, the École Polytechnique, but she got lecture notes from the great mathematician Adrien-Marie Legendre by writing and pretending to be Monsieur Antoine-Auguste Le Blanc. Marie submitted a paper as M. Le Blanc and Legendre was so impressed he tracked her down. On discovering she was a woman he became her sponsor.

Using a male pseudonym was the only way for some women to achieve what they wanted. How hard Marie must have fought to be herself. It was another kind of French revolution rather like that undertaken by **Amantine Lucile Aurore Dupin** in her desire to be herself. Amantine's name may not ring a bell. Her friends called her Aurore but you may be none the wiser until I tell you that she was more commonly known by the male pen name of **George Sand**. In her time George was more famous than Victor Hugo and Honoré de Balzac but neither of them had to change their name to be taken seriously.

George was born in 1804, a time when French law required any woman who wished to wear trousers to apply for a permit from the police. Sand wore trousers without asking anyone and it was considered scandalous. She did it, however, not to cause a scene, but to gain access to places otherwise forbidden to women – some libraries, museums and the pit of the theatre. She also, and I do hope you are sitting down, smoked in public.

George became one of the most significant writers of her time and through her work spent a lifetime arguing in favour of women's equality. At her funeral Victor Hugo declared,

> In this country whose law is to complete the French Revolution and begin that of the equality of the sexes, being a part of the equality of men, a great woman was needed. It was necessary to prove that a woman could have all the manly gifts without losing any of her angelic qualities, be strong without ceasing to be tender … George Sand proved it.

Neither Marie nor Aurore should have had to masquerade as men. Think what real freedom might have meant in terms of what they gave the world. I don't understand much of Marie-Sophie Germain's work. I do know that it included a great deal of critical work on something called the theory of elasticity. To me that sounds like something to do with the durability of pants but apparently it is very important. So important that it was used in the construction of the Eiffel Tower. When the tower was completed, the architects inscribed the names of seventy-two great French scientists under the first balcony. Marie-Sophie's name is not among them. Did those in charge forget? I mind terribly but I'm not sure she would have. She once said, 'It matters little who first arrives at an idea, rather what is significant is how far that idea can go.'

It's common on Bastille Day to say, *'Je lève mon verre à la liberté.'* (I raise my glass to freedom.) Here's to Marie and Aurore.

15 July 1885
Rosalía de Castro dies
Spanish novelist and poet, born 1837. De Castro was an incredibly significant writer in the Galician language, and among the greats of 19th-century Spanish literature. She helped bring about the cultural rebirth of the Galician language.

16 July 1899
Margaretta 'Meta' Riley dies
Born in 1804, Riley was an English botanist who studied ferns. She became the first female British pteridologist (a career no one mentioned at school). Riley worked with her husband and stopped her research when he died. She was also a poet, journalist and philanthropist, and enjoyed telling her recollections of the celebrations that followed the Battle of Waterloo.

17 July 1793
Charlotte Corday executed by guillotine
Marie-Anne Charlotte de Corday d'Armont assassinated Jacobin leader Jean-Paul Marat, who she thought had made the French Revolution too radical. She stabbed him with a kitchen knife while he was in the bath. At her trial she said: 'I knew that he [Marat] was perverting France. I have killed one man to save a hundred thousand.' She was executed aged twenty-four. After her death an autopsy was carried out to see if she was a virgin or whether she had shared her bed and her plan. She was virgo intacta.

18 July 1861
Kadambini Ganguly born
(Name in Bengali: কাদম্বিনী গাঙ্গুলী) Ganguly was the first Indian and South Asian female physician and surgeon to be trained in Western medicine. Along with **Chandramukhi Basu**, Ganguly

was one of the first female graduates in India and the entire
British empire. A women's and workers' rights activist, she
organised the Women's Conference in Calcutta 1906. Mother
of eight.

19 July 1965
Dame Evelyn Glennie born
Internationally renowned Scottish virtuoso multi-percussionist.
She gives over a hundred concerts a year, and is also a teacher.
Profoundly deaf since the age of twelve, she often performs
barefoot to feel the music. Glennie once corrected me when
I mispronounced her name. Total star. Watch her TED talk
'How to Truly Listen'.

20 July 1980
Maria Martinez dies
Native American potter and ceramicist, born 1887, in New
Mexico. She became internationally famous for her art and
craft inspired by traditional Pueblo techniques. Helped preserve
traditional Pueblo pottery as a cultural art. Her pieces are in
many museums, including the Smithsonian and the Metropolitan Museum of Art.

21 July 710
Shangguan Wan'er dies
Imperial consort to two emperors of the Tang dynasty of China,
born around 664. Poet, writer and politician. She was China's
de facto female prime minister to Empress Wu Zetian, the only
woman in more than 3,000 years of Chinese history to rule
in her own right (from 690 to 705). Shangguan was beheaded
when power changed hands. A tale of intrigue, sex and murder.

22 July 1849
Emma Lazarus born
American poet and essayist best known for her sonnet 'The New Colossus' ('Give me your tired, your poor, Your huddled masses yearning to breathe free') which is inscribed on the Statue of Liberty. Emma had Sephardic (Hispanic Jewish) heritage and campaigned for the defence of persecuted Jews. Her poems were widely praised. 'New Colossus' was written to help fundraise for the statue's pedestal. It played no role in the statue's unveiling and was not inscribed until long after her death.

More time-out fun

Honiton's Hot Pennies Day, Honiton, Devon
Three-day festival held on the first Tuesday after 19 July, which is specific. It has been an annual event since the 13th century. Opened, as only a British festival can be, with the town crier parading down the high street with a golden glove on the end of a flower-garlanded long pole declaring, 'Oyez, oyez, oyez. The glove is up. The fair has begun. No man shall be arrested, until the glove is taken down. God save the Queen.' People then throw hot pennies from windows above the street. It dates from a happy time when rich people used to throw money to the poor but amused themselves by making it too hot for them to pick up.

Tolpuddle Festival, Tolpuddle, Dorset
Held on the third weekend in July, the festival commemorates the Tolpuddle Martyrs, six local men who were convicted in

1834 for campaigning for fairer wages. They were sentenced to transportation to Australia but a mass protest led to them being pardoned and returned to their village. The annual event is a celebration of trade unionism. Music, speeches, beer.

23 July 1922
Jenny Pike born
Canadian photographer, Royal Canadian Navy servicewoman during the Second World War, darkroom technician. Pike was the only female photographer to help develop the first photos of the D-Day landings. Barbara Fosdick, former president of Ex-Service Women's Branch 182, said of Jenny, 'I think that my favourite memory of her is from the recent Remembrance Day parade, when all of the women were told they must march at the back of the parade. Jenny in her wrath was mighty to see. With fists clenched, she yelled, "We are women veterans, we will NOT march at the back, we're going to join the men where we belong." And we did.'

24 July 1954
Mary Church Terrell dies
American civil rights activist, author, teacher, lecturer on women's suffrage and rights for African Americans. Born in 1863, she was co-founder and first president of the National Association of Colored Women. Both of Terrell's parents were former slaves who then owned their own successful businesses. In 1884, Mary was one of the first African American women to receive a bachelor's degree. She led a successful campaign to stop segregation in public eating places and hotels in Washington, DC.

25 July 1865
James Barry dies
British military surgeon. Born Margaret Ann Bulkley around 1789. Barry lived as a man in order to be allowed to go to the University of Edinburgh Medical School and become a surgeon. Barry served in the army, becoming inspector general (equivalent to brigadier-general) in charge of military hospitals, the highest medical office in the British Army. He improved conditions for wounded soldiers and native inhabitants and performed the first successful caesarean section in Africa. Having lived fifty-six years as a man, James was found to be biologically female by the woman who laid out his dead body.

26 July 1969
Dame Tanni Grey-Thompson born
Grey-Thompson is a Welsh politician, television presenter, former wheelchair racer and Paralympic gold medallist. Born with spina bifida, she became one of the most successful disabled athletes in the UK: 16 Paralympic medals (11 gold, 4 silver, 1 bronze); 12 World Championship medals (5 gold, 4 silver, 3 bronze); 30 world records; won London Marathon six times.

27 July 1880
Malalai of Maiwand dies
Also known as Malala or 'The Afghan Jeanne d'Arc'. National folk hero of Afghanistan, born 1861. She rallied local fighters against British troops at the Battle of Maiwand on this day. She was there to help tend the wounded but when the Afghan army faltered and the flag-bearer was killed, Malalai took the flag and spurred the men on before being killed herself. The Pakistani-Pashtun women's rights activist **Malala Yousafzai** and Afghan activist-politician **Malalai Joya** are named after her.

28 July 1609
Judith Leyster born
Dutch Golden Age painter and genius. Almost forgotten because until 1893 all her work was attributed to Dutch painter Frans Hals or to her husband, artist Jan Miense Molenaer. She was possibly the first woman member of the artists' trade organisation, the Haarlem Guild of St Luke, but it could have been fellow artist **Sara van Baalbergen**. You can see Judith's work in the Rijksmuseum, Amsterdam; the Mauritshuis, The Hague; the Frans Hals Museum, Haarlem; the Louvre, Paris; the National Gallery, London; and the National Gallery of Art, Washington, DC.

29 July 1896
María L. de Hernández born
Mexican American women's rights activist. Also a broadcaster, she was the first female Mexican American radio announcer. Hernández fought against educational segregation and economic discrimination faced by women and children of Mexican descent. With her husband she co-founded the Orden Caballeros de América (Order of the Knights of America), which was dedicated to educating Mexican Americans about their rights.

30 July 1827
Susan Shelby Magoffin born
Magoffin was an American diarist and the first woman to write an account of travelling the Santa Fe Trail. Her diaries from 1846–47, a time when trade on the trail was at its high point, record important details of the Mexican–American War. This is the minutiae of history which is rarely captured – the conditions of travel, the people, the flora and fauna. She had a miscarriage on the way, at Bent's Fort, Colorado. She died after the birth of her fourth child.

31 July 1923
Stephanie Kwolek born
'I don't think there's anything like saving someone's life to bring you satisfaction and happiness.'
Kwolek is the American chemist who keeps us all safe every day thanks to her invention of Kevlar, 'a lightweight yet strong fiber to replace the steel used in tires'. Kevlar is stronger than nylon and five times stronger than steel by weight. It is used in more than 200 applications, including car tyres, aeroplanes, cables, bullet-proof vests and armoured cars.

AUGUST

'This morning, the sun endures past dawn. I realise that it is August: the summer's last stand.'

– **Sara Baume,** Irish author, born 1984

Weed Month

The Romans used to call this month *Sextillia*, which sounds like fun although it just meant 'sixth' because back then it was the sixth month of the Roman year. It was Emperor Augustus who thought he needed a month of his own and renamed it after himself. Augustus wasn't his name. It was an honorary title meaning 'Revered One'. He was Rome's first emperor and could pretty much do what he liked. He was also called Divi Filius (Son of a God) which gives you some idea of his power. Julius Caesar already had a month (July) named after him. That was thirty-one days long and August was only thirty, so Augustus nicked a day from February and added it to his month. Seriously.

Augustus was just nineteen when he raised an army and went to war against another Roman called Mark Antony for reasons I can't be bothered to go into. Some people died and the two boys settled the matter by Augustus having his sister marry Mark and him marrying Antony's stepdaughter. You'll be surprised to learn neither marriage lasted.

The two fellows went back to war and Mark Antony died, leaving Augustus feeling really free to name things after himself. The only thing I really like about Augustus is that he seems to have been a bit rubbish at fighting himself. He used to get sick the night before a battle. (It's quite the soap opera if you've got the time. Augustus married his daughter Julia off to his nephew, then to his best friend and finally to his stepson. In the end he banished her for sleeping with Mark Antony's son. I guess it can be a very hot month.)

The Anglo-Saxons called it *Weodmonath*, or 'weed month', because I guess the weeds go crazy this time of year in the northern parts.

Odd August facts
Leap years: August starts on the same day of the week as February.
Every year: August ends on the same day of the week as November.
August in the Northern Hemisphere is like February in the Southern Hemisphere.

Other names for August

Albanian: *Gusht*.

Vietnamese: *Tháng Tám*, meaning 'month eight'.

Croatian: *Kolovoz* – *kŏlo* ('wheel, cartwheel') + *vôz* ('cart load'), *vòziti* ('to drive').

Māori: *Hereturikōkā*. Third lunar month of the Māori year of which it is said, 'The warmth of the fire can be seen on the knees of people.'

AUGUST FESTIVALS

Air Guitar World Championships, Oulu, North Ostrobothnia, Finland

Annual August event since 1996. Based on the ideology: 'Wars would end and all the bad things would go away if everyone just played air guitar.' There are lots of rules of which my favourite is: 'The instrument must be invisible & must be a guitar.'

The Beñesmen or Beñesmer

Important harvest festival of the Guanches, the ancient inhabitants of the Canary Islands. Held during early August it is pretty much their new year, and also their name for the month. On that day the *tagoror*, or council of elders, would do their admin like dividing up tasks for the year and thanking the gods.

Lughnasa or Lughnasadh

A Gaelic harvest festival in Ireland, Scotland and the Isle of Man. According to the Irish, the festival was started by the god Lugh to commemorate his mother Tailtiu, who died of exhaustion after clearing the Irish land for agriculture. That would certainly do it to you.

The Twins Day Festival, Twinsburg, Ohio

This is the world's largest gathering of twins, held the first full weekend in August. (You can also be triplets or more but you do have to be a multiple at birth.) There are 'twin contests' which I don't think means two competitions happening at the same time. There's also a Seeing Double parade. The town used to be called Millsville but in the early 19th century a pair of identical twins, Moses and Aaron Wilcox, offered the town money if they changed the name to Twinsburg.

1 August 1980
Vigdís Finnbogadóttir becomes one of the world's first democratically elected female presidents

University French and drama teacher, born 1930. Finnbogadóttir was also artistic director of the Reykjavík Theatre Company, and an environmental and Icelandic culture activist. She became the fourth president of Iceland in 1980 and served until August 1996, making her the longest-serving elected female head of state of any country so far. She was the first single woman in Iceland allowed to adopt a child. Her motto: 'Never let the women down.'

2 August 1343
Jeanne de Clisson's husband executed, initiating her career as a privateer

Jeanne de Clisson, born 1300, was also known as Jeanne de Belleville and the Lioness of Brittany. On this day in 1343, Jeanne's husband, a Breton nobleman, was beheaded on the orders of Philip VI, King of France. Jeanne did what any woman might – swore retribution, outfitted three warships and began attacking French forces in Brittany. She became a privateer, a non-military person who engages in maritime warfare, and her flagship was named *My Revenge*. She hunted down any French ship in the English Channel and showed no mercy. She carried on privateering for thirteen years. She eventually remarried and settled down at the Castle of Hennebont, on the Brittany coast.

3 August 1902
Rabbi Regina Jonas born

Born in Berlin in 1935, she became the first woman to be ordained as a rabbi. Jonas was arrested by the Gestapo in

November 1942 and deported to Theresienstadt concentration camp, where she set up a suicide prevention service and helped organise concerts and lectures to distract others. In 1944 she was sent to Auschwitz, where she was murdered. Her work in the camps was largely forgotten until 1991 when she was 'rediscovered'.

4 August 1923
Mayme A. Clayton born
Clayton was a librarian and the founder, president and leader of the Western States Black Research and Education Center (WSBREC), the largest privately held collection of African American historical materials in the world. She used her own money to collect more than 30,000 rare and out-of-print books. The collection is now held in Mayme A. Clayton Library & Museum (MCLM), Culver City, California. It has 3.5 million items and includes a signed copy of **Phillis Wheatley**'s famous work of poetry, *Poems on Various Subjects, Religious and Moral*, from 1773 (*see* page 321).

5 August 1946
Dr Shirley Ann Jackson born
An award-winning theoretical physicist, Jackson was the first African American woman to earn a doctorate at MIT. She's brilliant on subatomic particles and Landau–Ginsburg theories of charge density waves in layered compounds, which for all I know about physics may be the same thing. I mean, I've got nothing on this, except she's amazing and in addition to her scientific achievements has raised a billion dollars for philanthropic causes. President of Rensselaer Polytechnic Institute. Highest-paid currently sitting US college president. Quite right.

6 August 1866
Zofia Daszyńska-Golińska born
Polish politician, suffragist, professor of demographics, who earned her PhD in 1891. She was also an early female senator in Poland. Member of the Little Entente of Women, an umbrella organisation for women's groups in the Balkans. Published more than eighty books.

7 August 2011
Nancy Wake dies
Also known as the 'Gestapo's Most Wanted', 'The White Mouse' and by her code name 'Hélène'. New Zealand nurse and journalist, born 1912. During the Second World War, Wake joined the French Resistance and then the Special Operations Executive (SOE). She helped Allied airmen escape to neutral Spain and, in June 1944, took part in a battle between Resistance fighters and a large German force. Afterwards she bicycled 500 kilometres to send a report to London. Her husband was captured and executed. The Gestapo called her 'The White Mouse' because of her ability to evade capture.

8 August 1856
Madame Vestris dies
British actress, opera singer and theatre manager, born 1797. She first found fame for what are known as 'breeches parts' (playing men) in opera because she had a low voice. She didn't stick with the posh stuff. When she took over the Olympic Theatre she became the first female actor-manager in London theatre. Here she presented burlesque and extravaganzas. She is very important in set design as she insisted on using real props, historically accurate costumes, and was the first to introduce the 'box set' where a whole room complete with

ceiling is presented on stage. It was all a high new standard for theatre. Check out pics of her as Don Giovanni. Campest thing you'll ever see.

9 August 1942
Aruna Asaf Ali launches Quit India Movement
Ali, born 1909, was an Indian educator, political activist and publisher. She was an active participant in the Indian independence movement, at one time arrested and held in solitary confinement. On 8 August 1942, Mahatma Gandhi made a speech in the Gowalia Tank Maidan in Mumbai calling on the British to leave immediately. The All India Congress Committee passed the Quit India resolution at the Bombay session. The major leaders were arrested and Aruna Asaf Ali presided over the remainder of the session. On this day she hoisted the Congress flag at the Gowalia Tank Maidan, which marked the beginning of the movement. In old age she was called the 'Grand Old Lady' of the independence movement. Post-independence she became Delhi's first mayor.

10 August 1387
Margaret I, Queen of Denmark, begins her reign
Margaret founded the Kalmar Union of the kingdoms of Denmark, Norway and Sweden. She was nicknamed 'the Lady King' and is probably the first great ruling queen in European history. Plus, you know, Danish, which is excellent. In 1396 she issued an ordinance demanding respect to, among other things, workers in the fields and women. She also distributed money to the women who had been 'violated and debased' during the wars between Sweden and Denmark.

11 August 1614
Lavinia Fontana dies
Italian painter, a famous portraitist of the Renaissance, born
1552. Fontana was one of the first women to execute large, publicly commissioned figure paintings and religious work. Studied
with her father. She created famous altarpieces including *Holy
Family with the Sleeping Christ Child* for El Escorial in Madrid,
completed in 1589. She was elected a member of the Roman
Academy, a rare honour for a woman. She also had eleven kids.
Eleven. I'm going to guess they all did a lot of finger painting
while waiting for dinner.

12 August 1898
Maria Klenova born
Russian/Soviet marine geologist, Klenova was first to fully
map the seabed of the Barents Sea. She helped found Russian
marine science and was the first woman scientist to do research
in Antarctica. She was the first female scientist to go ashore at
Macquarie Island (between New Zealand and Antarctica) and
helped to create the first Antarctic atlas.

13 August 1795
Maharani Ahilyabai Holkar dies
Warrior queen of the Maratha Malwa kingdom, India, born
1725. Her father, Mankoji Rao Shinde, was a village chief
who went against custom by educating his daughter. She was
spotted by the lord of the Malwa territory, Malhar Rao Holkar,
and he arranged for her to marry his son. It was 1733. She was
eight. Sadly, her husband died when she was twenty-nine, then
her father-in-law died. She was left as regent on behalf of her
son but then he died. She took the throne and was amazing.
She led her armies in battle using bows and arrows fitted to the

corners of the howdah of her favourite elephant. Her kingdom flourished under her thirty-year reign.

14 August 1791
Cécile Fatiman's vodou ceremony helps start the Haitian Revolution

Haitian vodou priestess, born 1771. Fatiman and her mother were both sold as slaves. On this day she took part in a vodou ceremony at Bois Caïman, considered to be one of the starting points of the Haitian Revolution, a successful slave rebellion to overthrow the French. A week later a thousand slaveholders were killed. She was said to have lived to be 112.

15 August 2006
Dame Te Atairangikaahu dies

New Zealand queen of the Kingitanga, born 1931. At forty years, hers is the longest reign of any Māori monarch. Her name meant 'the hawk of the morning sky', a title bestowed on her when she became queen. She worked to revitalise Māori culture and language and improve life for her people. The first Māori to be appointed a Dame Commander of the Order of the British Empire, and first ever appointee to the Order of New Zealand (her badge of the order bears the number one).

16 August 1225
Hōjō Masako dies

(Name in Japanese: 北条 政子) Born 1156, she was the wife of Minamoto Yoritomo, first shogun, or military dictator, of Japan. She married Yoritomo against her father's will and is said to have been largely responsible for her husband's success. It's a story with a lot of assassinations. After her husband's death she became a nun but not nun enough to go and live in a convent.

She carried on wielding so much power that she was called the *ama* ('nun') shogun.

17 August 1981
Mariama Bâ dies
Pioneer Senegalese author and feminist. Born in Dakar in 1929. Raised by her grandparents. Her grandmother didn't believe in girls' education but her grandfather sent her to school. This experience made her a critic of gender inequality at an early age. Later in life her divorce would leave her as a single parent of nine children. She wrote her debut novel aged fifty. *So Long a Letter*, about her frustration with the fate of African women, was translated into many languages.

18 August 1848
Camila O'Gorman executed
Nineteenth-century Argentine socialite of Irish descent, born in 1827 or 1828. O'Gorman was executed over a scandal involving her relationship with a 24-year-old Jesuit priest, Father Gutiérrez. They tried to elope but were kidnapped and returned to Buenos Aires. The Argentine dictator General Juan Manuel de Rosas (who had five kids of his own with the family maid) was determined to make an example of them. She was twenty years old and eight months pregnant when they both faced a firing squad. They were buried together in a single coffin as a final act of compassion. It's a great, if shocking love story. Rosas was eventually overthrown. He fled to England and lived out his days in Southampton.

19 August 1883
Coco Chanel born
French fashion designer born Gabrielle Bonheur Chanel. She grew up in an orphanage to become queen of Parisian haute

couture for almost six decades. Her designs were a huge influence in the shift away from the uncomfortable clothes of the 19th century. She believed, 'Luxury must be comfortable, otherwise it is not luxury.' By the late 1920s her salon employed more than 2,000 people. Chanel is famous for the creation of the Chanel suit and the 'little black dress'. Hers was the first major fashion house to launch a perfume – Chanel No. 5. All lovely and fragrant but she was also a secret agent for the Nazis which is hard to ignore.

 — 19 August —

National Aviation Day

'Flying is the best possible thing for women.'

– **'Baroness' Raymonde de Laroche**, the world's
first licensed female pilot, born 1882

Raymonde de Laroche was French and that was a splendid thing to be if you were a woman and wanted to fly in the early part of the 20th century. Her real name was Elise Raymonde Deroche, but she changed it to Raymonde de Laroche when she became an actress. She was the daughter of a Parisian plumber who loved all sport. It was after she saw Wilbur Wright demonstrate powered flight in 1908 in Paris that she determined to take to the skies herself. The plane she learned in only had one seat so she would sit in it while her instructor, Charles Voisin, shouted directions from the ground, which doesn't sound ideal. At first he forbade her from attempting to fly – she was only allowed to taxi across the airfield but she took off anyway. On 8 March 1910 de Laroche received the thirty-sixth aeroplane pilot's licence issued by the Aeroclub de France, the world's first organisation to issue pilot licences. It was the press who dubbed her 'Baroness'. On 18 July 1919 she was killed co-piloting an experimental aircraft.

When we hear about the history of flying, it is the Wright brothers, Wilbur and Orville, whose names reverberate down the years. They got their US patent for their 'flying machine' in 1906. If you grow up in America it is a well-known story, but the person often left out of the tale is **Susan Wright**, the boys' mother. She was born in 1831 in Hillsboro, Virginia, and grew up to attend college, which was most unusual for a girl at the time. She loved science and maths. Susan gave birth to seven kids but only five survived. She was mechanically minded and always making things for her children, including a sled with which she is said to have taught them the basics about wind resistance. When the boys had a mechanical problem with anything it was their mother they asked. Sadly, she died on 4 July 1889 of tuberculosis and never lived to see them fly, but she was the mother of flight.

Plenty of women have taken to the sky as aviators, or aviatrix as women pilots used to be called. In 1935 **Amelia Earhart** became the first person, male or female, to fly solo the 2,500 miles across the Pacific Ocean from Hawaii to California. I would have thought this was a nerve-racking enterprise, but Amelia was so relaxed during her eighteen hours in the air that she had time to listen to some opera on the radio. This diversion of hers links me to the first woman who ever took to the air.

Apart from Icarus's mythological flight no human being had ascended freely into the skies until 21 November 1783. It was in the market square of Annonay, a small village in the Ardèche in France, that two brothers by the name of Montgolfier demonstrated the world's first practical hot-air balloon. The idea for such an insane device is said to have come from women's dresses. Joseph Montgolfier had watched his wife airing her dresses in front of the fire. He noticed how the hot air currents made the dress material seem to balloon out and float. Perhaps heat, he thought, could also raise up some more substantial material.

The Montgolfiers' 500lb balloon was made of sackcloth and paper and held together with 1,800 buttons. I once owned a similar outfit myself. Attempts to fly had been made a couple of times before but these were with balloons tethered to the ground that carried non-human 'volunteers' – a sheep called Montauciel (Climb-to-the-sky), a duck and a rooster – but, in 1793, the brothers' vast bag carried two male volunteers into the air unconnected to the earth for twenty-five minutes while a great cheer went up from a crowd of well-wishers. It would spark a balloon craze, although not everyone was thrilled. When Le Globe, the first hydrogen-powered balloon, was sent up by French scientist Jacques Charles in Paris in 1783 it landed in the small French town of Gonesse, where the townspeople panicked. The thing fell from the sky and began fluttering about on the ground, at which point the locals attacked it with pitchforks before tying it to a horse's tail and dragging it through the streets.

Just a few months later it was time for the first woman to have a go. Here is the link to Amelia Earhart's flight. **Madame Élisabeth Thible** of Lyon was an opera singer. On 4 June 1784 she and a Monsieur Fleurant left the French soil in a balloon called La Gustave in honour of King Gustav III of Sweden, who was having a weekend away with King Louis XVI and Marie Antoinette, the way you do, and they all went to watch.

Maybe having an opera singer in the basket was like icing on the cake. I can tell you that Élisabeth went all out for the occasion. Dressed as the Roman goddess Minerva in a lace-trimmed dress and a feathered hat, she took off singing two duets from Monsigny's *La Belle Arsène*, a popular opera of the time. Not content with hitting the high notes, it is recorded that she also kept the balloon in the air by feeding the vital fire box during the forty-five-minute flight. Sadly, I lack further information about her. I have seen her described as the '*épouse délaissée*' (abandoned spouse) of a Lyon merchant, which is hardly how anyone wants to be remembered.

How brave she must have been. Indeed, it is what characterises all the early aviatrixes. Perhaps my favourite of all the female pioneers of the sky is **Bessie Coleman**. It's never good to begin a story at the end but, be warned, Bessie died because she was short which is terrible. What is astonishing is that she was born poor and obscure yet when she died (from being short) more than 10,000 people attended her funeral. Bessie was probably born on 26 January 1892 in Texas but like other women in history she also sometimes lied about her age.

She was a fine mix of African American on her mother's side and part Choctaw and Cherokee Indian on her father, George's. She grew up in Waxahachie, Texas. The family was large and poor, and Bessie walked four miles every day to a one-room school dreaming as she said of 'amounting to something'. In 1915, when she was twenty-three, she moved to Chicago and got a job as a manicurist in the White Sox barbershop. Her brother, John, returned from the war in Europe and told her that Frenchwomen were the best; that they were even allowed to fly aeroplanes. In that moment Bessie decided to become a pilot, but no white instructor wanted to teach a black person and no black pilot wanted to teach a woman. She needed to go to France to learn and, after a course in French, set off in November 1920, ready to parlez her way to be a pilot.

The flying course at the École d'Aviation des Frères Caudon at Le Crotoy in the Somme took ten months. Bessie completed it in seven. She was now the world's first licensed African American and Native American woman pilot. By the time she got back to America she was quite the celebrity. She began giving demonstrations of daredevil manoeuvres. She even gave a show in Waxahachie where she insisted that there was no segregation at the main gate. She became famous, giving lectures in black theatres, churches and schools, but plenty of the white newspapers ignored her and her life was not always easy.

Bessie could never quite afford the plane she wanted. On the evening of 30 April 1926 Bessie and her mechanic went up in her plane for a test run. Bessie was planning a parachute jump for the next day. Being too short to see over the edge of the cockpit, she took off her seatbelt to lean over and check where she would land. Someone had left a wrench in the plane after it had been serviced. The stray tool slid into the gearbox and jammed. The plane failed to pull out of a dive, it spun and, aged thirty-four, Bessie was thrown out to her death.

It would be another eighty years before Bessie was inducted into the National Aviation Hall of Fame in 2006.

Fabulous women. Oh, and who taught Amelia to fly? A woman called **Neta Snook**, born in 1896. Check her out.

I know I shouldn't fly because it damages the planet so instead I look at the work of the brilliant American artist **Georgia O'Keeffe** (*see* 15 November). She took to travelling the world in her seventies. Her view of the world from the seat of a plane changed her work forever. Her phenomenal paintings of the sky viewed from just above the clouds are another way to soar.

20 August 1836
Agnes Bulmer dies
English poet, born 1775, who is believed to have created the longest epic poem ever written by a woman. The 14,000-line long *Messiah's Kingdom* took over nine years to complete. It's about human salvation. I've had a go at reading it. I'm afraid I wouldn't bother. I think it's enough to know she did it, but good to know that *Wesleyan Methodist Magazine* described her as being a 'match for men' in her intelligence and interests. How kind.

21 August 1614
Countess Elizabeth Báthory de Ecsed dies
Hungarian noblewoman, born 1560. The most prolific female murderer of all time. So prolific I can't really give you an exact number of victims. Maybe 650. Despite this, her family were noble so she wasn't executed but imprisoned instead in her own castle (Čachtice Castle. Now a ruin in Slovakia). Apparently she started her spree with servant girls and then moved on to the daughters of lesser nobility. She also seems to have a bit of the vampire about her and maybe a hint of cannibalism, but you know how people exaggerate. There are those who say the stories about her were all a political conspiracy.

 — *21 August* —

World Fashion Day

'A smile is the ultimate accessory.'

– **Liz Claiborne**, fashion designer, born 1929

I am hardly someone to even mention the word 'fashion'. I've never really been interested. Given the choice I wear a plaid shirt in the winter, a Hawaiian one in the summer and jeans all year long. Lots of women like to dress up but I'm not one of them. The nearest I ever got to being a 'femme fatale' was when I was once in a very serious car accident. That doesn't mean I don't appreciate the importance clothes can play. For many women, what they look like in the mirror at home helps give them the confidence to stride out into the world and I get that.

It's hard to believe the struggle women had to be released from the corset and other confining garments of the Victorian era. Trousers have been around in the Western world since ancient times. Get on a horse in a robe and you soon find yourself thinking there must be something you could wear to stop the chafing. Persian and Asian horse riders knew this but at first the Greeks and the Romans thought trousers were ridiculous. It didn't take them long, though, to realise that no one can win a battle while their nether parts are being rubbed raw on a saddle. In ancient times trousers were worn by both sexes. There is a marvellous 2,500-year-old urn in the British Museum of an Amazon wearing fashionable-looking trousers and carrying a shield. Yet by the 18th and 19th centuries there was a misconception that trousers were a male garment, had always been a male garment, and the world would come to an end if women showed the shape of their legs. Laws were passed making it illegal for women to dare to wear such a thing.

In the 1850s, when the great French artist **Rosa Bonheur** wanted to wear trousers so that she might comfortably sketch outdoors, she had to get a police permit to do so. In fact, an old Parisian bylaw requiring women to ask permission from city authorities before 'dressing as men', including wearing trousers (with pleasing exceptions for those 'holding a bicycle handlebar or the reins of a horse'), wasn't officially revoked until 2013. The world still moves slowly, for it wasn't until March 2019 that a federal judge in North Carolina declared that a school's requirement that girls wear skirts was unconstitutional. How had it come to a court case? In 2020 my stepdaughter got most of her all-girls school (Grey Coats in London) to sign a petition requesting trousers as an option. The request was denied as it was not 'traditional'.

In so far as I am interested in clothes at all then it is as something that makes us feel better. For working women clothing has long been problematic, with a need for stylish but affordable clothing. Even a deadbeat like me can recognise how significant someone like the American fashion designer and businesswoman **Liz Claiborne** was in changing not only the style for work wear but how it is purchased. In 1976 Liz took her personal savings and launched her own company creating what I have learned are known as 'separates', which could be mixed and matched to make a wardrobe on a budget seem bigger than it was. She helped make career women feel confident and on the way she changed shopping forever.

From the beginning Liz was determined to do things differently. She insisted that department stores display her line of clothes in a section by themselves. It was the first time customers had been encouraged to select garments by brand name only in one place in the shop. Now you see it all the time. It was a huge success. Within ten years she had become the first woman to found a company that joined the *Fortune* 500 list of America's largest corporations. I love the sound of her. She wanted to stop what she saw as male hierarchies in the world of fashion, so all employees in her corporate directory were listed not in order of importance but alphabetically. She controlled meetings by ringing a glass bell and she loved to pose as a saleswoman to see what average women thought of her clothes. When she retired she established a foundation that distributed millions to environmental causes and nature conservancy projects around the world.

There's lots about the fashion world today that needs addressing – the imagery used to sell unnatural and unhealthy body shapes as desirable, the environmental cost, forced and trafficked labour and so on. At its best, though, it is great to feel good about yourself, however you choose to express that, and we should remember those in the past who have helped women and men be themselves.

I found an old bowler hat and I'm thinking of wearing it. What does it say about me? Just that I once saw *Mary Poppins* and liked Mr Banks best. Wear what you like. Be comfortable.

Great trouser wearers
1851: Elizabeth Smith Miller wore the 'Turkish dress' (a dress with trousers) to the New York home of **Amelia Bloomer**, who wrote a temperance journal called *The Lily*. The next month Bloomer announced to her readers that she had adopted the same outfit. She printed a description and a pattern to what became known as the 'Bloomer dress'.

1919: Luisa Capetillo – the first woman in Puerto Rico to wear trousers in public. She was arrested but the charges were later dropped.

1932: Marlene Dietrich shocked society when she appeared at the premiere of the movie *The Sign of the Cross* wearing a tuxedo, hat and patent leather shoes.

1969: Representative Charlotte Reid – the first woman to wear trousers in the US Congress.

2004: Hillary Clinton – the first woman to wear trousers in an official American First Lady portrait.

2009: In Sudan it is illegal to wear 'obscene outfits' in public. Thirteen women were arrested in Khartoum for wearing trousers. Ten of the women pleaded guilty and were flogged with ten lashes and fined 250 Sudanese pounds apiece.

2012: The Royal Canadian Mounted Police began to allow women to wear trousers and boots with all their formal uniforms.

2019: Virgin Atlantic began to allow trousers for its female flight attendants.

22 August 1664
Maria Cunitz dies

Born in 1610, Cunitz was an astronomer in Silesia (a historical region mostly in modern Poland). She is the most notable female astronomer of the early modern era. During the Thirty Years War she and her husband hung out in a convent where she had time to make astronomical observations and create tables to include all of the planets at any moment in time. These were published as *Urania propitia*. She corrected several of the great German Johannes Kepler's errors and became well known in Europe.

23 August 1971
Gretchen Esther Whitmer born
American Democratic politician serving as the forty-ninth governor of Michigan. Michigan Senate's first female Democratic leader between 2011 and 2015. She came to wider national and international attention in 2013, during a debate on abortion in which she shared her experience of being sexually assaulted. Elected governor in 2018, and earned high approval ratings for her handling of the Covid-19 pandemic.

24 August 1987
Ayesha Farooq born
(Name in Urdu: قوراف هشیئاع) Since 2013 Farooq has been Pakistan's first and only female combat-ready pilot. She flies missions in a Chinese-made Chengdu J-7 fighter jet alongside her twenty-four male colleagues in Squadron 20. There are nineteen women pilots in the Pakistani Air Force. 'Instead of looking up to role models, become one yourself.'

25 August 1988
Phyoe Phyoe Aung born
Student activist and former political prisoner from Burma (Myanmar). She was involved in the Saffron Revolution of 2007. She was arrested in 2008 and sentenced to four years in prison. After her release she became the general secretary of the All Burma Federation of Student Unions. Arrested again in 2015 for taking part in protests over a new National Education Law which activists claim restricts academic freedom. About 126 students were imprisoned, some of whom claim to have been tortured. Phyoe Phyoe Aung was released in April 2016.

26 August 1920

The 19th amendment, guaranteeing American women the right to vote, is formally adopted into the US Constitution

Crystal Eastman, born 1881, was an American lawyer, feminist, journalist and co-founder of the American Civil Liberties Union (ACLU). Shortly after the 19th amendment was adopted, Eastman gave a speech entitled 'Now We Can Begin', which clearly stated that the work of women's emancipation did not end with the amendment, it began.

> ... we must institute a revolution in the early training and education of both boys and girls. It must be womanly as well as manly to earn your own living, to stand on your own feet. And it must be manly as well as womanly to know how to cook and sew and clean and take care of yourself in the ordinary exigencies of life. I need not add that the second part of this revolution will be more passionately resisted than the first. Men will not give up

their privilege of helplessness without a struggle. The average man has a carefully cultivated ignorance about household matters – from what to do with the crumbs to the grocer's telephone number – a sort of cheerful inefficiency which protects him better than the reputation for having a violent temper. It was his mother's fault in the beginning, but even as a boy he was quick to see how a general reputation for being 'no good around the house' would serve him throughout life, and half-consciously he began to cultivate that helplessness until today it is the despair of feminist wives.

Crystal Eastman was once called the 'most dangerous woman in America'.

27 August 1942

First broadcast of Congress Radio, India

Dr Usha Mehta, born 1920, was a professor of political science, broadcaster and Indian freedom fighter. She took part in her first protest march aged eight. Mehta helped organise the Secret Congress Radio, an underground radio station that operated for a few months during the Quit India Movement of 1942. The first words broadcast on Congress Radio were hers, saying: 'This is the Congress Radio calling on [a wavelength of] 42.34 metres from somewhere in India.' The organisers had to move the station's location every day to avoid capture. The police found them on 12 November 1942. Mehta told them she was about to play the national anthem 'Vande Mataram' and made them wait till it was over before they could arrest her.

28 August 1665
Elisabetta Sirani dies
Italian Baroque painter and printmaker in Bologna, born 1638. A pioneering female artist who established an academy for other women. She was hugely successful, with many students (men and women) and portrait commissions. She died in unexplained circumstances at the age of twenty-seven. At first a maid was charged with her murder but not convicted. In a biography written in 1678 the author claimed Sirani died because she had never married and was lovesick, but most likely it was a ruptured ulcer. She was given an elaborate public funeral. Her 1658 *Self-Portrait as Allegory of Painting* is in the Pushkin Museum, Moscow. Magnificent.

29 August 1924
Dinah Washington born
American singer and pianist, 'Queen of the Blues'. Born Ruth Lee Jones. Probably the most popular black female recording artist of the 1950s. She did a show at the London Palladium where Queen Elizabeth II was said to be in the audience. She told the crowd: 'There is but one heaven, one hell, one queen, and your Elizabeth is an imposter.' She died of a heart attack aged just thirty-nine, yet she managed to find time to marry eight times.

30 August 1948
Alice Salomon dies
German social worker, born 1872. Founder of one of the first schools of social work. In 1906 she became one of the first women to receive a PhD from the University of Berlin, with a doctoral thesis on the inequality of pay for men and women doing equivalent work. She helped found the International Congress of Women in 1904. Exiled from Nazi Germany in

1939 because of her Jewish heritage and her political views, she went to the United States and lectured on social work administration. A university, a park and a square in Berlin are named after her.

31 August 1941
Marina Tsvetaeva dies

Russian/Soviet poet, born 1892. She was among the greats of 20th-century Russian literature but hers is a terrible story. She tried to save her daughters from the famine that followed the Russian Revolution of 1917 by placing them in a state orphanage, but her youngest died of starvation. Her husband was executed in 1941 on espionage charges and she committed suicide the same year. She had a deep love affair with the openly lesbian poet **Sophia Parnok**, which had a huge effect on both their writing. The work is wonderful.

And she gives us our Poem for August:

⤜ POEM OF THE MONTH ⤛

> *Amidst the dust of bookshops, wide dispersed*
> *And never purchased there by anyone,*
> *Yet similar to precious wines, my verse*
> *Can wait – its time will come.*

SEPTEMBER

'What dreadful hot weather we have!
It keeps me in a continual state of inelegance.'

– **Jane Austen**, English author, born 1775

Barley Month

In the Northern Hemisphere, September marks the beginning of autumn, while in the Southern it is spring. The name comes from the Latin *septem*, meaning 'seven'. It ought to be called November as *Novem* is Latin for 'nine' and September is the ninth month, but it was originally the seventh of ten months in the old Roman calendar and some people just don't like change.

The Anglo-Saxons called September *Gerstmonath*, meaning 'barley month', as this was when the crop was usually harvested.

Other names for September

Swiss: *Herbstmonat*, which means 'harvest month'.

Yiddish: *Oygust*.

Swazi: *iNyoni*.

Ojibwe: *Waabaagbagaa-giizis* (Leaves Turning Moon).

Forgettable things about September

1. It's the only month with the same number of letters in its name in English as the number of the month.
2. In any year, no other month ends on the same day as September.
3. Shakespeare never mentioned it in any of his plays.

Oktoberfest begins

Really?

Munich's famous Oktoberfest always begins in September because it has to finish on the first Sunday of October. The festival started on 12 October 1810, when Bavarian Crown Prince Ludwig married **Princess Therese of Saxony-Hildburghausen**, and locals celebrated in Munich. Everyone had such a good time they just kept going. (Therese seems to have been smart and helped run the place, but in 1848 Ludwig was forced to abdicate because he'd had an affair with the Irish actress **Lola Montez**. She's a cracker and totally worth reading about.)

ANCIENT ROMAN OBSERVANCES FOR SEPTEMBER

Ludi Romani (Roman Games)

4–19 September

A regular event which began around 367 BC. No idea what kicked it off. It'll be a conquest of some kind by a boy. It was held in honour of Jupiter and seems to have involved a lot of triumphal marching by military folk (*pompa*) and then a chariot race in which each chariot had a driver and a warrior. They would race along until the end, when the soldier had to leap out and finish on foot. A contest surely ripe for a return? There was also boxing and dancing (which go so well together) and in 364 they added plays, making it more like the Edinburgh Festival.

Epulum Jovis (Feast of Jove)

13 September
A fab feast for Jove/Jupiter, which was held during the *Ludi Romani*. Obviously, the gods were invited and they used to attend in the form of statues, which should have cut down on the catering but priests ate for them.

Ludi Triumphales (Triumphal Games)

18–22 September
These commemorated the victory of Constantine over Licinius at Chalcedon in 324. (Anybody?) I don't know much about it except there were forty-eight circus races, which sounds like clowns chasing each other but was actually chariots going round in circles. It was a busy time for whoever did the equivalent of a pit stop for chariots.

⤞ POEM OF THE MONTH ⤝

From *Nineteen Old Poems* by anonymous Chinese poet, from around 206 (translated by A. Waley)

A bright moon illumines the night-prospect;
The house-cricket chirrups on the eastern wall.
The Handle of the Pole-star points to the Beginning of Winter;
The host of stars is scattered over the sky.
The white dew wets the moor-grasses –
With sudden swiftness the times and seasons change.
The autumn cicada sings among the trees,
The swallows, alas, whither are they gone?
Once I had a same-house friend,
He took flight and rose high away.

He did not remember how once we went hand in hand,
But left me like footsteps behind one in the dust.
In the South is the Winnowing-fan and the Pole-star in the North,
And a Herd-boy whose ox has never borne the yoke.
A friend who is not firm as a great rock
Is of no profit and idly bears the name.

The 'Herd-boy' referred to in the poem is a star, used here 'never bearing the yoke' to imply a friend who is not a friend. This is one of a number of anonymous poems of the late Han period, characterised by the use of five-word lines (in Chinese) and the use of extreme economy and directness of language. These poems were believed to have been written by women. As Virginia Woolf said, 'I would venture to guess that Anon, who wrote so many poems without signing them, was often a woman.'

***

Festival of the month
World Testicle Cooking Championship, Ozrem, Serbia
Chef Ljubomir Erovic created this annual festival, held in early September, and has even written a cookbook called *Cooking With Balls*, which includes 'testicle pizza, battered testicles and barbecued testicles with giblets'. He says balls have aphrodisiac properties, especially sheep and stallion testicles. The festival motto is: 'Scots have their Scotch, the Swiss their cheese, and we, the Serbs, have balls.' Ozrem is fifty miles south of the capital Belgrade. The town is high up and small like a lot of ... well.

1 September 1843
Nadezhda Prokofyevna Suslova born
Russia's first female physician. Her parents gave both Nadezhda and her sister **Polina** a good education at home and then at boarding school. She went to the Medical Surgery Academy but in 1865 they stopped allowing women to study, so she went abroad and got her medical qualification in 1867. Nadezhda also wrote revolutionary stories that showed a feminist philosophy and caused her political trouble. She worked as a gynaecologist, gave out free medical care to the poor and built a school and library on her grounds for the local people. Polina became a writer.

2 September 1838
Queen Lili'uokalani born
The first female monarch of Hawaii to reign in her own right and last monarch of the Kingdom of Hawaii. Also a composer and musician. She was deposed in a coup led by American sugar planters on 17 January 1893. They established the Republic of Hawaii. Ninety-five per cent of the population objected and Lili'uokalani went to Washington, DC to plead their case, but five years later the islands were annexed to the US. In 1993 an 'Apology Resolution' was passed by the US Congress which recognised that '… the Native Hawaiian people never directly relinquished to the United States their claims to their inherent sovereignty as a people over their national lands …' In 2009 the Supreme Court ruled this resolution had no legal effect in any claim for Hawaiian independence.

3 September 1918
Fanny Kaplan executed
Born 1890, Kaplan shot Vladimir Lenin, believing he was a 'traitor to the revolution'. On 30 August 1918, Lenin was

leaving a Moscow factory when she fired three shots at him. It's an odd story as she was nearly blind. She was a teenager in turbulent times in Russia and became an anarchist aged sixteen. She was arrested following a bomb explosion and sentenced to 'eternal penal servitude'. Her sight was damaged while forced to do hard labour in a silver-mining camp in eastern Siberia. She was freed in 1917 and joined the Socialist Revolutionary Party. No one actually saw her fire the gun at Lenin, who survived. She was shot in a Kremlin park while truck engines drowned out the sound of gunfire.

4 September 1996
Joan Clarke dies
Born 1917, Clarke was a cryptanalyst and numismatist famous for codebreaking in the Second World War. She gained a double first degree in mathematics at Cambridge in 1933 but no woman was given a full degree. She was recruited to decoding operations at Bletchley Park, where she became deputy head of her section but couldn't progress because of her gender. She was paid less than the men. She was briefly engaged to Alan Turing, unfazed by his revelation of homosexuality. The full extent of her accomplishments remains unrecorded and unknown.

5 September 1939
Claudette Colvin born
Pioneer American civil rights activist, and nurse aide. Aged fifteen, in 1955, she refused to give up her seat for a white woman on a segregated bus in Montgomery, Alabama, nine months before the more widely known incident with Rosa Parks. She was arrested for her refusal. She had been mad that day, having written a school essay about blacks not being allowed to use department store dressing rooms to try on clothes. She was

unmarried, pregnant and didn't have 'good hair'. Black leaders did not think she would make a good representative for their case against segregation. She has said, 'Young people think Rosa Parks just sat down on a bus and ended segregation, but that wasn't the case at all.' Read her whole story. She wanted to be president. She would have been a great president.

6 September 1860
Jane Addams born
American suffragist, social reformer, social worker, public administrator and author. She suffered Pott's disease as a child, which caused a curvature in her spine and lifelong health problems. These prevented her from fulfilling her ambition to be a doctor. She is the founder of the social work profession in the US. Part of the 'settlement movement' providing housing for the poor. In 1910 Addams was the first woman to receive an honorary degree from Yale University. She was president of the International Congress of Women in The Hague in 1915. President of the Women's International League for Peace and Freedom (WILPF) and, in 1931, the first American woman to be awarded the Nobel Peace Prize.

7 September 1990
Clärenore Stinnes dies
German racing car driver, born 1901. She was the first person to circumnavigate the world by automobile, accompanied by Swedish cinematographer Carl-Axel Söderström. She did the driving in an Adler Standard 6 automobile, escorted by two mechanics in a vehicle with spare parts. The 29,000-mile trip took just over two years. When they got back, Söderström divorced his wife and married Clärenore.

8 *September 1879*
Eleanor Dumont dies
Born in 1829, Dumont was also known as 'Madame Moustache'
(she didn't pluck). Possibly born Simone Jules but changed her
name to sound French. Notorious gambler on the American
western frontier, especially during the California Gold Rush.
Opened a gambling parlour – Vingt-et-un – on Broad Street,
Nevada City, California, and was the only woman allowed in.
She was an accomplished card dealer. Men were drawn to the
place to see such an unusual sight as a woman dealing cards.
She left Nevada City when the gold dried up and travelled the
country gambling. In Bodie, California, she lost everything and
died of a morphine overdose.

9 *September 1949*
Tonita Peña dies
Born in 1893, Peña is also known as the 'Grand Old Lady of
Pueblo Art'. Her birth name was Quah Ah. Renowned Native
American Pueblo artist and teacher in the early 1920s and 1930s,
she was an instructor at the Santa Fe Indian School and the
Albuquerque Indian School. Considered the most influential
Native American woman artist of her time, she mostly worked
in pen and ink embellished with watercolour. When she died,
her husband followed Pueblo custom and burnt her remaining
paintings and personal effects.

10 *September 1749*
Émilie du Châtelet dies
French natural philosopher and mathematician, born 1706.
Her mother wanted her to be a nun, but her father helped her
gain an education. She once joined an intellectual discussion by
dressing as a man. She is best remembered for her translation

of, and commentary on, Isaac Newton's 1687 book *Principia* containing basic laws of physics. Her work made a profound contribution to Newtonian mechanics. In addition to her famous translations she also wrote philosophical work of her own. Partner and collaborator with Voltaire, which meant her own achievements have often been subsumed under his. She was a very respected thinker of her time. In 1738 she was the first woman to have a scientific paper published by the Paris Academy. She died in childbirth.

11 September 1995
Solveig Krey becomes the first female commanding officer of a submarine
Norwegian naval officer, born 1963. On this date she took command of the submarine *Kobben*, becoming the first female commanding officer of a submarine in the world. Also the first female commander of any Royal Norwegian Navy vessel.

12 September 1840
Mary Jane Patterson born
Patterson is believed to be the first African American woman to receive a Bachelor of Arts degree, in 1862. (The poet **Grace A. Mapps** graduated from a four-year college course in New York in 1852, but it is unclear if she was awarded a BA degree.) The daughter of a slave, in 1857 she went to Oberlin College, Ohio. Most women did a two-year diploma course but she joined the 'four-year gentleman's course in classics', which led to a BA degree. She became a teacher and then principal of a preparatory high school for African American youth in Washington, DC. After a decade in charge she was told that the school was now so big and successful that it needed a man to run it. She continued as a teacher for the rest of her life.

13 September 1944

Noor Inayat Khan dies

Also known as Nora Baker, Madeleine (SOE code name), Nurse (SOE call sign), Jeanne-Marie Renier (SOE alias). Born 1914, she was a British Second World War spy from an Indian Muslim family. She gave up her career as a writer to join the Special Operations Executive because, she said, 'I wish some Indians would win high military distinction in this war. If one or two could do something in the Allied service which was very brave and which everybody admired it would help to make a bridge between the English people and the Indians.' She was the first female wireless operator to be sent from Britain into occupied France to help the French Resistance. She was betrayed and captured. She was executed in Dachau concentration camp with fellow agents **Yolande Beekman**, **Madeleine Damerment** and **Eliane Plewman**. Her last word was reported as *'Liberté'*. She was posthumously awarded the George Cross and the Croix de Guerre with silver star. It's an extraordinary story. There is a bronze bust of her in Gordon Square Gardens, London.

14 September 1879

Margaret Higgins Sanger born

Sanger was an American birth control activist, sex educator, writer and nurse. She opened the first birth control clinic in the United States, and established organisations that evolved into the Planned Parenthood Federation of America. She helped to repeal the 1873 Comstock Act which made the distribution of information relating to the use of contraceptives illegal. She was arrested for her work. She promoted birth control as a way to prevent abortion. She is a controversial figure as she supported eugenics. Margaret got the funding Gregory Pincus needed to develop the first oral birth control pill. The money came from **Katharine McCormick** (*see* 15 September).

    — 15 September —

Battle of Britain Day

> *'I alone have dared to point out the dire need for air defence of London. You have muzzled others who have deplored this shameful neglect. You have treated my patriotic gesture with a contempt such as no other government would have been guilty of toward a patriot.'*
>
> – **Lucy, Lady Houston**, DBE, born 1857,
> in a 1932 telegram to then UK prime
> minister Ramsay MacDonald

In order to make it into the history books at all women have often had to outdo men. It's as though they have had to elbow their way on to the pages. Often it helped if their father thought them worth educating or, better yet, if the women themselves had money. Then all they needed was to make the world notice them. This is the story of a woman who changed history for Britain; who we ought to think about every Battle of Britain Day but, mostly, probably don't.

Lucy, Lady Houston, was rich. She was bold, she was patriotic and she didn't give a damn what anyone thought. Woe betide anyone who did not see things her way. Without her determination and courage Britain might never have won the Second World War. April 3rd marks the anniversary of the very first flight over Mount Everest in 1933. What has that got to do with Lady Houston? Well, she paid for the expedition and the long-term result was that Britain ended up with the Spitfire aeroplane, and you probably don't need a history lesson from me about why that was a good thing.

Before we get to the point where a two-seater biplane known as the Westland Wallace dared to soar over the highest mountain on the planet we need to go back a bit. Back to Lambeth in south London, near The Oval cricket ground, back to the year 1857 when Fanny Lucy Radmall was born into Victorian poverty. She was the ninth of ten children born to Thomas and Maria Radmall. You would think with that many siblings it would have been hard to have your voice heard, but Fanny would grow up to be the toast of Edwardian society and the richest woman in Britain.

Every photograph of the time shows that she was a beauty and, by the time she was sixteen, she was making the most of her good looks as a chorus girl called Poppy in the London theatre. It wasn't long before she attracted the attention of what used to be known as stage door Johnnies, men who hung around trying to date chorus girls. Before long she ran off with the already married brewer Frederick Gretton of the Bass family. I don't know what Mrs Gretton thought about it but Fred and Poppy eloped to Paris where they lived a high life of sin for ten years. The English hoi polloi mostly thought they were a disgrace, but the French had a different view and took them to their hearts. Poppy is described as being 'a beautiful young coquette, with ... impudent speech and a tiny waist, who became expert in Parisian fashions and manners'. She learned to speak French and made friends with Edward, Prince of Wales, who was also hanging out. Sadly, Poppy's beau died but not before he had bequeathed her £6,000 a year for life. That may not sound like a lot but when you remember this was 1882 then you realise that's about three quarters of a million pounds in today's money.

Poppy was set for life and returned to London as a sensation. She was wined and dined at all the top places and never went to a restaurant without knowing the colour of the décor so that her dress would not clash with the setting. She married again and then again, each time to society men.

She became Lady Byron and an ardent patriot. During the First World War she did what she could for the war effort, sending out footballs as well as matches to soldiers serving overseas, in boxes labelled 'A Match for Our Matchless Troops from Lady Byron', and ran a campaign entitled 'Give Him Socks'. Later, she opened a rest home for nurses who had served on the Western Front. Because of this Poppy was made a dame in her own right in 1917.

She became an active suffragette. She not only used her money for the cause, standing bail at one point for Emmeline Pankhurst, but was not averse to getting into the fray with her own unique style. She would drive to Hampstead Heath in her carriage, standing up in it when she got there to harangue visitors into writing to their MPs to demand 'justice' for women.

The death of her third and final husband, Sir Robert Paterson Houston, in 1926 left her the richest woman in the country. She used the money well. Everyone who knows anything about the Second World War knows how significant the Spitfire aircraft was. The predecessor to that aircraft was a single-engine racing seaplane known as the Supermarine S6. The design team were determined to create a high-speed aircraft that could transform the RAF, with its slow biplanes. When the Great Depression hit in 1931, the government of Ramsay MacDonald pulled the plug on financing the ongoing aviation research. Poppy was appalled. She saw aviation as key to the defence of Britain and she had the courage to put her money where her mouth was.

That year the Supermarine S6 had been due to take part in the prestigious Schneider Trophy, awarded to the world's fastest seaplane. Poppy was determined that Britain would not be left out, so she donated £100,000, about £3.5 million in today's money, to keep the work going, and the plane and the RAF crew flying it claimed victory. It was a move that would transform Britain's air defence. The design team gained the experience in producing high-speed aircraft without which they would never have been ready to fight off the Luftwaffe in 1940.

The flight over Mount Everest was a milestone in flight history. Even the Nepalese government recognised her generosity. A heart-shaped lake spotted from the air 6,000ft below the summit of Everest was named by Nepal's government the Lady of the Mountain in her honour.

Politicians, especially Labour ones, infuriated her. She published her own newspaper, the *Saturday Review*, so that she could say what she liked about the government. When Ramsay MacDonald's government refused her offer of £200,000 to strengthen the British Army and Royal Navy, she hung a huge electric sign decrying the prime minister in the rigging of her yacht and sailed it around Great Britain.

Although she died in 1936 her health regime sounds remarkably modern. It was eccentric for the time as she renounced 'tea, coffee, butter, bacon, meat, white bread and pastry, all alcoholic drinks and salt'. Sounds dull to me but she was certain it was the key to her health. She was obsessed with fresh air and sunshine, claiming that being nude in the open air had what she called 'prophetic powers' that were almost religious. On board her yacht, named *Liberty*, she would order the crew to go below so that she could promenade naked on deck.

On reflection, she held some right-of-centre views that I would have been appalled by but perhaps I have historical hindsight. In her day she was dazzling and daring. An activist and aviation pioneer. A philanthropist and, above all, passionate human being. When her old friend Edward VIII abdicated the British throne she was devastated. She took to her bed, refused to eat and, aged seventy-nine, passed away from a heart attack. Was she a bit mad? Absolutely. I love that. Live life to the full. Do what you can to make the world a better place and, above all, be unpredictable. We could do with more people like Poppy. A true eccentric who was once described as someone who provided 'a welcome break in the monotony of mass-produced humanity'. A remarkable woman who I expect most people have never heard of, but whose story is an inspiration to those of us who believe that whatever time we have ought to be lived to the full.

When the Second World War ended and Winston Churchill made his famous speech honouring 'the few' who had saved the country, Poppy was one of them but I wonder how many knew that?

15 September 1905
Katharine McCormick gets married instead of going to medical school
McCormick, born 1875, was the second woman to graduate from the Massachusetts Institute of Technology (MIT) when she earned a BSc in biology in 1904. She married a wealthy man, instead of becoming a doctor as she had planned, but at least she used his money for good. As well as her work on birth control, she supported the arts, medical research, and campaigned for women's suffrage. During the 1920s she smuggled

diaphragms to the US from Europe by sewing them inside her expensive clothes.

16 September 1887
Nadia Boulanger born

'Anyone who acts without paying attention to what he is doing is wasting his life. I'd go so far as to say that life is denied by lack of attention, whether it be to cleaning windows or trying to write a masterpiece.'

French composer, performer and conductor, Boulanger taught many of the leading composers and musicians of the 20th century. She was the first woman to conduct many major orchestras in America and Europe, including the BBC Symphony, Boston Symphony, Hallé and New York Philharmonic. Please also listen to her sister **Lili Boulanger**'s work, for example *D'un matin de printemps* (*Of a Spring Morning*).

17 September 1783
Nadezhda Durova born

Also known as Alexander Durov, Alexander Sokolov and Alexander Andreevich Alexandrov. A woman who, disguised as a man, became a decorated soldier in the Russian cavalry during the Napoleonic Wars. The first known female officer in the Russian military. Her memoir, *The Cavalry Maiden*, is one of the earliest autobiographies in the Russian language. In 1807 she left her husband and child and enlisted in the Polish Horse Regiment under the alias Alexander Sokolov. She fought in the major Russian engagements of the 1806–07 Prussian campaign and saved the lives of two fellow Russian soldiers. Tsar Alexander I learned she was a woman, promoted her to lieutenant and awarded her the Cross of St George. She continued to wear male clothing all her life and became a novelist.

18 September 1587
Francesca Caccini born
Italian composer, singer, lutenist, poet and music teacher of the early Baroque era. Also known as 'La Cecchina'. Her only surviving stage work, a 'comedy-ballet' entitled *La liberazione di Ruggiero*, is widely considered the oldest opera by a woman composer. She served the Medici court as their most highly paid musician.

 — 19 September —

International Talk Like a Pirate Day
Have a look online and you can find something to celebrate for every day of the year. This niche holiday was invented by two men in 1995 in the town of Albany, Oregon. They call themselves Ol' Chumbucket and Cap'n Slappy (I can't be bothered to use their real names) and they seem to have a romantic view of piracy as being less about death and more about people slapping each other on the back while crying, 'Ahoy, me hearties!', eyeing a treasure map and carrying a plastic sword. Why September 19th? It was Cap'n Slappy's ex-wife's birthday, which is as reasonable a date selection as any.

Years later this laddish idea is still going. They have their own website and everything, where they even give a nod to being gender equal. Under FAQs they list the question 'Can women be pirate guys?' and provide this comforting reply:

> They most certainly can. Being a pirate guy is a state of mind, not a matter of chromosomes. It's about bringing the spirit of pirate adventure into your daily life, and there's no reason women can't do that just as well or even better than

regular guys. Some women were blessed at birth with the ability to enjoy fishing and football and beer and gnawing on a plate of ribs, and some guys are lucky enough to be married to them.

Clearly I was not blessed at birth but that doesn't mean women haven't sailed the high seas and, according to the Albany boys, said 'Aaarrr!' a lot. If we know anything about girls taking the helm of a ship and shouting 'Avast behind!' then probably the most familiar names are those of **Mary Read** and **Anne Bonny**. Hard to find specific dates for them as they were both pirates, and pirates have not, historically, been keen on paperwork. I have a book on pirates and they are the only women in it. The author can't help himself but call them names like 'hellcats', 'banshees' and 'Amazons' instead of just telling us the story.

Mary Read was born sometime between 1670 and 1698 in London, England. It's a tale of intrigue and deception. Mary's mother had married a sailor. He went to sea where he was foolish enough to perish, leaving her with a baby boy. Fortunately her mother-in-law was rich and could support her. Unfortunately Mrs Read fell for another sailor, got pregnant and her first son died. In order to persuade the first, rich mother-in-law to continue her financial support, Mrs Read needed to pretend the first son never died, so she planned to give birth to another boy and pass him off as the original. That's when Mary came along. A female disappointment. Undaunted, Mrs Read dressed Mary as a boy and carried on fooling the poor but rich grandmother. In 17th-century Europe boys and girls dressed the same until they were five or six so it seemed like a plan. The ruse totally worked and old rich mum-in-law kept on supporting them till she died.

As it happens Mary loved being a boy and wanted to carry on, so she did the next logical thing in this strange tale – she joined the navy, then she joined the army, then the cavalry – ooh, she liked a fight. Unfortunately, while fighting, she fell in love with a Flemish soldier. Soon her camp mates were daring to suggest she was a homosexual so she told her beau the truth. He was thrilled. Getting any woman in a war zone was tricky at the best of times. It's a nice story. They got married and opened a pub in Holland, but before there could be a happy ending Mr Flemish up and died. Mary went back to what she knew. She dressed once more as a boy and headed to the West Indies on a merchant ship.

Meanwhile Anne Bonny was growing up in Ireland. For complicated reasons, she too was dressed up as a boy by her mother. It seems to have been a popular plan around then. Anyway, check out the whole story. It has more twists and turns than I have time for but suffice to say she ended up in the Bahamas where, aged sixteen, she eloped with a sailor called James Bonny.

Back to Mary, who you'll remember was at sea heading to the West Indies. En route, her ship was captured by pirates who happened to speak English. Well, so did Mary and this seems to have been enough to receive an offer to join the piratical crew, so she did. Eventually Mary and Anne would meet and both serve under Calico Jack, an English pirate captain in the Bahamas most famous, frankly, for his association with them. It did not end well. Jack's entire crew were eventually arrested and it says something about life on board that both women were able to 'plead their bellies', using pregnancy to stay their execution. Mary seems to have died in prison, possibly from complications after childbirth, while Anne simply disappeared.

Neither woman seems to have been a particularly remarkable pirate. The fascination is that they were women at all. Is that it for female pirates? Not at all. In fact, someone who is not even in my book on the subject is the most successful pirate of all time – **Ching Shih**, or **Madame Ching**, who ruled the China seas in the early 19th century. She was born in 1775 and seems to have been captured by pirates at the age of fifteen and set to work as a prostitute on a floating brothel. Clearly she was smart because by the time she was twenty-six, she owned the place and caught the eye of a notorious pirate called Cheng I. Cheng was a powerful man from a long line of pirates, but it wasn't enough to turn a young woman's head. Before she agreed to marry him Madame Ching insisted on a pre-nup. Equal shares in everything, all the booty, all the plunder, even the command from the ship's deck. She must have been something because he agreed and they married.

Together they created the most powerful pirate organisation in the world, known as the Red Flag Fleet. When Cheng died Madame Ching did not waste time. She took control of the Red Flag Fleet and of the South China seas. Two years later, an East India Company employee named Richard Glasspoole was captured by her pirates and he estimated that she had control of 800 large junks and 1,000 smaller ones. Compare this to the pirate Blackbeard, who is way more famous. In the same century he commanded just four ships and 300 pirates.

Her fleet was run with strict laws. Anyone failing to obey an order could be beheaded instantly. Perhaps the most interesting laws for a woman-led crew were the ones relating to sex. Any pirate who raped a female captive would be put to death. If the sex had been consensual, they would both die. Ugly female captives were released, although who was the judge of that I do not know.

The authorities tried to stop her gangs as they raided camps and ships, river towns and coastal villages, but no official or naval fleet was able to thwart her. In the end it was an offer of amnesty from the Chinese government that brought her reign to an end. In 1809 she surrendered, but not before she had done her usual brilliant deal. She was pardoned, the family was allowed to retain many ships for use in the salt trade, and some high-ranking pirates in her crew even got jobs in the Chinese bureaucracy. Madame moved to Macau and opened a gambling house ... and a brothel. Maybe that was for old times' sake. She died in her bed aged sixty-nine, having seen out her days in peace and quiet. The most successful pirate lord in history, a lady who ended her life a free woman. Not bad for a girl.

Addendum

I don't approve of the pirate life but while researching this piece I had a look at the town of Albany, Oregon, where the Talk Like a Pirate founders hail from. Among the town's archives I found **Abigail Scott Duniway**, born 1834, who I had never heard of and I am so glad I did. It was a lesson in the rewards of idle reading. Abigail's husband had poor business luck and then was permanently disabled in an accident, which left Abigail looking after him and their six kids. They moved to Albany, Oregon, where she opened a 'millinery and notions' shop. Her customers were mainly married women and Abigail began to become angry at their stories of injustice and mistreatment. Please read about her. She became an amazing advocate for women's rights, a newspaper editor and a writer. In 1872 she addressed Oregon's legislature to put forward the case for women's suffrage. She lived long enough to see Oregon become the seventh state in the US to pass a women's suffrage amendment in 1912. Governor Oswald West asked her to write and sign the equal suffrage proclamation. She was the first woman to register to vote in her county.

'Aaarrr!'

19 September 1889
Sarah Louise 'Sadie' Delany born

American teacher, author, activist. Delany was the first African American allowed to teach domestic science at the high-school level in the New York public schools. She graduated from Columbia University in 1920, gaining a masters in education in 1925. In 1993 she and her sister **Bessie** became famous when their oral history was published as a book, *Having Our Say: The Delany Sisters' First 100 Years*, which dealt with the trials and tribulations the sisters had faced during their century of life. The book was on the *New York Times* bestseller lists for 105 weeks. Bessie, who graduated as a dentist in 1923, lived to be 104. Sadie lived to be 109.

20 September 1898
Josefa 'Pepa' M. Llanes-Escoda born

Filipina civic leader, social worker, teacher, advocate of women's suffrage and founder of the Girl Scouts of the Philippines. She earned a masters degree in sociology from Columbia University in 1925. During the Second World War and the Japanese occupation of the Philippines, she and her husband Antonio supplied medicines, food, clothes and messages to both Filipino war prisoners and American internees in concentration camps. Both were arrested and executed in 1945.

21 September 2017
Evelyn Scott dies
Indigenous Australian social activist and educator, born 1935. Scott began working in the Townsville Aboriginal and Torres Strait Islander Advancement League in the 1960s. She was actively involved in campaigning for the 1967 Constitutional Referendum, which led to the inclusion of indigenous people in the national census. She chaired the National Council for Aboriginal Reconciliation in the late 1990s. Scott was the first Indigenous woman to receive a Queensland state funeral.

22 September 1862
The Emancipation Proclamation in the United States
The Emancipation Proclamation changed the legal status under federal law of more than 3.5 million African Americans in the Confederate states from enslaved to free. One of those freed was **Matilda McCrear**. A West African woman born around 1857, she was the last known living survivor of the transatlantic slave trade. She arrived in the United States on board *Clotilda*, the last known slave ship to have carried captives from Africa to the United States. She was a member of the Yoruba people. In her seventies, she made a legal claim for compensation for her enslavement, which was dismissed. She died in 1940.

23 September 1838
Victoria Woodhull born
Suffragist, politician, feminist, writer and the first woman to run for president of the United States. In 1872 Woodhull stood as presidential candidate for the Equal Rights Party, supporting

women's suffrage and equal rights; her running mate was black abolitionist leader Frederick Douglass. Together with her sister, **Tennessee Claflin**, they were the first women to operate a brokerage firm on Wall Street and the first to found a newspaper in the United States, *Woodhull & Claflin's Weekly*, in 1870.

24 September 1794
Jeanne Villepreux-Power born
Pioneering French marine biologist and, in 1832, inventor of the aquarium. She began her career as a dressmaker; in 1816 she created Princess Caroline's wedding gown when she married Charles-Ferdinand de Bourbon. Villepreux married an English merchant, James Power, and the couple moved to Sicily. It was here she began her natural history studies with the intention of creating an inventory of the island's ecosystem. She created three types of aquarium: a glass one for her study, a submersible glass one in a cage, and a cage for larger molluscs out at sea. Beginning in 1839 she published her findings. When she and James left Sicily in 1843 many of her records and drawings were lost in a shipwreck.

25 September 1900
Elizabeth Van Lew dies
American abolitionist and philanthropist, born 1818. Created and operated an extensive spy ring for the Union Army during the American Civil War. When her father died she and her mother freed the family's slaves nearly twenty years before the law required it. She used all of her inheritance to purchase and free some of their relatives. During the war, she helped prisoners escape and passed on information about Confederate troop movements to Union commanders. She hid escaped Union prisoners and Confederate deserters in her own house.

She was the first person to raise the United States flag in Richmond, Virginia. She became postmaster general of the city. Many southerners regarded her as a traitor and she was ostracised. '[I am] held in contempt & scorn by the narrow minded men and women of my city for my loyalty ... Socially living as utterly alone in the city of my birth, as if I spoke a different language.'

26 September 1649
Katharyne Lescailje born
Dutch poet, translator and publisher. One of the most successful female Dutch poets of the second half of the 17th century. She and her sisters inherited their father's publishing business in Amsterdam and continued to run it after his death. She specialised in political poems but also wrote plays. In 1731, her collected works were posthumously published. Her poetry occupied three large volumes of nearly 1,000 pages.

27 September 1871
Grazia Deledda born
Italian writer, novelist and the first Italian woman to receive the Nobel Prize in Literature, in 1926. She wrote about life on her native island of Sardinia. Her first novel, *Fiori di Sardegna* (*Flowers of Sardinia*), was published in 1892. She was prolific, writing, on average, a novel a year. She had a pet crow called Checcha.

28 September 1938
Rosario Ferré born
Writer, poet, academic, she acted as First Lady of Puerto Rico for her father between 1970 and 1972. She published her first writing aged fourteen, and became one of the leading women authors in contemporary Latin America. She gained her BA and

PhD in the US. She won international awards for her writing. Her novel *House on the Lagoon* was written in English.

29 September 1848
Caroline Yale born

American teacher who revolutionised the teaching of hearing-impaired students. She worked at the Clarke School for Hearing and Speech in Northampton, Massachusetts, for sixty-three years, including thirty-six years as principal from 1886. She collaborated with Alexander Graham Bell and his father, Alexander Melville Bell, on the development of her phonetic system and teaching methods. She established a teacher-training department at Clarke, providing teachers for the deaf in thirty-one US states and nine foreign countries.

30 September 1900
Tilly Devine born

English-born organised crime boss in Sydney, Australia. She and her Australian husband Jim Devine left their son with Tilly's parents when they left London to live in Australia. Together they became narcotics dealers, brothel owners and crime gang members. The New South Wales Vagrancy Act 1905 prohibited men from running brothels but not women. The Devines' establishment had different kinds of prostitutes – elite 'call girls' for politicians, businessmen and overseas guests of significance; 'tenement girls', hard-up young working-class women who resorted to casual prostitution; and 'boat girls', older female prostitutes who served sailors or working-class men. Tilly became very rich. She was convicted 204 times and served many jail sentences for prostitution, violent assault, affray and attempted murder. Her life is a colourful read.

Calling the mare

Raucous fun from medieval England. September was harvest month and hard work but that didn't mean there wasn't time for teasing. Farmers would race each other to beat their neighbours gathering in the crop. When you were done, the last sheaf of the harvest would be made into a straw horse and lobbed on to the neighbour's place while shouting, 'Mare, Mare!' I think it was supposed to suggest wild horses were on their way to eat what was left in the field. The farmer who received it would pass the horse on when he was done and so on and on to the last in the harvest race. The last farmer kept the straw mare for a year to show he was slowest. I can't think of a way to make this sound more fun.

OCTOBER

'I've always loved October so much, haven't you?
I can see why it's called the Month of the Angels.'

– Eva Ibbotson,
Austrian-born British novelist, born 1925

Winter Full Moon Month

The Anglo-Saxons said that winter began on the first full moon in October and called the month *Winterfylleth* or *Þinterfylleþ* (which is the same but jollier spelling). It's the tenth month of the year but you won't be surprised to learn it's named after the eighth one in the old calendar of Romulus (*c.*750 BC) – from the Latin and Greek *ôctō*, meaning 'eight'. You know how you forget sometimes to move with the times.

Other names for October

Albanian: *Tetor*.

Cherokee: *Duninvdi*, meaning 'month of the harvest moon'.

Arabic (Libya): *At-tumūr*.

Basque. *Urri*.

Useless trivia
More US presidents were born in October than in any other month.

OCTOBER FESTIVALS

The Phuket Vegetarian Festival, Phuket, Thailand

Also known as the Nine Emperor Gods Festival, Thetsakan Kin Che.

The festival is held across Thailand and other Southeast Asian countries, but the biggest celebration is in Phuket. It takes place each year during the ninth lunar month, which has a habit of shifting but fundamentally we're talking about October. It's a nine-day vegan frenzy which for a meat-eater like me is hard to imagine. Anyway there are parades and music plus, you know, a lot of veg and … protein products. Play your cards right and you can watch a man put a sword through his cheek, as ritualised mutilation is an important aspect of the celebrations. It's about spirit-cleansing and one of the rules is that pregnant women or women with their periods shouldn't take part or even watch any ceremonies. You can eat, though.

Drink to the Romans

The Romans celebrated 11 October as *Meditrinalia*, which sadly is not as popular anymore. It was a time to celebrate the new vintage of the year. A bit like Beaujolais Nouveau Day in France (though that is celebrated in November). Anyway, time to raise a glass to health, longevity and wine, which not everyone these days puts in the same sentence.

⤞ POEM OF THE MONTH ⤝

Common Dust by Georgia Douglas Johnson

And who shall separate the dust
What later we shall be:
Whose keen discerning eye will scan
And solve the mystery?

The high, the low, the rich, the poor,
The black, the white, the red,

And all the chromatique between,
Of whom shall it be said:

Here lies the dust of Africa;
Here are the sons of Rome;
Here lies the one unlabelled,
The world at large his home!

Can one then separate the dust?
Will mankind lie apart,
When life has settled back again
The same as from the start?

Johnson was born in Atlanta, Georgia, in 1880, and became a poet of the Harlem Renaissance. This poem is a marvellous reminder that, where we are all ultimately heading, there will be nothing to divide us.

1 October 1847
Annie Besant born

London-born women's rights activist, orator, philanthropist, prolific author of over 300 books and pamphlets. Besant was an ardent supporter of both Irish and Indian self-rule. She founded Banaras Hindu University, and fought for workers' and women's rights and freedom of thought. Besant was arrested for publishing an American book on birth control, which cost her custody of her kids. Her friend George Bernard Shaw considered Besant to be 'The greatest orator in England'. Her work in India is extraordinary. She was president of the Indian National Congress for a year. She became the adoptive mother of Jiddu Krishnamurti, who she claimed was the new Messiah and incarnation of Buddha (though he did not agree). It's a lot for a mum to load on their kid.

2 October 1963
Maria Ressa born
Ressa is a Filipina-American journalist, author and co-founder of *Rappler*, an online news service. She has spent two decades working as a lead investigative reporter in Southeast Asia for CNN, and is a pioneer in combating fake news. On 15 June 2020, a court in Manila found her guilty of cyberlibel in an act widely seen as a politically motivated attack on free speech. In April 2019, she was included in *Time*'s '100 Most Influential People in the World'.

3 October 1996
First performance of *The Vagina Monologues*
The play opened in New York City on this day, with a limited run. In 2001 it sold out New York's Madison Square Garden, raising $1 million for groups working to end violence against women and girls. It was written by **Eve Ensler**, playwright, performer, feminist, my friend and activist. It has now been performed in 140 countries. Ensler founded the V-Day movement to stop violence against women and girls. It has raised over $100 million and furthered education worldwide.

3 October 1990
Reunification of Germany
The word German comes from Old French meaning 'of the same parents or grandparents', so it seems mad that Germany was ever divided as its very name is one of family unity. Today 3 October is a national holiday in Germany, and commemorates the anniversary of reunification when the Federal Republic of Germany (West Germany) and the German

Democratic Republic (East Germany) got back together after too long a separation. This was not when the Berlin Wall came down, but the day reunification was complete.

There are shedloads of fabulous German women who have changed the shape of the world. Probably the first who comes to mind is **Hildegard of Bingen**, born 1098. She was a nun who, as well as her preaching, theological studies and convent-running duties, also found time to be an artist, author, composer, pharmacist, poet and the founder of German scientific natural history.

4 October 1957

Launch of Russia's Sputnik satellite

The Americans tried to catch up but their TV-3 satellite crashed on 6 December 1957. Time to think of **Gladys West**, born in 1930 to an African American farming family. She became a mathematician known for her contributions to the mathematical modelling of the shape of the Earth, and her work on the development of what would eventually become the Global Positioning System (GPS). She is said to still prefer a paper map. 'When you're working every day, you're not thinking, "What impact is this going to have on the world?" You're thinking, "I've got to get this right."'

5 October 1973

Milunka Savić dies

Serbian war heroine, born 1888, who fought in the Balkan Wars and in the First World War. She became the most decorated female combatant in the entire history of warfare. Savić was responsible for incredible acts of bravery and heroism but died penniless and mostly forgotten. She served dressed as a man and was only 'discovered' on her tenth mission, when she got shrapnel in her chest. She once captured twenty-three enemy soldiers single-handed.

6 October 1820
Jenny Lind born
Lind was a world-famous Swedish opera singer, also known as the 'Swedish Nightingale'. She toured Europe and America to great acclaim. Her American tours earned a fortune and she used the money to endow free schools in Sweden. She retired to England where she was a professor of singing at the Royal College of Music in London. There is a plaque to her in Poets' Corner, Westminster Abbey.

7 October 1977
Felicity Aston born
Aston is an English explorer and former Antarctica climate scientist. In 1996 she was part of the first all-female team in the Polar Challenge race across Arctic Canada, and ten years later she was part of the first all-female British expedition across the Greenland ice sheet. In 2009 she was team leader of the Kaspersky Commonwealth Antarctic Expedition where seven women skied to the South Pole. And in 2011 she became the first person to ski alone across the Antarctic landmass using only personal muscle power, and the first woman to cross the Antarctic landmass alone. It took her fifty-nine days to cover the 1,084 miles. 'It was clear to me that the success of my expedition had not depended on physical strength or dramatic acts of bravery but on the fact that at least some progress – however small – had been made every single day. It had not been about glorious heroism but the humblest of qualities, a quality that perhaps we all too often fail to appreciate for its worth – that of perseverance.'

8 October 1907
Polina Denisovna Osipenko born
Soviet military pilot. In 1937, she set three world records for altitude. She was co-pilot with **Valentina Grizodubova** and **Marina Raskova** when they performed a non-stop flight between Moscow and the Sea of Okhotsk in 1938, setting a new distance record for non-stop flights operated by women. The flight had to crash-land as they ran out of fuel. All three survived and they became the first women awarded the title Hero of the Soviet Union. Osipenko was killed in 1939 during a routine flight.

 — October —

National Cookbook Month
(It's an American thing but why not?)

> *The FAIR, who's Wise and oft consults our BOOK,*
> *And thence directions gives her Prudent Cook,*
> *With CHOICEST VIANDS, has her Table Crown'd,*
> *And Health, with Frugal Ellegance is found.*
>
> *– The Art of Cookery, Made Plain and Easy*
> *(which far exceeds anything of the kind yet*
> *published),* **Hannah Glasse**, born 1708

When Hannah Glasse died on 1 September 1770 we lost the mother of modern cookbooks. Her work was intended to teach people how to produce something edible in the kitchen using plain language which, and this was radical, even servants would understand. *The Art of Cookery, Made Plain and Easy* was first published by subscription in 1747. You could also buy a copy at 'Mrs. Ashburn's China Shop' at the corner of Fleet Ditch in London, which is where Hannah hailed from. At first no one knew of Hannah's involvement. The book was published as being the work of 'A Lady', but even this was too much for the English writer Samuel Johnson, who is said to have declared, 'Women can spin very well, but they cannot make a good book of cookery.'

The book was a triumph in Britain and swiftly made its way into any 18th-century home wanting to know the right end of a ladle. The book contains a number of firsts – the first to mention trifle with jelly in it, the first mention of 'Hamburgh sausages' and piccalilli, and the first recipe for Yorkshire pudding. A 1774 edition of the book included one of the first recipes in English for an Indian-style curry. In the American Colonies copies of Glasse's work could be found on the kitchen shelves of Benjamin Franklin, Thomas Jefferson and George Washington.

Some of the recipes were rich, to say the least, with a pumpkin pie that included a glass of Malaga wine, seven eggs and half a pound of butter. Why, it makes your arteries harden at the thought. The importance of the book is that it opened up the world of cooking to the 'ordinary' person or, as Glasse put it, '… my Intention is to instruct the lower Sort'. Among the instructions you can find the thing I think is most critical for any budding chef – a recipe for chicken soup.

> Take an old Cock, or large Fowl, flea it, and pick off all the Fat, and break it all to Pieces with a Rolling-pin, put it into two Quarts of Water, with a good Crust of Bread, and a Blade of Mace …

It's a perfectly good recipe although I rather stopped paying attention after the thought of fleaing an old cock. Add to this

Hannah's instructions on how to 'force the inside of a rump of beef' and you begin to feel something illegal is in the air. There is also a listing entitled 'The French way of dressing partridges', which I imagine involves them wearing a beret and a stripey jumper. Where the cookbook differs from any modern work of its kind is that there are no weights and measures included. The world would have to wait till **Eliza Acton** produced clearer recipes in 1845, and in the US it was another fifty years before the marvellously named **Fannie Farmer** (*see* 15 January) introduced more exact ingredients.

Ask the average person to name a woman cookery writer and most likely the answer will be 'Mrs Beeton', who in 1861 published *Mrs Beeton's Book of Household Management*. It's a marvellous book although very little of it was her original work. She was indebted to another woman, who has been left at the wayside of history. **Eliza Acton** was born in Sussex, England, in 1799. She too was focused on the domestic reader when she produced *Modern Cookery for Private Families*. It was Eliza who came up with the now commonplace idea of listing ingredients and telling you how long something took to cook. It too contains a number of firsts – how to cook Brussels sprouts and even make spaghetti – and she happily included a chapter on foreign food. It even had jokes, with her recipe for Publisher's Pudding containing cognac, macaroons, cream and almonds because it could 'scarcely be made too rich'.

The early part of Acton's career focused on the education of young ladies in her own school. She became a poet and in 1826 printed her first poetry collection, which was reprinted within the month. Meanwhile, she worked on her cookery book, which was intended as a functional helpmate for the English middle classes. The book was so good that many writers stole freely from it.

Eliza was a pioneer in the change she brought to everyday kitchens but, by the turn of the century, women were not content to be confined to the kitchen. Suffragists were on the march and cookbooks themselves became part of the movement. In 1886 *The Woman Suffrage Cook Book* was published. It started a trend of peppering recipes with propaganda for the Great Cause. Among the first to buy a copy was the novelist **Louisa May Alcott**, who would go on to become the first woman registered to vote in her hometown.

To the modern mind it may seem odd to publish something ostensibly intended to tie women to the stove, but it's important to remember that for most women at the time there was no freedom to control their own life. They had no money, couldn't vote, and so it was necessary to disseminate political messages where they could. In a way, it also thumbed the nose at anyone who said a woman couldn't be political and look after her family at the same time. The 1909 *Washington Women's Cook Book* opened with the couplet:

> 'Give us the vote and we will cook
> The Better for a wide outlook.'

A fan of Alcott's work will recall that in *Jo's Boys,* the final book of her *Little Women* series, she describes a tableau in which:

The first figure was a stately Minerva; but a second glance produced a laugh, for the words 'Women's Rights' adorned her shield, a scroll bearing the motto 'Vote early and often' hung from the beak of the owl perched on her lance, and a tiny pestle and mortar ornamented her helmet.

Read these suffrage cookbooks and you will find a host of contributions from extraordinary activists like Chicago obstetrician and gynaecologist **Alice Bunker Stockham** and **Anna Ella Carroll**, a politician and lobbyist who wrote many pamphlets criticising slavery and who freed her slaves when Abraham Lincoln was elected president.

Partly through the cookbooks women learned how to organise, publish and fundraise. Some also helped women feel better. The *Suffrage Cook Book* published in Pittsburgh in 1915 included satirical recipes such as 'Pie for a Suffragist's Doubting Husband', whose ingredients were listed as:

1 qt. milk human kindness

8 reasons:
War
White Slavery
Child Labor
8,000,000 Working Women
Bad Roads
Poisonous Water
Impure Food

Mix the crust with tact and velvet gloves, using no sarcasm, especially with the upper crust. Upper crusts must be handled with extreme care, for they quickly sour if manipulated roughly.

The mention of 'white slavery' is uncomfortable but the intent is clear. Cookbooks like those of Eliza Acton helped give women confidence in their domestic sphere, but when standing in a kitchen it is worth remembering that there can also be feminism in food.

9 October 1830
Harriet Hosmer born
'I honor every woman who has strength enough to step outside the beaten path when she feels that her walk lies in another; strength enough to stand up and be laughed at, if necessary.'
Neoclassical sculptor, considered to be probably the first female professional sculptor. She pioneered a process for turning limestone into marble and lived in a fascinating expatriate colony in Rome. Hosmer was from Massachusetts and determined early on to be a sculptor. When she was denied access to Boston Medical School to study anatomy she moved to St Louis and took classes there. She had to go to Rome to be allowed to work with live models. In Italy she hung out with Nathaniel Hawthorne, Bertel Thorvaldsen, William Makepeace Thackeray, Georges Eliot and Sand, Elizabeth Barrett and Robert Browning at Casa Guidi. For twenty-five years she was romantically involved with Louisa, Lady Ashburton.

10 October 1870
Louise Mack born
Australian poet, journalist and novelist, born in Tasmania. Mack was the first female war correspondent, reporting for the *Evening News* and London's *Daily Mail* from the front lines during the First World War. At risk of being shot as a spy in German-occupied Antwerp she disguised herself as a mute hotel maid. She went on to publish sixteen novels and write for the *Sydney Morning Herald*.

11 October 1854
Adela Zamudio born
Also known as Soledad (Solitude). Bolivia's most famous poet, founder of the feminist Bolivian movement, campaigner for

the legalisation of divorce, teacher. Zamudio wrote about the social struggles of Bolivia. She was condemned for refusing to teach religion at the school she ran. Her birthday is celebrated in Bolivia as the 'Day of Bolivian Women'.

12 October 1904
Ding Ling born
Pen name of Jiang Bingzhi, one of the most celebrated Chinese authors of the 20th century. Born in Hunan province, she fled to Shanghai after refusing to follow tradition and marry the man chosen to be her husband. Her eventual partner, the poet Hu Yepin, was executed by the Kuomintang government in 1931. She was placed under house arrest between 1933 and 1936 for her work in the communist revolutionary cause. She criticised the Communist Party's attitude to women and had to apologise. During the Cultural Revolution she spent five years in jail and then spent twelve years doing manual labour on a farm before being 'rehabilitated' in 1978. Despite this she authored more than 300 works.

13 October 1862
Mary Kingsley born
English ethnographer, scientific writer and explorer of West Africa. Kingsley was another woman who got her education from her father's library. When her parents died, she took her inheritance and set off for the west coast of Africa, which was unheard of for a single woman. She lived with local people and often travelled alone. Kingsley canoed up the Ogooué River in Gabon, collecting specimens of fish previously unknown to Western science, three of which were later named after her. She criticised Christian missionaries and their work for taking away African culture without any real benefits in return. She

later toured England, giving lectures about life in Africa. Kingsley worked as a nurse in the Second Boer War, where she died of typhoid aged thirty-seven. Responded to repeated questions about travelling in Africa without a husband by answering: 'I am looking for him.' She never found him.

14 October 1972
Zoya Akhtar born
Indian film director and screenwriter, born in Bombay. Trained in filmmaking at NYU, Akhtar is one of the few female Bollywood directors. Her films include *Luck by Chance*, *Zindagi Na Milegi Dobara*, *Dil Dhadakne Do* and *Gully Boy*.

15 October 1917
Marion O'Brien Donovan born
American inventor and entrepreneur, who is best known for developing the first waterproof disposable nappy, or diaper. She trained as an architect at Yale University, where she was one of only three women in the graduating class of 1958. She invented the waterproof nappy using a shower curtain because she was fed up with the mess from her baby daughter. Donovan was granted twenty patents between 1951 and 1996.

16 October 1891
Sarah Winnemucca dies
Northern Paiute author, activist and spokesperson from Nevada. Born Thocmentony, meaning 'Shell Flower', in 1844. She became an advocate for the rights of Native Americans when her mother and several members of her extended family were among twenty-nine Paiutes killed in an attack by the US cavalry in 1865. After the Bannock War, Paiute people were interned in what was described as a 'concentration camp' in

Yakima, Washington. Sarah travelled to Washington, DC, to lobby for their release.

17 October 1956
Mae Jemison born
American engineer, physician and former NASA astronaut. In 1992 Jemison became the first black woman to travel into space. She took with her a photo of **Bessie Coleman** (*see* page 220), the first black woman to fly an aeroplane. Jemison is also the first real astronaut to appear on the TV series *Star Trek*. She is now a professor-at-large at Cornell University. Only about 10 per cent of people who have travelled to space have been female. NASA officials estimated female astronauts would need 'a makeup kit and 100 tampons for a 1-week flight'.

18 October 1852
Gertrude Käsebier born
American photographer known for her images of mother-hood, her portraits of Native Americans and her promotion of photography as a career for women. She went to art school aged thirty-seven after having three kids. She had an unhappy marriage and expressed herself in photography. See her 1915 photograph *Yoked and Muzzled – Marriage*, a picture of two oxen yoked together where one is trying to stand and the other to lie down. Her photographs of the Sioux tribe from Buffalo Bill's Wild West Show are in the Smithsonian.

---

18 October 1929
The British Privy Council voted that women were persons
There was a group of women in Canada in the 1920s who were known as 'The Famous Five'. **Emily Murphy, Irene Marryat**

Parlby, Nellie Mooney McClung, Louise Crummy McKinney and **Henrietta Muir Edwards** were all suffragists who advocated for women and children. They brought a case in Henrietta's name asking the Supreme Court of Canada to answer the question: 'Does the word "Persons" in Section 24 of the British North America Act, 1867, include female persons?' It was an important matter. If women were legally considered persons then they could be appointed to the Senate. On 24 April 1928, Canada's Supreme Court summarised its unanimous decision that women were not such 'persons'. The five did not give up and the matter went to a higher authority – the British Judicial Committee of the Privy Council. They came to a different view. Turns out we are people after all.

 — October —

Black History Month

This should not just be a month but a part of history woven through all education.

Sometimes you read about an incident from the past and the hurt from it continues to reverberate. You can feel it in your soul. In 1963 a man called Medgar Evers was living in Jackson, Mississippi. He was a Second World War veteran, a civil rights activist and the state's field secretary for the civil rights organisation called the National Association for the Advancement of Colored People, or NAACP. Medgar campaigned to end the segregation of public facilities and expand opportunities for African Americans. On 12 June 1963 he was murdered in his own driveway by a white supremacist. I won't dignify his murderer by naming him but the man was tried twice for the crime without conviction. Medgar's wife **Myrlie** did not give up; she

fought for justice not just for her husband
but as an activist for others. She became
chairwoman of the NAACP and I first heard
her name in 2013, when she delivered the
invocation at the second inauguration of
Barack Obama.

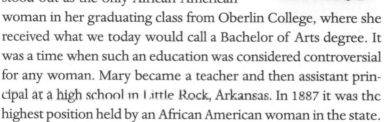

There are so many names no one
mentioned when I was at school. No
one ever talked to me about **Mary
Burnett Talbert**, who ought to be an inspiration to us all. Born in 1866 in Oberlin,
Ohio, she must have been something
because by the time she was twenty she
stood out as the only African American
woman in her graduating class from Oberlin College, where she
received what we today would call a Bachelor of Arts degree. It
was a time when such an education was considered controversial
for any woman. Mary became a teacher and then assistant principal at a high school in Little Rock, Arkansas. In 1887 it was the
highest position held by an African American woman in the state.

The treatment of African Americans in her lifetime was gruesome. The Southern, so-called Jim Crow laws excluded them
from political, economic, public and educational spheres of
influence. Mary used her position to speak out. She was a gifted
orator and began to travel, lecturing across the US and in eleven
European countries, educating her audiences about oppressive
conditions in African American communities and the need for
legislation to effect change. She helped lay the foundations for
civil rights activism in America. I was never taught her name.

Nor was I taught to look more closely at any history.
Examine the very white Tudor times a little more thoroughly
and you will discover **Catalina de Cardones**, who was black and

for twenty-six years served Catherine of Aragon as her Lady of the Bedchamber, and **Mary Fillis**, an independent black seamstress, baptised in London in 1597. No one mentioned them. Head to the Industrial Revolution and you will discover **Dido Belle Long** – the first black aristocrat in Britain. We need these stories so that we can see the past as the complicated tapestry of human experience it actually is, where everyone ought to be able to find role models and inspiration.

I was five when Martin Luther King Jr led the Great March on Washington in 1963. It's a story that is not simple either, for the women involved were not treated well. My heart breaks for the activist **Anna Hedgeman**, who had helped organise the event, personally recruiting 40,000 participants and making sure everyone had food and water. Despite this she was not allowed to march at the front and not allowed to speak. When Dr King declared, 'I have a dream', she cried and scribbled on her programme how she wished he had said, '*We* have a dream.' After Dr King's famous address, he and all the male leaders of the march were invited to the White House. Not one of the women who was there, including the legendary **Rosa Parks**, was asked to go with them.

Myrlie Evers never gave up the fight for her murdered husband. It would not be until 1994 that enough evidence was finally produced to send the murderer to prison. He had lived for more than three decades as a free man but don't mess with a determined woman.

Much of what lies behind us in human history is very ugly indeed but that doesn't mean we shouldn't face it and try to understand how it influences the present. Too much of the past lies in silence. Now is the time to speak up.

19 October 1850
Annie Smith Peck born
American mountaineer and adventurer. Passionate suffragist and renowned lecturer. She wanted to attend Brown University, Rhode Island, like her father and brothers but was refused admission because of her gender. She finally got a place at the University of Michigan. In 1886 she was the first woman to attend the American School of Classical Studies at Athens. She began mountaineering about the same time, and was criticised for wearing trousers while climbing. The northern peak of the Peruvian Cordillera Blanca mountain chain, Huascarán, was named Cumbre Aña Peck in her honour. In 1911, aged sixty-one, Peck climbed one of the five peaks on Coropuna in Peru and placed a 'Votes for Women' banner at the summit.

20 October 1936
Anne Sullivan Macy dies
American teacher, born 1866, best known for being the instructor and lifelong companion of **Helen Keller** (*see* 27 June).

21 October 1904
Isabelle Eberhardt dies
Swiss explorer and author, born 1877. As a teenager she published short stories under a male pseudonym. Aged twenty, Eberhardt moved to Algeria, dressed as a man and converted to Islam. She would eventually adopt the name Si Mahmoud Saadi. She advocated feminism and decolonisation; the French thought she must be a spy or troublemaker. Hers is a great story of a unique individual. She was killed by a flash flood aged twenty-seven.

22 (possibly 23) October 1844
Sarah Bernhardt born

Also known as 'The Divine Sarah'. The greatest French actress of the later 19th century and still one of the best-known figures in the history of theatre. The illegitimate daughter of a Dutch courtesan and unknown father who rose to unrivalled international fame. Her voice was said to be remarkable in its beauty. She appeared throughout Europe, the US and Canada. She played several 'trouser' parts, including Hamlet in Paris and London in 1899. In 1915 her right leg was amputated following a stage accident. She continued on visiting soldiers at the front during the First World War, carried in a chair.

23 October 1778
Kittur Chennamma born

A rani (queen) of the Nayakas of Keladi in Kittur, India. She is an Indian national heroine; one of the first female freedom fighters to resist British colonisation. She is said to have fought fiercely but was eventually imprisoned in Bailhongal Fort, where she died. Her legacy is still commemorated in Kittur, during the Kittur Utsava festival held between 22 and 24 October every year, which commemorates her victory over the British East India Company.

24 October 1975
Icelandic women's strike

On this day the women of Iceland went on strike for twenty-four hours to 'demonstrate the indispensable work of women for Iceland's economy and society' and to 'protest wage discrepancy and unfair employment practices'. No paid work, housework or child rearing was done. Ninety per cent of Icelandic women took part. Iceland's parliament passed a law guaranteeing equal pay the following year.

25 October 1923
Beate Sirota Gordon born
Gordon was a women's rights advocate and performing arts director. Born in Austria, and brought up in Japan, she earned a US degree in modern languages in 1943. During the Second World War she monitored overseas radio in Japanese for the US government. In 1945 she became an interpreter and translator with the General Headquarters of the Allied Forces in Japan. Aged twenty-two, she was the only female member of a committee tasked by General Douglas MacArthur with drafting a new Japanese constitution. She personally composed two articles – one that enshrined egalitarianism as a basic legal principle and another that improved the status of women in particular. She went on to become director of performing arts for the Japan Society in New York City, and received the Order of the Sacred Treasure from the Japanese government in 1998.

The 'Red October' Russian Revolution
The 'Red October' Russian Revolution of 1917, which established the Soviet regime, did not occur in October. At least, not by the Gregorian calendar. The 1917 revolution occurred on 7 November, but, at that point, Russia was using the Julian calendar, which marked that date as 25 October.

26 October 1902
Beryl Markham born
English-born Kenyan aviation pioneer, racehorse trainer and author. Markham was the first person of either sex to fly solo,

non-stop, across the Atlantic from Britain to North America. She was one of the first bush pilots. She married three times and had notable affairs. She was friends with the Danish writer **Karen Blixen** (*see* 17 April), taking up with Blixen's lover Denys Finch Hatton after Karen. Her excellent memoir, *West with the Night*, was published in 1942. It was reprinted in 1983 and became a bestseller, saving her from poverty.

27 October 1917
Twenty thousand suffragists march on Fifth Avenue in New York City demanding the right to vote
One of them was **Komako Kimura**, born 1887, a prominent Japanese suffragist, actor, theatre manager, lecturer and magazine editor. Her work shaped the women's rights and women's suffrage movement in Japan. She performed in over 500 plays, including performances at Carnegie Hall and on Broadway.

28 October 1897
Edith Head born
American costume designer who, between 1949 and 1973, won a record eight Academy Awards for Best Costume Design. She worked with almost every top female star in Hollywood. Her final Oscar was for her work on *The Sting*.

29 October 1808
Caterina Scarpellini born
Italian astronomer and meteorologist. Caterina began her work as assistant to her uncle, Abbe Feliciano Scarpellini, director of the Roman Campidoglio Observatory. Caterina became the editor of *Corrispondenza Scientifica*, a bulletin publishing scientific discoveries. She carried out her own observations six times a day, discovered a comet in 1854 and established a meteoro-

logical station in Rome in 1856. She compiled the first Italian meteor catalogue and was the only observer in Rome of the Leonid meteor shower in 1866.

30 October 1756
Lydia Taft becomes the first known woman to legally vote in colonial America

On this day Taft, born 1712, voted in a town meeting in the New England town of Uxbridge in Massachusetts Colony. Women were not allowed to vote in colonial America. **Margaret Brent** of Maryland Colony had tried to assert property rights and vote in 1647 but she was refused. Lydia's vote was a proxy on behalf of her deceased husband and not-yet-adult son.

31 October 1876
Natalie Clifford Barney born

American playwright, poet and novelist who held a celebrated salon as an expatriate in Paris for more than sixty years. She brought together writers and artists from around the world and formed a 'Women's Academy' (L'Académie des Femmes) to promote women's writing. She was openly lesbian and thought the scandal was a good way to stop unwanted heterosexual attention.

Annual Emma Crawford Coffin Races and Festival, Manitou Springs, Colorado
Held on the weekend nearest to Halloween.

Here is an odd story and an event that is definitely on my 'to do' list. Manitou Springs was founded in 1872 as a 'scenic health resort'. Located around a natural spring in the Rocky Mountains, it was quite the restful place. In 1889 a young woman named Emma Crawford came here hoping to find a cure for her tuberculosis. She was in love with a civil engineer on the Pikes Peak Cog Railway named William Hildebrand and she told him how much she loved the place. If she died, declared Emma, she wanted to be buried on top of Red Mountain. William seems to have been a good guy because Emma did die and he, and eleven other good folk, carried her coffin up the 7,200ft slope and buried her near the summit. So far so good. Sadly, in 1929, after years of soil erosion from the pounding weather, Emma and her coffin came lose and raced back down the mountainside.

In 1994 the town was looking for a unique selling point for tourists and invented the Emma Crawford Coffin Memorial Races. Every year they put the 'fun' into 'funeral' with a full day of coffin racing. About seventy teams of five (Emma and four costumed 'mourners') race in pairs down the street. There is a Coffin Cup plus a chance to win 'Best Emma', 'Best Entourage' and 'Best Coffin' during the parade.

I don't know any more about Emma except I guess, in a weird way, she does live on, which had been the plan.

NOVEMBER

'November always seems to me the Norway of the year.'

– **Emily Dickinson**, American poet, born 1830

Sacrifice Month

I am confident you have the hang of this by now. This is the eleventh month of the year but the name comes from the Latin for nine (*novem*) because it used to be the ninth month on the Roman calendar and we just can't move on.

For the Anglo-Saxons it had a rather more chilling name – *Blōtmōnaþ*. *Blót* is the term for 'sacrifice' in Norse paganism. It was like an exchange with the gods – I give up something to you, oh mighty god, and in return I'd like good weather or a baby, luck in battle, that kind of thing. Anyway, this is the month for it. Mostly the gods seem to have wanted dead cows, which was fine as that led to loads of feasting. The Anglo-Saxon scholar Bede (I don't feel we've had enough of him) said, 'Blod-monath is the month of immolations, for it was in this month that the cattle which were to be slaughtered were dedicated to the gods.'

Other names for November

Finnish: *Marraskuu*, which means 'month of the dead'.

Cantonese: *Sahp yāt yuht* – *sahp* is ten, *yuht* is month. I think *yāt* is one but I need to work on my Cantonese.

Xhosa: *NgeyeNkanga*, meaning 'month of the small yellow daisies'.

Breton: *Miz du* – *miz* means 'month'; *du* seems to mean 'black', which is not exactly cheerful.

Pointless trivia
November begins on the same day of
the week as March every year.

FESTIVAL OF THE MONTH

The Giant Omelet Celebration, Abbeville, Louisiana

Early November

That's just how Americans spell omelette, I'm afraid. I'm fine with that. I grew up in America and have had to fight the urge to call this an *Almanack* not an *Almanac*. For nearly forty years the town of Abbeville, Louisiana, has had a two-day annual festival celebrating with a massive omelette cooked in a 12ft frying pan. They got the idea from the French town of Bessières, which does the same thing but every Easter. Apparently Bessières started cracking that many eggs originally because Napoleon happened through with his army, all of whom were hungry.

The rough recipe

5,000 eggs
50lb onions
75 bell peppers
4 gallons onion tops
2 gallons parsley
1½ gallons cooking oil
6½ gallons milk
52lb butter
3 boxes salt
2 boxes black pepper

15lb Louisiana crawfish tails
Tabasco (to taste)

⇢ POEM OF THE MONTH ⇠

Figs from Thistles: First Fig
by Edna St Vincent Millay

My candle burns at both ends;
It will not last the night;
But ah, my foes, and oh, my friends –
It gives a lovely light!

I discovered Edna St Vincent Millay late in life yet feel I should always have known about her. There is a photograph of her from 1914 standing under a magnolia tree, which was taken in Mamaroneck, New York. This is the very town I grew up in. I went to Mamaroneck High School but no one ever mentioned her or any other female poets that I can think of, yet Edna was one of the most successful and respected writers in America. She wrote plays, opera librettos and poetry. She was a master of the sonnet but those who knew her say it was her personality more than her poetry which held the attention. It is said that she was a riveting performer. She got her unusual middle name from a New York hospital that saved her uncle's life and as a child called herself Vincent. It was an early life of poverty but she always wanted to write. As an adult she was openly bisexual and actively feminist and her wonderful celebratory poem 'Figs from Thistles' was considered controversial. In 1923 she received the Pulitzer Prize for Poetry yet she is largely forgotten. **Nancy Mitford** wrote a biography about her. Go find her. It's worth it.

1 November 1918
Leola N. King becomes America's first female traffic cop
On this day she was assigned to duty at 7th and K Streets in Washington, DC. She looked fabulous in her uniform. Please check her out online. For some reason she carried a gun, which suggests traffic was rougher than you think. All the pictures also tell me she was the 'wife of Cap. E. H. King, med. capt.', which seems irrelevant.

2 November 1261
Bettisia Gozzadini dies
Gozzadini, born 1209, was a jurist who lectured at the University of Bologna from about 1239. She is thought to be the first woman to have taught at a university. As a young woman she dressed as a man but no one knows if that was choice or necessity. On 31 May 1242 she gave the oration at the funeral of the Bishop of Bologna, Enrico della Fratta. She died following a flood. Her writings are lost.

3 November 1324
Petronilla de Meath burnt at the stake
De Meath, born around 1300, was the maidservant of **Dame Alice Kyteler**, a wealthy 14th-century noblewoman and the first person recorded as being condemned for witchcraft in Ireland. Kyteler was accused of practising witchcraft to make her money and get rid of her husbands. Her weirdest charges were of 'cutting up animals to sacrifice to demons at crossroads' and having sex with a demon named 'Robin Artisson'. Petronilla was charged as an accomplice, flogged and burnt at the stake. Dame Alice escaped and fled the country.

— *November 1620* —

What about the Pilgrim Mothers?
Women and recorded history
There is no finer story about how women get left out of history than that of the founding of the United States. There is a rock in the town of Plymouth, Massachusetts, which, rather unimaginatively, is known as Plymouth Rock. It is a large boulder with the date 1620 carved into it. This is said to be the very rock where the Pilgrim Fathers stepped off their frankly hideous journey to found America, having journeyed for more than two months on the heaving waters of the Atlantic in an elderly sailing vessel called the *Mayflower*. This tale does not work for me. I want you to imagine – it was November. The boat was tiny, with 102 passengers on board and thirty crew. Among the passengers was a woman who gave birth. At that angle. There had been terrible storms and the already old, wooden boat was falling apart. If the ship's captain, one Christopher Jones from Harwich, had docked his creaking vessel alongside a great big, bad old boulder it would've been the last thing he did.

But here is how history comes to be written down and then literally set in stone. In 1741, 121 years after the *Mayflower* had supposedly arrived at this spot, a 94-year-old church elder named Thomas Faunce declared that he knew the precise boulder on to which the *Mayflower* pilgrims first stepped when disembarking. Bear in mind that Faunce's own father had arrived in the US two years after the *Mayflower*, so he hadn't been there either, but nevertheless Thomas declared his father had told him this marvellous piece of history. The town carried the old man down to the shore in a chair and, weeping, he pointed to the rock, which I don't think had the helpful date carved on it at the time. An old man who wasn't there when history happened pointing to a rock that his father had once pointed to who also hadn't been there. Bound to be right. That is history in a nutshell – the recollections of old men who weren't there in the first place. It was Jane Austen who wrote, 'I often think it odd that history should be so dull, for a great deal of it must be invention.'

What we do know for sure is that while the Founding Fathers of America were on board the boat the famous Mayflower Compact was created. This is not an early make-up mirror but a document in which the passengers agreed to conduct their lives through majority rule. Seems a simple and pleasing idea. As noted, there were 102 passengers on board, and the Compact was signed by forty-one of them. No children, fair enough, but none of the seventeen women on board signed either. Nor did any of the thirty crew, but two 'indentured servants' did get included. This is heralded as the beginning of democracy. A famous painting by Jean Leon Gerome Ferris is often used to illustrate this moment, although it was painted 300 years later. In it one woman was allowed to watch history being made as long as she didn't stop knitting. We don't know her name. We know the names of all the men in the picture but not her. Women are at the sidelines of so much history.

Nearly 78 per cent of the women would die during the first winter in Plymouth, a far higher percentage than for men or children. Not surprising. They nursed the sick so got sick themselves and they continued to live in the cramped and unsanitary conditions of the boat for four months after they arrived. Much better to have been out in the fresh air felling trees.

'When you look at history you are confronted by the startling and disturbing fact that women are the greatest race of underdogs that the world has ever known.' That's not my rather gloomy view but that of **Margaret Cavendish**, Duchess of

Newcastle (*see* Poem of the Month in April). Margaret declared, 'The truth is, we [women] live like bats, or owls, labour like beasts, and die like worms.'

So history gives us women at the sidelines, brilliant women who have been forgotten or misremembered, and Margaret Cavendish's analysis about women's lives through history sadly resonates – from wife-beating to witch-hunts, genital mutilation to the use of rape as a weapon of war, lots of it is not a pretty picture.

4 November 1883
Minnie D. Craig born
American legislator. Craig was the first female speaker of a state House of Representatives in the United States. She was elected to the North Dakota House of Representatives in 1923, just three years after women won the right to vote, and encouraged women to become politically active. 'Women are naturally given to detail ... If they weren't, they couldn't make pies or sew dresses. Men don't like details. Because of woman's training ... she's more thorough than man and right there she has a splendid opportunity for politics.'

5 November 1607
Anna Maria van Schurman born
Dutch painter, engraver, poet and highly educated scholar. Van Schurman was taught at home by her father alongside her brothers. She spoke fourteen languages. In 1634 she challenged the exclusion of women from the University of Utrecht,

leading to permission for her to attend lectures. In 1636 she became the first woman to study at a Dutch university, sitting behind a screen so the male students couldn't see her. In *The Learned Maid or, Whether a Maid may be a Scholar* she advocated female education.

5 November 1935
Monopoly goes on sale for the first time
The story of Monopoly is a sadly typical one for female inventors. The game was invented in 1903 by an American woman, **Lizzie Magie**, who was trying to explain a theory about tax.

She called it The Landlord's Game and took out a patent. In 1932, an out-of-work man called Charles Darrow played the game at a friend's house. He decided to make his own version and sold it to Parker Brothers, telling them he had invented it out of boredom. He and the games company made millions. When Parker Brothers learned the truth about the invention they bought Magie's copyright for a pittance. She sold it because she thought the game would help educate people. For years she was never mentioned in relation to the game.

6 November 1901
Kate Greenaway dies
Greenaway, born 1846, was an English Victorian artist and writer, known for her children's book illustrations. Between 1858 and 1871 she studied graphic design and art at South Kensington School of Art, the Royal Female School of Art, and the Slade School of Fine Art. She started her career by making greetings cards. See her bestselling book, *Under the Window*.

7 November 1961
Andrea Jenkins born
American policy aide, politician, writer, performance artist, poet and transgender activist. On 7 November 2017 Jenkins became the first African American openly transgender woman elected to public office in the US. She received more than 70 per cent of the vote to represent the eighth ward on the Minneapolis City Council.

8 November 1875
Qiu Jin born
Chinese revolutionary, feminist and writer. Qiu was executed after a failed uprising against the Qing dynasty which had ruled for three centuries. She is considered a national heroine in China. She was a feminist, speaking out about freedom to marry, to be educated, and campaigning for the abolishment of the practice of foot-binding. She was beheaded in her home village, aged thirty-one.

9 November 1914
Hedy Lamarr born
Austrian-American actress, inventor and film producer. Lamarr acted in thirty films, including the 1933 Czech movie *Ecstasy* in which she became the first movie actress to appear completely naked. In the same film she became the first woman in film history to simulate an orgasm on screen. She and composer George Antheil invented an early version of 'frequency-hopping spread spectrum', which was an early stage in the development of Bluetooth technology. She also helped improve aviation designs for Howard Hughes.

10 November 2008
Miriam Makeba dies
Also known as 'Mama Africa'. South African singer, born 1932. One of the world's most prominent black African performers of the 20th century. She grew up in a segregated black township outside of Johannesburg. She introduced Xhosa and Zulu songs to Western audiences and sang songs that were critical of apartheid. Please listen to *An Evening with Belafonte/Makeba*.

11 November 1926
Maria Teresa De Filippis born
Italian pioneer racing driver, and the first woman to race in Formula One. She participated in five World Championship Grands Prix, beginning in 1958. She was five foot two and had to have extra padding in her driver's seat to reach the pedals.

12 November 1648
Sor Juana Inés de la Cruz born
'Who has forbidden women to engage in private and individual studies? Have they not a rational soul as men do? ... I have this inclination to study and if it is evil I am not the one who formed me thus – I was born with it and with it I shall die.'
Also known as Sister Joan Agnes of the Cross, she was a Mexican child prodigy, writer, philosopher, composer, poet, nun and protofeminist. She inherited her grandfather's library and taught herself. Sister Joan joined a nunnery aged twenty so she could study, and began writing about love, feminism and religion. She encouraged intellectuals to meet with her. She wrote what is considered the first feminist manifesto, which led to her condemnation by the Bishop of Puebla. Having fallen out of favour, she was forced to sell her collection of books and devote herself to the poor. She died the following year, in 1695, of the plague.

13 November 1897
'Tilly' Edinger born

German-American palaeontologist, and the founder of paleo-neurology – the study of brain evolution. Edinger began to lose her hearing as a teenager and as an adult could not hear without hearing aids. She discovered that mammalian brains left imprints on fossil skulls, allowing paleoneurologists to discern their anatomy. She had to work in secret when the Nazi Party's 'racial laws' targeted the Jewish population. She fled to the United States, where she published *The Evolution of the Horse Brain* in 1948. Tilly bones, thickened bones on the vertebral columns of some fish species, are named in her honour. She was killed when she was hit by a car she didn't hear approaching.

14 November 1817
Policarpa Salavarrieta executed for high treason

Also known as 'La Pola', born 1795. Policarpa Salavarrieta was an alias. We do not know her real name. She was a heroine of the Colombian independence movement, seamstress and spy for the revolutionary forces during the Spanish Reconquista of the Vice-royalty of New Granada. She spied by offering to do sewing in the homes of royalists. She was captured and executed for high treason. She refused to kneel for the firing squad, yelling, 'I have more than enough courage to suffer this death and a thousand more. Do not forget my example.' When they began shooting she turned to face them. The Day of the Colombian Woman is commemorated on the anniversary of her death.

15 November 1887
Georgia O'Keeffe born

'Mother of American modernism'. If you don't know her paintings of enlarged flowers or New Mexico landscapes, treat yourself. In 2014, O'Keeffe's 1932 painting *Jimson Weed* sold for $44,405,000, which was more than three times the previous world auction record for any female artist. A bucket-list stop – the Georgia O'Keeffe Museum in Santa Fe.

16 November 1625
Sofonisba Anguissola dies
Italian Renaissance painter, born around 1532. She was apprenticed to local painters in Cremona, which was rare if not unheard of for a woman. Michelangelo was a fan. She became an official court painter to the king, Philip II. Her self-portraits make you feel she might speak directly to you.

17 November 1558
The reign of Queen Elizabeth I begins
Queen Mary I of England dies and is succeeded by her half-sister, Elizabeth I of England, beginning the Elizabethan era. I'm not that interested in royals but Liz I was a corker. She ruled till 1603, during which time there was, among other things:

- A renaissance in the arts (Shakespeare obvs. But also music and art).
- Defeat of the Spanish Armada.
- Successful circumnavigation of the globe.
- The establishment of the Royal Exchange, the first stock exchange in England.

18 November 1939
Margaret Atwood born
Award-winning Canadian writer. Her books include *The Edible Woman* and *The Handmaid's Tale*. I once had to do a double act with her. She was hilarious.

— *19 November* —

World Philosophy Day

'No one is free who has not obtained the empire of himself.'

– **Pythagoras**, father of philosophy, born *c.*570 BC

I quote Pythagoras because I can't seem to find the words of **Elena Cornaro Piscopia** recorded in English. I would have preferred to quote her as, in 1678, she became the first woman to receive a PhD degree as a Doctor of Philosophy. Nevertheless it is not Dr Piscopia who I can readily find but the old pa of philosophy instead. I am fascinated by philosophy. The word is from the Greek *philosophia*, 'love of knowledge or pursuit of wisdom', and how wonderful to have the time to do just that, to sit and think, but I have a busy life, kids, grandkids, career, a dog that needs worming, and there are few moments to consider what I think about things, what matters to me and where I am in my life. It takes time to 'obtain the empire' of yourself. I am old enough now to know a little. I like chocolate better than I thought I did, five o'clock does not seem too soon to me for a beer and I have the pointless yet comforting understanding that my knees may not work well anymore but I am at least too old to die young which is … something.

I never thought of philosophy as a career, partly because I never sat still long enough and then, when I was older, the kids were too noisy. There are plenty of women philosophers in history but ask anyone to name a philosopher at all and the boys tend to nail the top positions. Indeed, when BBC's Radio 4 did a poll, no woman made the top twenty. I suspect this absence is entirely to do with time. Being a philosopher mostly requires a life of privilege. You can't be gazing at your navel if you need to get dinner on the table. Throughout recorded history boys on the whole have had fewer household commitments.

Pythagoras, the so-called 'father of philosophy', is generally agreed to have been a Greek fellow from 2,500 years ago who clearly had plenty of leisure time, as you may recall he obsessively measured triangles as well. He did get married and have kids but, rather like the British politician Boris Johnson, no one is sure how many because the philosophy of domestic life does not seem to have been his focus.

Pythagoras came from money, which helps. Through the ages few women have found themselves in a position where they have the resources to think deep thoughts. Women who did manage it needed to be exceptional like Elena Cornaro Piscopia, who was born in 1646. She was Italian. Born in Venice, which is nice. When she was thirty-two, she became one of the first women, if not the first, to receive an academic degree from a university, and certainly the first to receive one as a Doctor of Philosophy.

Her father was part of the Venetian nobility – there's that money thing again – and early on he wanted his daughter Elena to make a good marriage, but her only interest was studying. She was by any standard a child prodigy. She soaked up education. By the time she was seven she was familiar with Latin, Greek, French and Spanish, and would go on to master Hebrew and Arabic. She studied maths, philosophy and theology. Learned to play the harpsichord, the clavichord, the harp and the violin, and used these skills to compose music. Then she discovered physics, astronomy and linguistics.

Her fame as a scholar spread. Between 1669 and 1672 she was elected to seven academies in five cities, becoming the director of the Accademia dei Pacifici, the Academy of the Peaceful, where she delivered formal, academic lectures.

On 25 June 1678 she received her degree in philosophy, having spoken for an hour in classical Latin and explained difficult passages selected at random from the work of Aristotle. It must have been a scary affair. Her exam had attracted so much interest the university had had to move the event to Padua Cathedral, where professors, students, senators and invited guests from universities all over Italy gathered to see the spectacle of an accomplished woman.

She continued to study but in 1684, aged just thirty-eight, she died of tuberculosis. In her short life she had had quite an effect. Her death was marked by memorial services in Venice, Padua, Siena and Rome. Memorial volumes of tributes to her were published and her statue was placed in the University of Padua, whose governors changed its statutes from then on to allow women to graduate. Go to Vassar College in Poughkeepsie, New York, one of the first elite women's colleges in the United States, and you can see Elena's graduation ceremony depicted in a magnificent stained-glass window, the Cornaro Window, installed in 1906 in the Thompson Memorial Library.

I think philosophy matters. It can provide an analysis of the world and how we live in it which is not ordered by dogmatic religion. Human beings need answers. That's been true ever since someone first stepped out of a cave, looked up at the stars and thought, 'Hmm, I wonder where I fit in all this?' Thoughtful consideration of big questions seems so much more preferable to the short bursts of Twitter pontification that teach us nothing.

We could do with a brilliant mind like that of Elena Cornaro Piscopia at the moment to help us make sense of the world. It is time for a new philosophy of how we treat the planet and each other. It is a worrying time but as Pythagoras himself said, 'Concern should drive us into action and not into a depression.'

Pythagoras. Father of philosophy. You know who taught him? **Themistoclea**, a priestess at Delphi. In the first half of the 3rd century AD. Diogenes Laërtius wrote a biography of Pythagoras in which he declared that it was Themistoclea who taught Pythagoras his moral doctrines. A woman. I know, right? Who knew? The great **Hypatia of Alexandria**, another astonishing female thinker who died in 415, declared, 'Reserve your right to think, for even to think wrongly is better than not to think at all.'

Now that would make a very good tweet.

19 November 1835
Lakshmi Bai born
Rani (queen) of the Maratha state of Jhansi in North India, a leader of the Indian Mutiny of 1857–58 and a symbol for Indian nationalists of resistance to the British Raj. She was brought up with the boys in the royal court and became an excellent sword fighter and horsewoman. When she was twenty-two the British tried to take over the kingdom. She was proclaimed regent and organised the troops against the British. It's a great tale of daring. She died in combat dressed as a man.

20 November 1914
Vinnie Ream dies
American sculptor, born 1847, best remembered for her sculpture of Abraham Lincoln in the rotunda of the Capitol in Washington, DC. She was an amateur who got the commission

aged just eighteen, the first woman to win such an assignment from the federal government. In 1875 she beat prominent male artists to win a $20,000 government commission to create a bronze statue of Admiral David G. Farragut. Cast from the propeller of the naval hero's flagship, it stands in Farragut Square, Washington, DC. She gave up sculpture for many years because her husband didn't like it.

21 November 1631
Catharina Questiers born
Questiers was a Dutch poet, dramatist, engraver. Along with **Cornelia van der Veer** and **Katharyne Lescailje** (*see* 26 September) she was the most successful female Dutch poet of the second half of the 17th century. Her second play starred Amsterdam's first professional actress, **Ariana Nozeman**.

22 November 619
Khadijah bint Khuwaylid dies
Commonly known as Khadija and often referred to by Muslims as 'Mother of the Believers', born 555. She was the first wife and first female follower of the Islamic prophet Muhammad, and a successful businesswoman in her own right. Khadijah proposed to Muhammad when he was twenty-five years old and she was forty. She was a highly intelligent philanthropist and is revered by billions to this day.

23 November 1534
Beatriz Galindo dies
Also known as 'La Latina' because of her skill in Latin. Spanish writer, humanist and a teacher of Queen Isabella of Castile and her children, born around 1465. She taught Catherine of Aragon, the future wife of Henry VIII of England, and Joanna

of Castile, the future wife of Philip of Habsburg. One of the most educated women of her time. One of the first women to be active in public life during the Renaissance.

24 November 1815
Grace Darling born
Grace's father was the lighthouse keeper at Longstone Lighthouse on Longstone Rock in the outer group of the Farne Islands off the Northumberland Coast, England. When steamship *Forfarshire* foundered during a storm, Grace and her dad rowed out to help, taking an oar each through the raging sea. They saved nine people. Both were awarded honours. Grace was awarded an RNLI Silver Medal, the first woman to receive such recognition. Queen Victoria sent her £50. Grace became a celebrity and didn't like it. She died of tuberculosis, aged twenty-six.

25 November 1960
The Mirabal sisters assassinated
María Teresa Mirabel, born 1935: *'Perhaps what we have most near is death, but that idea does not frighten me. We shall continue to fight for that which is just.'* On this day the Mirabal sisters, Patria, Minerva and María Teresa of the Dominican Republic, were assassinated. They all opposed the dictatorship of Rafael Trujillo and were involved in clandestine activities against his regime. In their honour, the United Nations General Assembly designated 25 November the International Day for the Elimination of Violence against Women.

26 November 1792
Sarah Grimké born
American abolitionist widely held to be the American mother of the women's suffrage movement. Born into money in South

Carolina, she wanted to be an attorney but this was not allowed as it was 'unwomanly'. Her father had slaves and, from the age of twelve, Sarah taught them Bible class but was not allowed to teach them to read, as that had been illegal in South Carolina since 1740. She secretly taught Hetty, her personal slave, and got into terrible trouble. She became an outspoken advocate for education and suffrage for African Americans and women. *'I ask no favours for my sex. All I ask of our brethren is that they will take their feet from off our necks.'*

 — *26 November 1867* —

First British parliamentary vote cast by a woman (yes, really)

> *'I refuse to barter my freedom to act according to my conscience, while my health permits me to fight on.'*

– **Adelaide Knight**, British suffragette, born 1871

Ask even the ardent student of women's history and they might tell you that no woman voted in a British parliamentary election until after 6 February 1918, when the Representation of the People Act was passed, giving women the vote for the very first time. To be honest it wasn't much of a law. Putting a cross on a ballot paper was deemed complex, so any woman giving it a go needed to be supremely qualified and mature. She had to be over thirty years of age and own property, or at least have the good sense to live with someone who did. This left 60 per cent of the female population unable to register to vote but I suppose it was a start.

Yet on 26 November 1867, more than half a century before that partial enfranchisement of women, shopkeeper **Lilly Maxwell** cast a vote at a Manchester by-election. She became the first woman known to have voted at a parliamentary contest since the 1832 Reform Act had specifically limited the franchise to 'male persons'. Lilly was a suffragist but she also had her own shop where she sold crockery and candles. Weirdly, she's also listed as selling 'red herring'. Actual red herring but I don't know if mentioning that is a red ... Had she been a man with such a business then, because rates were paid to the local council, he would have been entitled to vote. A suffragist named **Lydia Becker** heard about Lilly's shop and persuaded her to try to vote. Lilly thought this was a marvellous idea, so on the day of the vote she and Lydia marched to Chorlton Town Hall for Lilly to change history.

The Englishwoman's Review wrote of Lily: 'It is sometimes said that women, especially those of the working class, have no political opinion at all. Yet this woman, who by chance was furnished with a vote, professed strong opinions and was delighted to have a chance of expressing them.'

Lydia carried on trying to persuade any woman who was the head of a household to apply for their names to be put on the electoral register. Eventually this went to court, where the judge ruled that women could not vote whatever their financial circumstances. I love how brave Lilly must have been as she marched to the town hall with just her pal and her pride to accompany her. It is the courage of those women that still echoes.

Lots has been written about the key women who brought about the much-needed change to the voting laws and that's great, but I'm always looking for the women I don't know about. I know the names of many women who fought for the right to vote but I long to bring the most marginalised to the fore. I realise there is a whole gap in my knowledge of women in history who triumphed over adversity while dealing with a disability. There are so many ways to be sidelined in society and those people are always harder to find in history, so I thought I would highlight two, perhaps lesser known, suffragettes who had physical challenges and to whom we owe a debt of gratitude.

Adelaide Knight was born in London's East End in 1871, a time when the area was one of deep poverty. I don't have any more specific dates than that, all I know is that she was described as frail and born with deformed thumbs. She suffered some accidents in childhood that left her in poor health and with impaired mobility, so that she needed a stick or crutches to get about. Adelaide had little education, leaving school at twelve or thirteen, but that didn't mean she wasn't smart. Her fellow activist **Annie Kenney** described her as 'extraordinarily clever'.

Adelaide must also have been a bold soul for, in 1894, she married Donald Adolphus Brown, the son of a Jamaican Royal Navy officer. A so-called 'mixed race marriage' was not exactly welcomed in British society. He must have been quite the guy because when they took their vows he also took her name, and they set about a life which included shared domestic chores.

Adelaide became known as an outspoken advocate for the rights of poorer women as she joined the suffrage movement. By 1906 she was secretary of the Women's Social and Political Union's branch in Canning Town. She was militant and unafraid of the consequences. When she and three other activists, **Annie Kenney**, **Teresa Billington** and **Jane Sparborough**, attempted to get a meeting with the then Chancellor of the Exchequer, Herbert Asquith, she was arrested and sentenced to six weeks in Holloway jail. The quartet would be the first of hundreds of suffragettes who were eventually imprisoned there. She had been offered a sentence of giving up campaigning for one year but could not take it.

By now she and Donald had children. She wrote to him from prison declaring, 'What can I do, Daddy? To draw back will encourage this intimidation. Can I count on your full support? It will be agonising to be away from you and our children, but with your help I can face this.'

Her health was poor in prison but nevertheless she is said to have sung the socialist anthem 'The Red Flag' every morning and even scratched the lyrics into her cell windowsill with a hairpin. Adelaide would eventually lose faith in the WSPU and become a founder member of the Communist Party of Great Britain, a passionate campaigner for equal rights for all regardless of gender, physical health or race. Many of the first suffragettes came from the middle classes. Without Adelaide the voice of London's working-class women might not have been heard. Adelaide and Donald's daughter, **Winifred Langton**, wrote a memoir of her parents entitled *Courage*.

The language we use around disability has changed and the world is better for it but back in the early years of the suffrage movement **Rosa May Billinghurst** was known as the 'cripple suffragette'. She was born in Lewisham, London, in 1875. She too did not come from money. Those were the days when polio might take the life of a child. Rosa survived it but the disease left her unable to walk. She wore leg-irons and mostly got about either on crutches or using a modified tricycle wheelchair. Rosa joined the WSPU in 1907 and, despite her disability, took part in the WSPU's march to the Royal Albert Hall in June the following year. She decorated her hand-propelled 'invalid' trike with coloured WSPU ribbons and 'Votes for Women' banners. In 1911 she founded the Greenwich branch of the WSPU and became its first secretary.

Rosa seems to have had no hesitation in using her wheel-chair for publicity purposes. She was arrested by the police after they tipped her out of her trike. She was helpless but is said to have known it didn't reflect well on them as a story.

I love the image of her, her crutches lodged either side of her tricycle as she charged against any opposition. In March 1912 she went to Holloway for the first time, sentenced to one month's hard labour for smashing a window on Henrietta Street in central London. It's a marvellous story of her and the Glaswegian suffragette, **Janie Allan**, working in cahoots, with Rosa apparently hiding a ready supply of stones under the rug that covered her knees. Prison officials did not know what to do with Rosa and never found her any hard labour to get on with. On 8 January 1913 she was sentenced once more, this time eight months for damaging letters in a postbox. She went on hunger strike and was force-fed along with other suffragettes.

She spoke at meetings, she chained herself to railings and, on 21 May 1914, took part in the mass deputation of suffra-gettes to petition King George V, where once more the police deliberately tipped her out of her wheelchair. When the 1918 law was passed she decided her fighting days were over. She lived to be seventy-eight and left her body to science.

Working-class women, women of colour and disabled women have often been erased from history in general. The least we can do is not make the same mistake when we write about women's suffrage.

Some men who have been in charge while women waited to vote

Charles the Bad
Charles the Bald
Charles the Mad
Charles the Simple
Ethelred the Unready
Ferdinand the Inconstant
Hakim the Mad, Ruler of Egypt
Henry the Impotent
Ivan the Terrible
Louis the Fat
Louis the Quarreler
Louis the Sluggard
Otto the Idle
Pedro the Cruel
Selim the Grim, Sultan of Turkey
Stephen the Fop

27 November 1911
Fe del Mundo born

Filipino pioneer paediatrician and founder of the first paediatric hospital in the Philippines. She was National Scientist of the Philippines. The death of her older sister, who had wanted to be a doctor for the poor, spurred del Mundo to her career choice. During the Japanese occupation of the Philippines she cared for child internees detained at the University of Santo Tomas internment camp for foreign nationals, where she became known as 'The Angel of Santo Tomas'. In 1957 she sold her home and possessions to fund her own paediatric hospital. Among other things she devised an incubator made out of bamboo to use in isolated communities with no electricity.

28 November 1947
Gladys Kokorwe born

Speaker of the National Assembly of Botswana. Kokorwe began her career as a typist and clerk in the civil service, rising up to be chief executive of the Kgatleng District. She was elected to the National Assembly in 1994. In 2008 Kokorwe became the first parliamentarian in Botswana to have a private member's bill become law. Her bill aimed to better protect victims of domestic violence, and was passed into law as the Domestic Violence Act.

29 November 1910
Elizabeth Choy born

Teacher and politician, best known as a Second World War heroine. During the Japanese occupation of Singapore, Choy risked her life by smuggling supplies and messages to British prisoners of war held at Changi jail. In 1943 she and her husband were arrested. She endured terrible, repeated torture but refused to give them names of her co-workers.

30 November 1952
Sister Elizabeth Kenny dies
Founder of physiotherapy, born 1880. Kenny was a self-trained Australian bush nurse who developed a new approach for treating polio victims. Her controversial methods of muscle rehabilitation became the foundation of physiotherapy. She set up and supervised a temporary hospital in Queensland to care for victims of the 1918 flu pandemic.

The Monkey Buffet Festival, Phra Prang Sam Yot Temple, Lopburi, Thailand
Last Sunday in November
The Thai people have great respect for the monkey. This dates back to the time about 2,000 years ago when a divine prince called Rama was trying to rescue his wife, Sita, from the clutches of a demon lord. He managed it but only with the help of the monkey king, Hanuman. To mark this rescue, on this day a banquet is laid on among the ruins of the Phra Prang Sam Yot temple. *Lopburi* means 'monkey town' and thousands of macaques live in the area, which is thought to bring good luck. Dancers in monkey costumes open the proceedings and then the monkeys are left to enjoy nearly two tons of food. Apparently, the amount of food on offer can make the monkeys a tad unruly. In fact, they had a bit of a turf war during the coronavirus pandemic of 2020. Tourists stopped coming with their usual treats and the temple monkeys fought the street monkeys over a single yoghurt cup. Apparently it stopped traffic.

DECEMBER

'Roasting turkeys! Rich mince pies!
Cakes of every shape and size!'

– **Louise Bennett Weaver** and **Helen Cowles LeCron**,
'December', *A Thousand Ways to Please a Husband*
with Bettina's Best Recipes (1917)

Yule Month (which is exciting)

The Anglo-Saxons called this time *Ġēolamonaþ* (Yule month) as they headed to celebrations of the winter solstice, the end of the long nights and the return of the sun. On Christmas Eve they celebrated *Mōdraniht* or *Modranicht* (Night of the Mothers or Mothers Night). Head back to the 5th century AD and female deities the *Matres* (mothers) and *Matronae* (matrons) were in charge in northwestern Europe. You see them depicted in art of the time. Usually in threes with someone holding some fruit.

All this is mostly forgotten now but we remember the Roman calendar with the word 'December' meaning, of course, the tenth month even though it's twelve and so on ...

In the Northern Hemisphere the winter solstice occurs around 21 or 22 December and lots of cultures take this as a time to party or have rituals. Around this time of year you can rush from one festivity to another, celebrating over a span of a few weeks Christmas, Hanukkah, Kwanzaa, New Year, Pongal, Yalda and plenty of other festivals of light. Treating this as a special time of year is nothing new. Head to the prehistoric wonder that is Stonehenge and you will find it laid out to carefully align with the winter solstice sunset. That's a lot of heavy rocks to move just to get a good sightline, so it must have been important.

Other names for December

Kashubian: *Gòdnik.*

Abkhaz (a northwest Caucasian language spoken mainly in Abkhazia, an autonomous republic in Georgia): *Ԥxynčkǝyn.*

Cornish: *Mys Kevardhu*.

Central Dusan (Malaysia): *Tulan Momuhau*, which means 'scarecrow month'.

DECEMBER FESTIVALS

Mount Popa Nat Festival, Myanmar

Early December

Spirits worshipped in Myanmar and neighbouring countries in conjunction with Buddhism are called *nats*. On the full moon of the month of Natdaw (December) people gather for the Mount Popa Nat Festival. Mount Popa (flower mountain) is an extinct volcano, home to thirty-seven of the most important *nat* spirits. Climb 777 steps to the top of the volcano and you reach an amazing monastery, Popa Taungkalat. *Nats* have been worshipped on the mountain for at least a thousand years. There is a shrine in the monastery containing statues of the most important *nats*, most of whom were humans who suffered a violent death. The festival lasts for five days, with ceremonies guided by the traditional spirit mediums (*nat kadaw*, or spirit's wife), who are almost always transvestites. Being a spirit wife is one way for transvestites to escape censure in a deeply conservative country.

The Chichibu Yomatsuri (Night Festival), Chichibu, Japan

2–3 December

A 300-year-old festival with ornate floats of lanterns, tapestries and gilded wood carvings pulled through the streets to the city hall. Lots of music and fireworks. Try *amazake* (sweet rice wine).

⇥ POEM OF THE MONTH ⇤

A Hymn to the Evening
by Phillis Wheatley

Soon as the sun forsook the eastern main
The pealing thunder shook the heav'nly plain;
Majestic grandeur! From the zephyr's wing,
Exhales the incense of the blooming spring.
Soft purl the streams, the birds renew their notes,
And through the air their mingled music floats.
Through all the heav'ns what beauteous dies are spread!
But the west glories in the deepest red:
So may our breasts with ev'ry virtue glow,
The living temples of our God below!
Fill'd with the praise of him who gives the light,
And draws the sable curtains of the night,
Let placid slumbers sooth each weary mind,
At morn to wake more heav'nly, more refin'd;
So shall the labours of the day begin
More pure, more guarded from the snares of sin.
Night's leaden sceptre seals my drowsy eyes,
Then cease, my song, till fair Aurora rise.

The only date I have for Phillis Wheatley is that she died on
5 December 1784. It's impossible to write a short precis of her
life. She needs a whole book. The first African American woman
to publish a book of poetry. Born in West Africa in around 1753,
she was sold into slavery at the age of seven or eight and transported to North America. She was purchased by the Wheatley
family of Boston, who taught her to read and write. They realised she was a talented poet. In 1773 she went to London to
find a publisher for her work. I mean, it's an astonishing story.

Please read more about her. George Washington thought she was tremendous.

1 December 1723
Susanna Centlivre dies

Also known as Susanna Carroll, born at some point between 1667 and 1670. She was an English poet, actress, and often cited as the most successful female playwright of the 18th century. If you ask someone to name an early woman writer for the English stage then **Aphra Behn**'s (*see* page 90) name is the one likely to come up. Susanna hardly ever gets a mention. She seems to have left home and joined a team of strolling actors with whom she often played boys. She began to write to earn a living, and became very successful writing poems, books and plays. Much of her work was political.

2 December 1923
Maria Callas born

American-born Greek soprano, also known as 'La Divina'. One of the most renowned and influential opera singers of the 20th century. She endured much scandal in her personal life but remains the definition of opera star and is still one of classical music's bestselling vocalists.

3 December 1842
Ellen Swallow Richards born

American industrial and safety engineer, environmental chemist, teacher and feminist. Richards laid the foundation for the new science of home economics, applying chemistry to the study of nutrition. She was the first woman admitted to the Massachusetts Institute of Technology and later its first female instructor. Richards became the first woman in America accepted to any school of science and technology and, in 1870, the first American woman to obtain a degree in chemistry.

4 December 1884
Dewi Sartika born
National hero of Indonesia and education pioneer. Sartika campaigned for education for Indonesian women. In 1904 she founded the first school for women in the Dutch East Indies. She was diabetic and died from a leg wound while evacuating from Bandung, which was under siege from the Dutch during the Indonesian War of Independence in 1947.

 — 4 December —

International Day of Banks
There are lots of reasons I didn't go into banking. The main one is that I was never very good at sums. Tell me that two negatives make a positive and it feels like some kind of Buddhist saying about character building from bad luck. Right now I imagine there are people in government offices doing nothing but sums and I realise how glad I am that I didn't go into banking. To be fair, I know nothing about it. My image of that world is based entirely on the big building where Mr Banks, the father of Michael and Jane, in *Mary Poppins*, worked. Full of men carrying umbrellas while sporting a bowler hat and a creased brow from doing so much adding up.

I realise it's not quite like that but historically the world of finance has been seen as a boys' preserve. Probably the easiest way to get into banking is to be born into a family that owns one.

That's what happened to **Angela Burdett-Coutts**, born 1814. There is a big English bank called Coutts, it's the eighth oldest bank in the world, and Angela had the good sense to be born into the family that owned it. In her lifetime the bank was known as Thomas Coutts and Co., named after Angela's maternal grandfather. He appears to have been a marvellous character. First he married a servant called Elizabeth, although some people think she was called Susannah, that's how little attention is paid to the way women are recorded in history. A year after Angela was born Elizabeth died. Thomas remarried, which happens, except he married again four days after Elizabeth's funeral.

By now he was nearly eighty. He chose as his new wife an actress, **Harriet Mellon** (or Harriot, again records vary). She was thirty-seven and a beauty. It was a splendid scandal. Actresses were the lowest of the low. I love the sound of her – the daughter of strolling players, she lived the high life in both London and Brighton, throwing legendary parties. Thomas died and Harriet got all the money. Bear in mind, Angela was her step-granddaughter but there must have been something about her that made Harriet decide she was the one who ought to get everything. So when Harriet departed to the great cocktail party in the sky, Angela inherited about £1.8 million. In today's money that would be very nice but you have to understand that in 1837 it was eye-watering. The equivalent of £160 million in modern spending. Angela had been born Angela Burdett. All she had to do to get the money was take the name Coutts. She did, as Burdett-Coutts. Overnight Angela became the richest heiress in England.

She owned the best part of a bank and you might think she sat down with some ledgers and got on, but these were Victorian times and she was not allowed to do business. Instead, she became one of the greatest philanthropists Britain has ever known. She set up life with her old governess to ward off suitors and began helping the poor. I mean, a lot. She gave so much to the disadvantaged in London's East End that her name became Cockney rhyming slang for 'boots'. She was a patron of the arts, funded David Livingstone's expeditions across Africa and helped to found both the NSPCC and the Royal Marsden Hospital. In 1871 she became the first woman to be created a baroness in her own right as thanks for her incredible generosity. When she died, 30,000 people came to pay their respects.

I think Angela should have been allowed to run the bank and certainly there are women who have done just that in difficult times. Shortly after the end of the American Civil War an African American woman called **Maggie Walker** was born in Richmond, Virginia. Her mother, Elizabeth, was a former slave who was widowed in Maggie's childhood. Elizabeth worked as a laundress and, as a youngster, Maggie would help her deliver clean clothes. It was not a life of luxury but Maggie would grow up to be the first African American woman in the United States to charter a bank and serve as its president.

Aged fourteen, Maggie joined a local group called the Independent Order of St Luke, which had been founded to help care for the sick and make sure even the poor had a decent burial. Maggie loved it. She climbed up the ranks of the order and eventually took charge of the organisation. Under her leadership, it would grow in size from just over a thousand members to 100,000. Her focus was on the need for economic independence, something she saw as critical to improving the lives of African Americans. She was determined to see her community gain financial security, and business ownership. She declared, 'Let us put our money together; let us use our money; let us put our money out as usury among ourselves, and reap the benefit ourselves.'

She spread the word, speaking across the United States and founding the *St Luke Herald*, a weekly newspaper that highlighted the social, economic and legal injustices experienced in the black community. She used it to organise a strike against the Richmond streetcar system in protest against its rules of segregation. She became focused on ways to improve the financial independence of the African American community, even setting up her own insurance scheme to provide members with disability and life insurance in the face of terrible legislation-backed anti-black prejudice.

White-owned banks proved reluctant to accept deposits from an African American benevolent society, so in 1903 she started her own bank, the St Luke Penny Savings Bank, where she served as the first president. Later, when the bank merged with two other banks to become the Consolidated Bank and Trust, she served as chairman of the board. Under Maggie's leadership it survived the Great Depression when so many other financial institutions failed. Today it is the oldest, continuously operated African American-owned bank in the United States. Later in life she became disabled and used a wheelchair, becoming an example for people with disabilities. It wasn't all roses in her life. She suffered depression and alcoholism, but there is a statue to her on Broad Street in her hometown of Richmond. It's ten feet tall which feels about right.

I don't understand maths but I do understand courage. The current pandemic is highlighting the sort of financial inequalities that Maggie would have known only too well. Maybe we can do things differently when we wake from this dystopian dream. Wouldn't that be great? At least we could try. As the American screenwriter and actress **Elaine May** once said, 'The only safe thing is to take a chance.'

5 December 1941
Amrita Sher-Gil dies

Sher-Gil, or Shergil, was a pioneer painter of the modern movement in Indian art. She was born in Hungary but the family moved to India when she was a child. I love the fact that she was expelled from her convent school for declaring she was an atheist. She trained in Paris in the 1930s and there are both Western and Indian influences in her vibrant art. She is one of India's most celebrated modern artists and the Indian government has declared her work as National Art Treasures. She died aged twenty-eight, possibly following a botched abortion.

6 December 1925
Louisa Keyser (Dat So La Lee) dies

Celebrated Native American basket weaver, born around 1829. A member of the Washoe people in northwestern Nevada. Many museums of art and anthropology preserve and display her baskets – including the Smithsonian National Museum of the American Indian and the Metropolitan Museum of Art in New York. She met her art dealers, Amy and Abram Cohn, around 1895, probably when she was hired to do laundry.

7 December 1878
Yosano Akiko born

Pen name of Shō Iō. Japanese author, poet, pioneering feminist, pacifist and social reformer. The critics didn't like her first volume of poetry because it didn't promote traditional Japanese values for women. She saw women as active, not passive, in every aspect of their lives including sex. She was accused of 'corrupting public morals'. She had thirteen kids, of whom eleven survived. Yosano has come back into popularity in recent years.

8 December 587
Fredegund dies
Queen consort of Chilperic I, the Merovingian Frankish king of Soissons. Fredegund served as regent from 584 to 597 before her son came of age. She is a good example of someone whose reputation is based more on what men said about her than on facts. Gregory of Tours depicted her as ruthlessly murderous and sadistically cruel. He even reported that she tried to murder her own daughter using a treasure chest. Whatever the truth, it is a fabulous soap opera of assassinations, adultery and jealousy. The death of Fredegund's nemesis Brunhilda is particularly gruesome.

9 December 1961
Tanzania declares independence
Bibi 'Titi' Mohammed was a Tanzanian politician of Muslim descent, born 1926 and known as 'Mother of the Nation'. She considered herself a freedom fighter for Tanzanian independence. She influenced the writing of the new constitution and saw to it that women had a place in the government. Mohammed created the All African Women's Conference. She was nicknamed 'Titi' because of her large bosom.

10 December 1815
Ada Lovelace born
The only legitimate child of Lord Byron and his wife, Annabella. Lovelace became a mathematician and writer and is considered among the world's first computer programmers. She worked on Charles Babbage's proposed mechanical general-purpose computer, the Analytical Engine, and realised the machine could do more than pure calculation. She published the first algorithm to be carried out by such a machine.

11 December 1876
Eliza Suggs born
Suggs was a 19th-century American author, the daughter of former slaves. She was born with brittle bone disease and grew to only thirty-three inches tall. She was offered money to appear as a sideshow or museum 'oddity' but she had other plans. Her sisters would carry her to school in a special chair to prevent her bones continuously breaking. In 1906 she published a book called *Shadows and Sunshine*, which shone a light on her parents' lives as former slaves, and her own story as a disabled black woman.

---

11 December 1919
The Boll Weevil Monument is dedicated in Enterprise, Alabama

If you haven't seen this work of art then it is hard to describe. In downtown Enterprise, at the intersection of Main and College, stands a white marble statue of a Greek woman, more than thirteen feet tall, holding a fifty-pound bug above her head. It's a boll weevil which, in real life, is smaller than your little fingernail but here is reproduced in giant form. The monument was erected by the citizens to show their immense appreciation of what this small insect did to influence the prosperity of the local agriculture and economy. This is surprising, for the boll weevil is a pest. Indeed, as far as I know, this is the world's first commemoration of an agricultural pest.

The boll weevil likes to eat cotton. A lot of cotton. And when it came to town the town decided to diversify into farming peanuts, which the boll weevil is less keen on. The peanuts were a triumph and the people duly showed their gratitude to the bug that made it happen. The original statue has been replaced by a replica as naughty people kept trying to steal the weevil.

My favourite statue of a woman.

12 December 1821
Phoebe Hessel dies

Born 1713, Hessel is best known for disguising herself as a man to serve in the British Army, probably to be with her lover. She served as a soldier in the West Indies and Gibraltar. Her gender was discovered when she was stripped to be whipped. She lived to be 108. In old age, she was a street hawker on a corner in Brighton, Sussex, near the Pavilion. Then in 1808 the Prince Regent granted her a pension of half a guinea a week.

13 December 1871
Emily Carr born

Canadian artist and writer inspired by the indigenous peoples of the Pacific Northwest Coast. One of the earliest chroniclers of life in British Columbia. I have a postcard of her 1929 painting *The Indian Church* on my study wall. She didn't start her best work till she was fifty-seven. Hurrah.

— 14 December 1898 —

Ann Cole Lowe born

When it was announced in the summer of 1953 that Jacqueline Bouvier was to marry John F. Kennedy the world went mad. She was a high society gal marrying into one of the most distinguished families in America. When they married it was considered the social event of the season. Jackie, as I feel relaxed enough to call her, wore a fabulous 'you shall go to the ball' white wedding dress made of ivory silk taffeta. I say that like I know what I'm talking about. All I know is, it was a gorgeous dress which any fairy godmother would have been thrilled to have conjured up. In fact, it was made by Ann Lowe, the first African American to become a noted fashion designer. Ann was born in Clayton, Alabama, at a time when the oppressive Jim Crow laws were still in operation. She learned to sew from her mother and grandmother. She got married in 1912 but, when her husband demanded that she give up her work as a seamstress, she packed up her needles and left. She took their son and moved to New York City, where she enrolled at S. T. Taylor Design School, but this was 1917, the school was segregated, and she had to attend classes in a room by herself. Nevertheless, she graduated and in 1919 opened her first dress salon in Tampa, Florida. It was a triumph and within ten years she was back in New York City designing for the top stores. In 1946, she designed the dress that Olivia de Havilland wore to accept the Best Actress Oscar for *To Each His Own*, but the gown was credited to someone else.

Ann knew she needed to work for herself, so she and her son opened Ann Lowe's Gowns on Lexington Avenue in 1950. It was an instant success and high society flocked to her. The dress she made for Jacqueline Bouvier to float down the aisle was stunning. It remains one of the most iconic wedding-day looks of all time. The story behind it, though, makes anyone who has ever sewn anything shudder. For two months, Lowe and her team worked on the fifty yards of silk taffeta creating the elaborate folds that make the gown so unique. They were ten days away from the wedding when there was a flood in their studio and everything – the wedding dress and those of the bridesmaids – was ruined.

Ann rolled up her sleeves. Bought more fabric, hired more staff and worked night and day to recreate the wonder she had already made once. She never told anyone and she ended the commission $2,000 in debt. You can imagine her exhaustion as she arrived to deliver the dresses. An exhaustion that must also have been mixed with pride. She had delivered on time. When she got to the house a member of staff told her to use the service entrance in the back. Ann looked him in the eye and replied that she would rather take the dress back. Carrying her creations, she walked in the front door.

Every newspaper in the country wrote about the frock in exquisite detail. No one credited Ann. Most painful of all, when the bride herself was asked who designed the dress, she reportedly responded, 'A colored dressmaker did it.' I think there is a nice end to this story. Years later when Ann was losing her sight and had fallen into debt, an anonymous benefactor stepped in to help financially. She always believed it was Jackie Kennedy.

15 December 2011
Paula Hyman dies

American social historian, teacher, writer, born 1946. Hyman pioneered the study of Jewish women's history and was the president of the American Academy for Jewish Research. In 1972 she was the co-author of *Jewish Women Call for Change*, which advocated for the full equality of women within Conservative Judaism. Hyman was joint editor (with Deborah Dash Moore) of the two-volume historical encyclopedia, *Jewish Women in America*.

16 December 1901
Margaret Mead born

American cultural anthropologist. Mead made twenty-four field trips among six South Pacific peoples, publishing the bestseller *Coming of Age in Samoa*, and *Growing Up in New Guinea*. In her later works, including *Male and Female*, she argued that male and female characteristics were shaped by cultural conditioning rather than biology. She spoke about the fluidity of human sexuality back in 1933. 'The kind of feeling which you have classified as "homosexual" and "heterosexual" is really "sex adapted to like or understood temperaments" versus "sex adapted to a relationship of strangeness and distance".'

17 December 1957
Dorothy L. Sayers dies

English crime writer, playwright, essayist, linguist and poet, born 1893. Sayers is best known for her mysteries featuring English aristocrat and amateur sleuth Lord Peter Wimsey, but she thought her best work was her translation of Dante's *Divine Comedy*. In it she guides the reader brilliantly from heaven to hell.

18 December 1922
Esther Lederberg born
Professor of microbiology and immunology, Lederberg was a pioneer of bacterial genetics who collaborated with her husband. He got the Nobel Prize for their work.

19 December 1915
Édith Piaf born
French singer-songwriter, cabaret performer and film actress. Piaf was one of France's most famous stars, with an utterly unique style. She specialised in 'torch' songs. Check out 'La Vie en rose' or 'Non, je ne regrette rien'.

20 December 1859 (or thereabouts)
Elsie de Wolfe born
'I opened the doors and windows of America, and let the air and sunshine in.' Also known as Lady Mendl, de Wolfe was an American actress and interior decorator. She was one of the first interior designers. She had a marriage of convenience to English diplomat Sir Charles Mendl but her lifelong companion was Elisabeth Marbury, the pioneering American theatrical and literary agent. According to *The New Yorker*, 'Interior design as a profession was invented by Elsie de Wolfe.' I read that she died in France and her ashes were placed in a common grave when the lease expired, at Père Lachaise Cemetery in Paris. I hope that's not true. She'd have hated that.

21 December 1892
Rebecca West born
'I myself have never been able to find out precisely what feminism is: I only know that people call me a feminist whenever I express sentiments that differentiate me from a doormat, or a prostitute.' Also

known as Dame Cicily Fairfield, West was a British author, journalist, literary critic and travel writer. Her work ranged from
novels to coverage of the Nuremberg trials. In 1947 *Time* magazine called her 'indisputably the world's number one woman
writer'. She espoused feminist and socialist causes. During the
Second World War she housed Yugoslav refugees in her home.
In 1980 West was living in an apartment adjacent to the Iranian
embassy in London when it was attacked. She had to be evacu-
ated, aged eighty-seven.

22 December 1868
Katharina Paulus born

Paulus was a German aerial acrobatics performer who used to
parachute out of hot-air balloons. She invented the first col-
lapsible parachute, as well as the drag chute, where one small
parachute opens to pull out the main parachute. Paulus made
about 7,000 parachutes for the German forces during the First
World War. Her husband was killed in a joint jump when his
parachute failed to deploy

23 December 1754
Queen Aliquippa dies

Queen Aliquippa was an influential Iroquois leader during
the early part of the 18th century but details are hard to find,
including when she was born. A Native American woman
who had an enduring impact on history yet we know so little
about her. In 1749 the French explorer Celeron, travelling
down the Allegheny River, wrote, 'The Iroquois inhabit this
place and it is an old woman of this nation who governs it.
She regards herself as a sovereign. She is entirely devoted
to the English.' This devotion to the English was critical in
the French and Indian War which eventually led to English

control of most of North America, which led to the American Revolution etc., etc.

24 December 1843
Lydia Koidula born
Pen name of Lydia Jannsen, Estonian poet. Koidula's father published the first national Estonian language newspaper and her earliest writing was for him. Because she was a woman her work was published anonymously. At the time, Estonia was part of the Russian empire, and the Estonian language was seen as that of the oppressed indigenous peasantry. As the first person to write original plays in Estonian, Koidula is seen as the founder of Estonian theatre and a voice of the nation.

      — 25 December —

Religion

> *'Christmas always rustled. It rustled every time,*
> *mysteriously, with silver and gold paper, tissue paper and*
> *a rich abundance of shiny paper, decorating and hiding*
> *everything and giving a feeling of reckless extravagance.'*

> – **Tove Jansson**, Finnish author, born 1914

For many in the West, December is all about heading towards Christmas. For some it is a celebration of their Christian faith, while for others it is about worshipping the gods of retail. This whole book has been about allocating calendar dates and it is worth bearing in mind that selecting 25 December to mark the birth of Jesus had more to do with convenience than fact. The

Gospel writers Matthew and Luke may have noted the circumstance of the nativity, but neither one of them took the time to refer to a calendar. I've had a look at what theologians nearer the time of the event thought and old dudes like Clement of Alexandria placed the occasion on 18 November, but also suggested 20 May or 6 or 19 January. I'm going to suggest he wasn't sure. It wasn't until more than 300 years after Christ's birthday that everyone settled on 25 December. It was an easy date to pick as it was the winter solstice in the Roman calendar and everyone tended to party then anyway.

Whatever your particular faith or lack of, it's an interesting day to consider what we believe and why when it comes to religion. Human beings have had one form of belief system or other for at least a hundred thousand years. Religion exists in every culture, with more than 85 per cent of the world's population embracing some sort of faith in a life greater than themselves and I get that. At their core, these convictions help bring a sense of order to what can otherwise feel a chaotic world. Religion also helps us form larger social groups, held together by a common view of our place in the world. Our belief systems provide comfort that somewhere, someone at least has a plan.

Religion is unique to humans and some kind of religious practice is found in pretty much all human cultures. Once the *Homo sapiens* brain developed enough then people started wondering what we were all doing here. Anatomically, modern humans emerged about 120,000 years ago, but it takes a while for ritual behaviour to be established. There is a cave in the Tsodilo Hills of Botswana which the local people, the San, call 'The Mountain of the Gods'. Here you will find the largest collection of rock paintings in the world. In it lies a six-metre-long rock shaped like a snake. It has a gash for a mouth and hundreds of notches carved in it by hand which give the impression of movement. Beside it were discovered thousands of elaborately made artefacts more than 70,000 years old. Something was going on. Something ritualistic. A snake, a python, is part of the San's creation myth. It is an ancient belief that it was from this slithering creature that we all descended. It was the ceaseless circling of the snake in search of water that was said to have made the hills. So believing in something outside ourselves is ancient but belief is also about living in the present. For many of us, let's be honest, much of our religious observance takes place around the dinner table and I like the fact that even our earliest ancestors got together to share food. Mind you, chimpanzees and bonobos do that too, so I'm not sure what it says about us lot.

There are many religions around the world and the interesting thing that they all have in common is that, on the whole, women don't do all that well out of them. Most religions give men a higher status than women and are rougher on women who stray from any of the rules. Women may be exalted as mothers, but at the same time they are required to be submissive to the Church and men in general. Leadership is often restricted to men, with the patriarchy firmly in place in the bulk of organised religion. The ranks of the faithful are dominated by women but it's the boys who tell them how to behave.

Gods tend to be male and it is the boys who seem to be in closest touch when it comes to writing things down. The result is a strange silencing of women. In the Bible, for example, women only speak just over 1 per cent of the total words in the book. Jesus' mother Mary who, let's face it, had an extraordinary time which I would love to hear about, says just 191 words.

Historically, it's interesting how few women have been responsible for beginning a school of faith and there's a really simple explanation. Let me give you a quick Buddha biog: thousands of years ago he was born into money and privilege as a member of the aristocracy in ancient India. He grew up to marry a princess called Yaśodharā and together they had a son named Rāhula. According to tradition, Rāhula was born on the day that Buddha decided to go off and lead a life of austerity. In fact, the name Rāhula is said to mean 'a fetter on the path to enlightenment'. Those of us who are parents all know the feeling of being tied down by the kids but Buddha went anyway, leaving Mrs Buddha to pick up all the childcare. I think, particularly at the moment, there are women who would have had a problem with his decision. It's no wonder so few women have ever started a religion. They're far too busy looking after the kids.

There are some splendid feminists who feel the gender gap in religion needs addressing. For two decades **Zainah Anwar**, a Muslim feminist from Malaysia, ran a group called Sisters in Islam (SIS), a worldwide organisation that aims to promote the rights of women within the framework of Islamic belief and universal human rights. It is a group that has caused controversy, with the Pan-Malaysian Islamic Party (PAS) calling for members of SIS to be 'rehabilitated'. In the 1970s feminists in the Jewish community formed Ezrat Nashim (Women's Courtyard), gathering information about the status of women in Judaism and working towards challenging inequalities. The name itself referred to the place where women were seated separately in synagogues. **María Pilar Aquino** is a feminist historian whose work focuses on the issues of liberation for Latino women, while **bell hooks** (also known as Gloria Watkins) has examined spirituality for black women from a Buddhist perspective.

Lots of religions start out with good intentions. I studied Islamic law at university and at its core found much to commend it, yet the Taliban interpretation of the Qu'ran is what led to **Malala Yousafzai** getting shot for daring to want an education. The founder of Sikhism, Guru Nanak, stated in 1499 that we should not 'consider women cursed and condemned, when from women are born leaders and rulers'. The theory of gender equality is in place from the outset yet today women make up less than 20 per cent of the central governing body, the Shiromani Gurdwara Parbandhak Committee, and are not permitted to help carry the sacred scriptures to and from the Golden Temple.

The only present-day religion founded by a woman that I can find is the Church of Christ, Scientist, which was the 'discovery' of the American **Mary Baker Eddy**, born 1821. She argued that sickness could be cured by prayer and that much disease was about wrong-headed thinking rather than a genuine physical malady. While not exactly a feminist, Mrs Eddy (as Christian Scientists refer to her) did believe in women's suffrage and she attempted to lay down the rules with absolute equality of the sexes, embracing the concept of God as Father-Mother. We are all, however, human and her beliefs in the power of prayer did not stop her allegedly having something of a morphine habit.

I have no faith at all but am sometimes jealous of those who do. I think it must be a great comfort. Sadly, I read too much history and can't shake off the moments when women as a group have been sidelined by the faiths to which they belonged.

Of course, the other option on 25 December is to go and celebrate Takanakuy in the Chumbivilcas Province of Peru. *Takanakuy* is a Quechuan word which I've found translated as 'when the blood is boiling' or 'to hit each other'. Basically, it's a fighting festival. In places like Santo Tomás, Cuzco and Lima, this is a fabulous festive day of dancing, drinking, colourful costumes and the settling of old grievances with a public fistfight. Everyone is welcome to land a punch – men, women, young, old. I mean, it couldn't be more egalitarian. It's a great way to get rid of social tensions for another year. There's loads of drinking, which sounds just like British festivities. Lots of families in the UK get together at Christmas, consume alcohol and then fight, but those battles are often passive-aggressive with buckets of silent resentment. The advantage of this Andean shindig is that it all seems so much more upfront. You even get to wear a kind of Peruvian ski mask called a *uyach'ullu* so no one can tell it's you throwing the punches. I never know what to wear this time of year. This sounds perfect. Happy Takanakuy everyone.

26 December 1780
Mary Somerville born
'I resented the injustice of the world in denying all those privileges of education to my sex which were so lavishly bestowed on men.'
Scottish science writer and polymath, Somerville was known as 'The Queen of Science'. She was nominated with **Caroline Herschel** as the first female members of the Royal Astronomical Society. Somerville was a suffragist and hers is the first signature on a huge petition organised by John Stuart Mill in 1866 to give women the right to vote. She owed much of her education to her father's library. She refused to take sugar in her tea as a protest about slavery. Among her works were *On the Connexion of the Physical Sciences*, *Physical Geography* and *Molecular and Microscopic Science*.

27 December 1980
Nadia Anjuman born

Anjuman was an Afghan poet. When the Taliban captured her home city of Herat in 1995, all schools for girls were closed in northwestern Afghanistan. Anjuman joined other local women attending an underground educational circle called the Golden Needle Sewing School, where women would receive education while pretending to sew. She continued to write and, when the Taliban were displaced, went to Herat University. She published a popular book of poetry, *Gul-e-dodi* ('Flower of Smoke') followed by *Yek sàbad délhoreh* ('An Abundance of Worry'). She wrote about the oppression of women. In 2005 her husband beat her to death when she wanted to go out. He was convicted, but later forgiven by Anjuman's father who was promised the murderer would stay in prison for five years. Anjuman's husband was released a month later. Her death was ruled a suicide.

28 December 1722
Eliza Lucas born

American plantation manager of her father's lands and busines woman. She changed agriculture in colonial South Carolina, where she developed indigo as a cash crop which would eventually represent more than a third of the colony's exports. She had five children. Her 'letter-books' of the time provide wonderful detail of colonial life in the mid-18th century. Hers is one of the most complete collections of writing from 18th-century America.

29 December 1885
Nadezhda Udaltsova born

Russian artist, painter and teacher. Udaltsova was a leading figure of the pre-revolutionary Russian avant-garde. The Stalinist era led to her marginalisation in Soviet art. Her husband, the painter

Aleksandr Drevin, was arrested on political charges and executed in 1938. She did powerful work, especially her cubist paintings. I love *Typewriter Girl*.

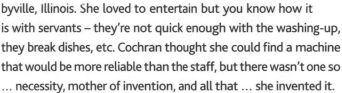

29 December 1886
The dishwasher is patented

The dishwasher was invented by a woman called **Josephine Cochran**, born 1839, and I for one will always be grateful. I'm not sure about some of the background to this. Cochran was a wealthy woman living in Shelbyville, Illinois. She loved to entertain but you know how it is with servants – they're not quick enough with the washing-up, they break dishes, etc. Cochran thought she could find a machine that would be more reliable than the staff, but there wasn't one so … necessity, mother of invention, and all that … she invented it.

She was methodical – measured all the plates, cups, saucers, and then went out into her shed and made wire compartments to fit all the different bits of crockery. These she put inside a wheel on top of a copper boiler, and used a motor to turn the wheel while hot soapy water squirted from the bottom of the boiler and fell back down on the dishes. Triumph.

She showed the dishwasher at the 1893 Chicago World's Fair where she won a prize. Restaurants and hotels thought it was marvellous. Ordinary folk not so much. The standard dishwasher didn't really become a thing until the 1950s, but that may have been to do with access to the amount of hot water the machine needed. Not one to rest, Cochran also founded a company to manufacture her invention. The company would grow up to became KitchenAid®.

30 December 1889
Peggy Hull born
Pen name of Henrietta Deuell, an American journalist who
covered the First and Second World Wars. Hull was the first
female correspondent accredited by the US War Department.
She always dressed in her own version of military garb.

31 December 1881
Elizabeth Arden born
Canadian-American businesswoman who built a legendary cosmetics empire. Arden opened her first salon in 1910. Nineteen
years later she owned 150 salons worldwide, with hundreds of
products sold in twenty-two countries. She was the sole owner
and one of the wealthiest women in the world. In addition to
being an entrepreneur, Arden was a dedicated suffragette. In
1912 she marched for women's rights and provided the red lip-
stick – a sign of solidarity – worn by the 15,000 suffragettes who
marched with her.

Why not end the year with ...
fireball whirling, Stonehaven, Aberdeenshire, Scotland
Stonehaven is a small fishing town in the northeast of Scotland where it can get very cold this time of year. To combat
this and see the year out, just before midnight on 31 December about thirty locals (men and women) parade through the
streets twirling enormous balls of fire about their heads. Naturally, they are accompanied by bagpipers. They get to the
shore's edge and chuck the fireballs into the North
Sea. This happens no matter what the weather.

That's it. I can't believe I've ended on balls.

A Final Word

Writing was invented about 5,000 years ago and once that turns up you begin to get recorded history, a history entirely dependent on the whims of those putting pen to paper. If writers didn't record an event or a life, then it wasn't deemed important and might soon be forgotten. Of course, human beings at their core haven't changed very much and often what someone bothered to note down was of interest only to them.

Take the great city of Pompeii, for example. It is incredibly well preserved (being buried in ash will do that) and thus we can find not just an extraordinary ancient Roman ruin but graffiti. Yep. It was a thing back in AD 79. The oldest piece of wall-scribbling says simply 'Gaius was here'. I think it's a boy thing to want to write such a thing. There are declarations of love, schoolboy insults, pictures of phalluses (obvs), adverts, laundry lists and maxims like: 'The smallest evil, if neglected, will reach the greatest proportions.'

As President Trump and Twitter will attest, writing things down is a way of getting noticed and you don't even need to be clever. On average, 500 million tweets are sent worldwide per day. That's a lot of words but, rather like the Pompeii graffiti, most of it doesn't mean anything.

For generations women have been left out of history. What half the population did or thought was not deemed worthy of attention and it's still true today. According to the World Economic Forum, the most recent study of who we hear about in the news generally found that just 24 per cent of people seen, heard or read about in the media were women. It's true for other sources of information. The online encyclopedia Wikipedia has a serious gender issue. It's not just that women aren't being input, in some cases they are actively being taken out.

Take **Donna Strickland**, for example. Born in 1959, she is an optical physicist at the University of Waterloo in Canada. Former president and fellow of the Optical Society. Recipient of a Sloan Research Fellowship. According to quantum physicist Avik Dutt, her work 'pushes the boundaries of how short and how intense light we can produce, [and] it has myriad applications in eye surgery, chemistry, industrial laser machining, and biology and medicine in general'. Sounds like she knows her stuff. On 28 March 2018, someone submitted an article about Strickland to Wikipedia, which did not have a page for her. The article was refused by a volunteer editor because they said Strickland lacked the necessary criteria to be included. She wasn't important enough to be notable. She finally got her page but only after she'd won the Nobel Prize.

Whole swathes of the world are being excluded from the historical record, and if we don't do something about it then this present capturing of history will become accepted as unchangeable fact. We can all do something about it. Sign up and start editing Wikipedia. Every voice can make a difference. This book is a tiny dent in the subject matter. If you think I've got it wrong then, please, gather an almanac of your own. Capture the stories of the women in your life who may otherwise go unnoticed in the passage of time.

Be active.

Write the wrongs of history.

Acknowledgements

This almanac had its origins in the great UK pandemic lockdown of 2020, which began on March 23. A few days before I had been filming the BBC series *QI*. As we left the studio for what we thought would be a three-week stay at home, one of the producers of the show, Alex Bell, and I agreed we ought to make something to keep people entertained. The next day my wife, Debbie, and I began shooting a series of talks we called *VoxTox*, which I wrote and presented, Deb recorded and Alex edited. They focused on women's history, and we would go on to make more than fifty of them on our own YouTube channel, which was watched round the world. From those chats this book grew, so my gratitude to Alex and Debbie is huge.

Had it not been for the lockdown I would never have found the time to put this together, but it has been an amazing solace in the midst of the sadness at the loss of friends, shared anxiety and missing my family beyond all measure. It was a great escape to spend my days educating myself, and I want to thank all those who helped me. My sister, Jeni, is a wonderful writer in her own right, and I could not have kept track of everyone in this book without her astonishing spreadsheet and insight. I am lucky to have her in my life. Thanks also to my friend and agent, Cathryn Summerhayes, who made the book happen; my editor, Pippa Wright, who has become a friend and helped me see the wood for the trees; and Catherine Riley, Lorraine Jerram and Clare Hubbard, who spotted the errors the rest of us missed. Thank you to all the women in this book, whose extraordinary lives I have relived in my research. They have made me laugh and cry and long to share them with others.

Finally, my wife, Debbie, once more. It turns out three months or so entirely on our own is not nearly enough. She is the light and love of my life. Thank you.

Index